DESKTOP PUBLISHING WITH WORDPERFECT

FOR 5.0 AND 5.1

DESKTOP PUBLISHING WITH WORDPERFECT

Roger C. Parker
Version 5.1 Revisions by Robert W. Harris

VENTANA PRESS

Desktop Publishing With WordPerfect For 5.0 and 5.1

Library of Congress Cataloging-in-Publication Data
Parker, Roger C.
Desktop publishing with WordPerfect: For 5.0 and 5.1 / Roger C. Parker, --2nd ed.
p. cm.-- (Ventana Press desktop design series)
ISBN 0-940087-47-2
1. Desktop publishing. 2. WordPerfect (Computer program)
I. Title. II. Series.
Z286.D47P34 1990
686.2'2544536--c20 90-34751
CIP

Cover design: Holly Russell, Chapel Hill, NC

Book design: Karen Wysocki, Ventana Press

Desktop publishing: Laser Image Corporate Publishing, Durham, NC

Linotronic output: Azalea Typography, Durham, NC

Technical Editor: Robert W. Harris, Durham, NC

Editorial Staff: Marion Laird, Terry Patrickis, Jeff Qualls, Elizabeth Shoemaker

Second Edition, Sixth Printing

Printed in the United States of America

Ventana Press, Inc.
P.O. Box 2468
Chapel Hill, NC 27515
919/942-0220
919/942-1140 Fax

AUTHOR'S ACKNOWLEDGMENTS

I used to think that Acknowledgments were an empty formality. But that's not so. *Desktop Publishing with WordPerfect* proves, once again, that books are the result of a team effort. It takes more than an author to bring a book to life. *Desktop Publishing with WordPerfect* simply would not have happened without the encouragement and support of Andy Bangs, Larry Daywitt, Bill Gladstone, William McKinley and—most important—Jeff Sandine.

I'd also like to thank Elizabeth Woodman for her uncanny ability to read between the lines of my manuscript and intuitively understand what I was struggling to say. Hats off, also, to Karen Wysocki who refined my vision of what *Desktop Publishing with WordPerfect* should look like and gave it life.

The real heroes of this book, of course, are my wife, Betsy, and my children—Christopher, Zachary and Ryan—who frequently put up with an absentee husband and father in order to allow me to "write without guilt" till sunrise.

Thanks also to WordPerfect's unparalleled Customer Support Group, who always answered my questions with patience, enthusiasm and tact.

The publisher wishes to express appreciation to the following individuals who assisted in the production of this book:

Jeff Acerson, Robert Harris, Rebecca Mortenson, Cheryl Shelly and Richard Wilkes.

TRADEMARKS

ABOUT THE AUTHOR

Roger C. Parker is owner and president of The Write Word, Inc., an advertising and marketing consulting firm based in Dover, NH. He is the author of *Looking Good in Print: A Guide to Basic Design for Desktop Publishing, The Makeover Book: 101 Design Solutions for Desktop Publishing,* and *Newsletters from the Desktop: Designing Effective Publications with Your Computer*, all published by Ventana Press. He also wrote *The Aldus Guide to Basic Design* (Aldus). His clients include Apple Computer, Aldus, Bitstream, Hewlett-Packard, Microrim and Yamaha.

The author may be reached at

The Write Word, Inc.
466 Central Avenue, #3
Dover, NH 03820
603/742-9673

CONTENTS

INTRODUCTION

With the introduction of WordPerfect's powerful new Version 5.1, word processing will never be the same. While traditional word processing changed the way you organize and generate information, WordPerfect changes the way you present it by integrating desktop publishing features into its program.

You now can produce professional-looking printed materials.

Compare this: with this:

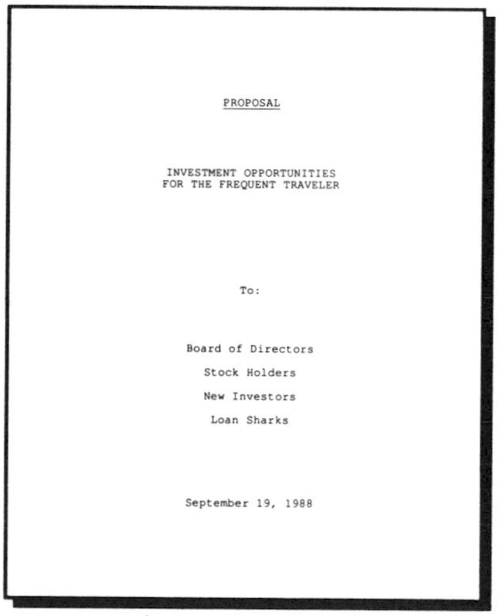

PROPOSAL

INVESTMENT OPPORTUNITIES
FOR THE FREQUENT TRAVELER

To:

Board of Directors

Stock Holders

New Investors

Loan Sharks

September 19, 1988

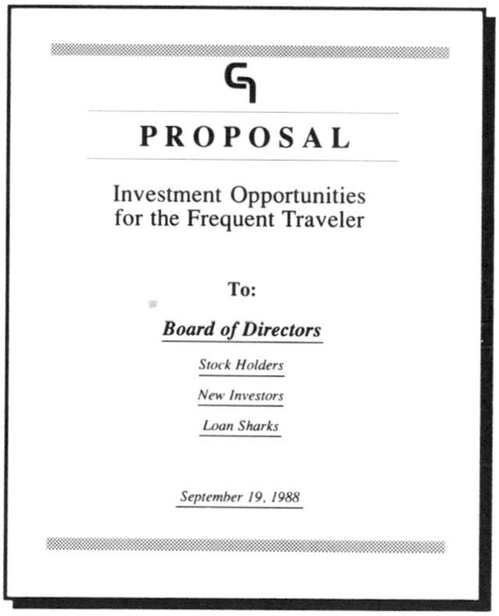

PROPOSAL

Investment Opportunities
for the Frequent Traveler

To:

Board of Directors

Stock Holders

New Investors

Loan Sharks

September 19, 1988

WordPerfect removes the barriers between writing and page layout—the arrangement of copy on a page. Once the domain of graphic artists and designers, the appearance of the printed page is now in your control.

Your documents can feature

- Multiple typefaces, type sizes and type styles.
- Graphic elements such as rules, boxes, reverses and screens.
- Charts, graphs, illustrations and other artwork—even scanned photographs created with other software programs!

Everyone wants their printed materials to be as attractive and persuasive as possible—and WordPerfect's flexible graphics features are a natural extension of its powerful word processing capabilities.

Why Your Documents Should Look Their Best

Professional-looking printed materials, built around a carefully chosen selection of typefaces and type sizes, are easier to read. Readers grasp your message more quickly and give more credibility to what you say.

In addition, multiple-column documents, which use a variety of type sizes, often are more cost-effective because they accommodate more type and thus require fewer pages. Finally, raw information takes on new meaning and is greatly enhanced when translated into charts and graphs.

Without getting in your way, WordPerfect makes it easy to place words on a page as effectively and efficiently as possible, making your printed materials more persuasive, more attractive and easier to read.

Who Should Read This Book?

Who will really benefit from these desktop publishing features? If you create proposals, newsletters, brochures, books, training manuals or other projects where the success of your communications is based on clarity, consistency and readability, WordPerfect can provide the solution to many of your design needs. And *Desktop Publishing with WordPerfect* shows you how to use these features to make your documents look their best. Enhancing the appearance of your printed materials has never been so easy or cost-effective.

Veteran and new users may find that WordPerfect's new graphic features eliminate the need to purchase a more expensive desktop publishing program. By integrating page layout capabilities with word processing, WordPerfect eliminates the need to invest time learning a second program in order to enhance the appearance of your documents.

In addition, WordPerfect eliminates time-consuming file transfers between word processing and page layout programs when you're designing a document. With WordPerfect you can format and design your document while entering text.

However, if your job involves designing sophisticated, single-page projects, such as posters or complicated magazine advertisements, WordPerfect isn't a substitute for dedicated page layout programs. Art directors and graphic designers may become frustrated by its lack of typographic niceties. In other words, WordPerfect offers the capabilities necessary for producing all but the most design-intensive projects.

In short, WordPerfect gives word processing a new respectability. No longer must documents generated via word processing be monotonous in appearance. With its desktop publishing capabilities, WordPerfect can generate documents that present a professional image to your clients, customers and readers.

WordPerfect Versions

Many people now use the newest WordPerfect software, Version 5.1. But other users have decided to stay with Version 5.0 for a while longer because it still meets their needs. So to accommodate the widest audience, *Desktop Publishing with WordPerfect* is written for users of both versions. The descriptions and instructions in the book are the same for Versions 5.0 and 5.1, except as noted in the text.

If you're still using WordPerfect 5.0, you may be considering upgrading to the newer program. Version 5.0 introduced desktop publishing features to WordPerfect users; but Version 5.1 includes some useful new features, such as pull-down menus, mouse support, control over leading and more flexible table construction.

Whether you upgrade to 5.1 or stay with 5.0, *Desktop Publishing with WordPerfect* will guide you through the features that will help you produce effective printed materials.

What's Inside

Desktop Publishing with WordPerfect teaches you how to use WordPerfect 5.0 and 5.1 to produce better-looking documents that reflect well on you and your business.

Section One, "Mastering the Printed Page," will help you become acquainted with WordPerfect's desktop publishing features. You'll learn how to add graphic elements (such as rules, boxes and screens), work with multiple columns and use stylesheets to speed up page formatting. You'll also learn how to integrate illustrations (graphics files) created with other programs, as well as make the most of the various typeface options available with your laser printer.

Section Two, "Design Tips and Tricks," puts the basics you learned in the first section to work, providing numerous examples of basic graphic design skills needed to produce attractive, persuasive documents.

How to Use This Book

If you're not familiar with WordPerfect's desktop publishing features, read Section One carefully, particularly Chapters 1 through 6. More advanced users will want to read Chapters 7 and 8, which cover macros and stylesheets.

If you already know about WordPerfect's graphics capabilities, you may want to review Section One quickly and concentrate on Section Two, which offers invaluable tips and techniques for creating specific types of documents using WordPerfect.

Use this book as a work tool, tagging pages and making notes. You'll want to refer to key passages repeatedly as you encounter similar design challenges with your various projects.

How Well Should You Know WordPerfect?

Desktop Publishing with WordPerfect was written to complement WordPerfect's program documentation, not as a substitute for it. You should already know the basic WordPerfect commands, such as how to

- Enter, delete and move text.
- Print, retrieve and save files.
- Format text, create line spacing, and add headers, footers and page numbers.

This book was written with the assumption that your computer and printer are up and running, that you're comfortable with WordPerfect as a word processing program and, finally, that you're ready to forge ahead, learning how to create better-looking documents.

Hardware/Software Requirements

Obviously, you must have a copy of WordPerfect Version 5.0 or 5.1; previous versions don't include desktop publishing features.

In most cases, WordPerfect doesn't require the purchase of additional hardware or software. Nor do you need an operating environment like Microsoft Windows.

However, WordPerfect's new features may provide the catalyst you need to upgrade your computer and printer. For example, because WordPerfect is a large, multi-disk program—and contains an even more comprehensive spelling checker and thesaurus—you'll find that a hard disk is a near-necessity. If you don't have one, now would be an excellent time to add one, thereby avoiding tedious "floppy-swapping."

Likewise, if you don't have a laser printer, you may want to consider this worthwhile investment. If you already have one, you'll probably find that now is the time to increase the number of fonts (type families) you have available.

Whether you choose font cartridges or downloadable disk-based fonts, the ease with which WordPerfect handles fonts lets you add many new design elements to your documents.

Font cartridges (plug-in circuit boards designed for certain brands of laser printers) contain a specific number of typefaces, type sizes and type styles. They're the easiest and least expensive way to add visual variety to your publication.

Downloadable fonts—or "soft" fonts—are alphabet and number sets on floppy disks that you transfer to your hard disk. Downloadable fonts offer the most flexibility, giving you a virtually unlimited choice of typefaces, type sizes and type styles. WordPerfect has a unique "font-swapping" feature that preserves printer memory and lets you include up to 250 typefaces, type sizes and type styles on a single page.

If you're using WordPerfect 5.1, you may want to consider purchasing a mouse. This device makes it easier to select commands, block text, move the cursor and perform other routine tasks. A mouse is a good investment because it can also be used as an input device in a wide variety of software, including drawing programs.

WordPerfect's ability to smoothly integrate graphics files may motivate you to round out your software programs with additional chart, graphics or drawing programs. You may even want to invest in your own image scanner.

Because WordPerfect now does so much, you might find it worthwhile to upgrade your monitor and enjoy a clearer on-screen representation of your page layouts.

The money you save because you won't have to buy page layout software may allow you to buy many of these important enhancements that can save time and greatly improve your finished documents. If you're serious about improving the look of your printed materials, I strongly recommend that you invest in the tools that will make your job easier—and less expensive in the long run.

All Aboard

Version 5.0 or 5.1 and *Desktop Publishing with WordPerfect* provide the tools you need to savor the creative design and page layout features of one of the world's most advanced word processing programs.

Eventually, WordPerfect will introduce new, improved versions that will do the job even better—integrating word processing and page layout functions more easily and less expensively. However, don't succumb to the "I'll-wait-for-the-next-train" syndrome. Those who wait will have a harder time catching up than those who are already on board.

By learning WordPerfect's desktop publishing features now, you'll be better able to take advantage of future upgrades. While those on the platform are waiting to catch up, you'll be that much farther down the track.

Roger C. Parker
Dover, New Hampshire

SECTION ONE

MASTERING THE PRINTED PAGE

CHAPTER 1

GETTING STARTED

Producing professional-looking documents was once a tedious and expensive process, involving many different steps and missed deadlines. Revisions and last-minute changes were costly and often resulted in further delays. And managing all of it could transform you overnight into a candidate for an Excedrin commercial.

But now, desktop publishing is an inexpensive alternative to the traditional methods of document production. Desktop publishing is the activity of creating near-typeset quality printed materials in your own office. By using a laser printer and sophisticated word processing software, you can produce attractive, persuasive documents that convey a professional image.

WordPerfect's new desktop publishing features let you incorporate basic graphic design techniques into your newsletters, brochures, training books and other printed materials. You now have the power at your fingertips to perform such sophisticated formatting functions as creating multiple columns, choosing from a variety of typefaces, drawing lines and boxes, using graphics and more.

Before you plunge into the details involved in creating camera-ready documents (material you send to the printer) with WordPerfect, let's look at the features and enhancements that give WordPerfect its desktop publishing capabilities.

Previewing the Printed Page

WordPerfect's VIEW DOCUMENT command [SHIFT-F7, 6] takes the guessing game out of formatting (or designing the page layout of) your publication. VIEW DOCUMENT lets you preview on your computer screen how your advertisement, brochure or newsletter will look when it's printed.

You can evaluate your publication at three different levels of magnification, giving you the option of seeing the overall appearance of the page or focusing on smaller, selected areas in greater detail.

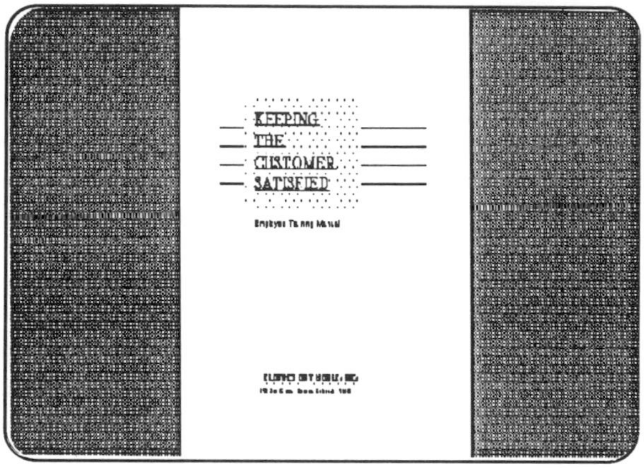

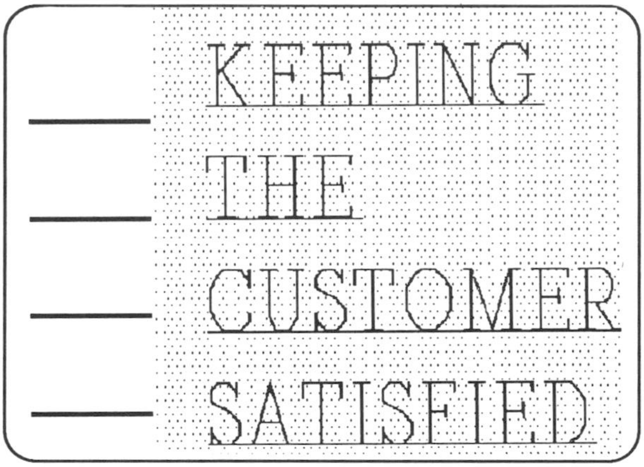

You can even view facing left- and right-hand pages—known as "spreads."

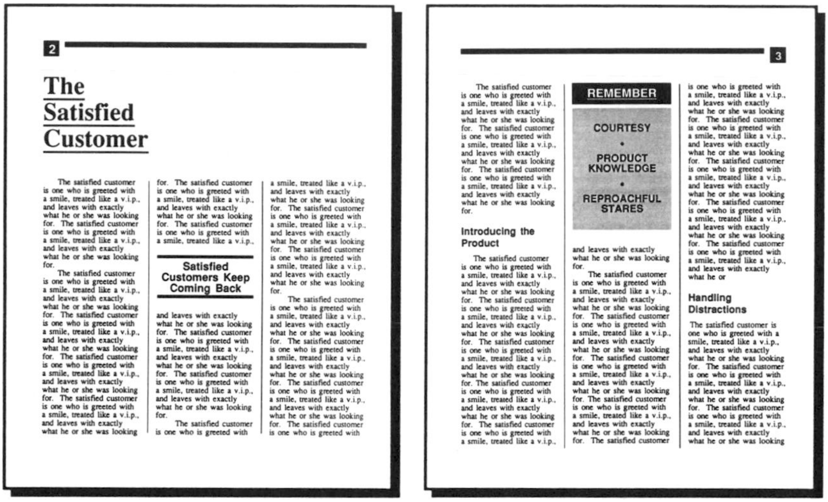

Because readers rarely encounter just one page at a time, the ability to look at spreads is an extremely important feature. WordPerfect's facing-pages feature helps ensure that left- and right-hand pages don't "fight" each other when viewed side by side.

Looking at WordPerfect's Codes

One of WordPerfect's most popular features has been its "clean screen." Your words, and only your words, are visible on the screen. Formatting codes are hidden in the background and become visible only when you activate the REVEAL CODES command [ALT-F3].

By using REVEAL CODES, you can see at a glance which typeface and type size you're using, and whether you're using boldface or italic type. If you have a color monitor, typeface and type attributes (features) become even more visible.

In WordPerfect 5.1, you can change the size of the Codes window. So, if you want it to take up less of the editing screen, you can go into the [SHIFT-F1] (FORMAT) menu and then select 2 (DISPLAY), 6 (EDIT-SCREEN OPTIONS) and 6 (REVEAL CODES WINDOW SIZE). Then you can enter the number of lines you want displayed.

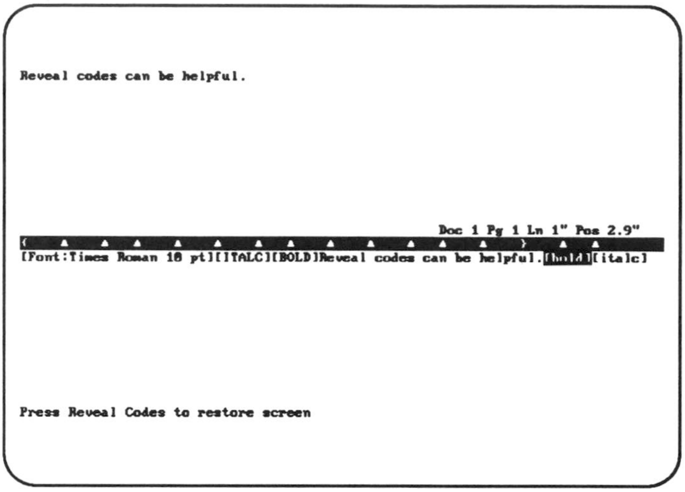

In earlier versions of WordPerfect, you couldn't edit (change) these codes while they were visible on your screen. WordPerfect now lets you edit while in REVEAL CODES mode, which simplifies formatting documents.

If you add the Hercules RamFont card (described in Appendix B), you can actually see accurate representations of the various type attributes as you apply them!

Using Rules and Boxes

WordPerfect allows you to add rules—or lines—and boxes of any length and width anywhere on the page.

Rules and boxes are the basic building blocks of graphic design. They let you organize the various sections—or departments—of your publication in an attractive, logical way. They also add to the visual appeal of your publication, help readers separate one feature from another and emphasize important ideas.

For example, WordPerfect makes it easy to add pull-quotes to your publication. Pull-quotes are short excerpts that summarize adjacent body copy and are usually set in large type inside boxes.

You also can add sidebars—short features set in boxes that elaborate on or relate to adjacent text. Depending upon the printer you use, you can even create boxes containing reversed headlines—white type on a black or screened background.

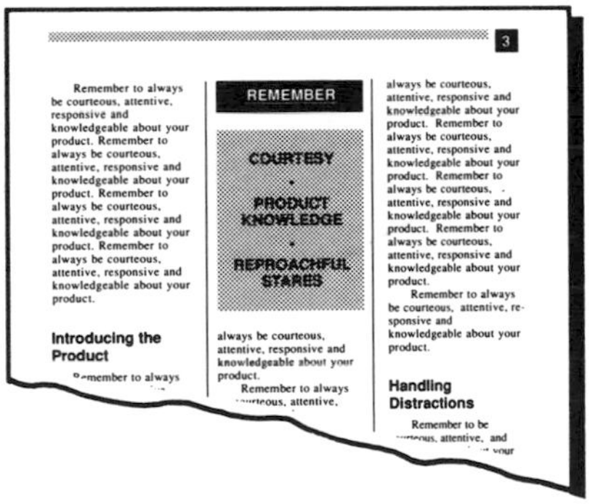

Adding Graphics to Your Documents

WordPerfect makes it easy to add—or import—charts, graphs and illustrations previously created with specialized drawing or image-scanning programs.

You can even place scanned photographs in your publications.

After graphics have been added, they can be made larger or smaller. In addition, you can distort them by increasing their height relative to their width, or vice versa.

Important parts of an imported graphics file can be emphasized by cropping—moving the chart or illustration within its environment to eliminate unimportant elements.

You can rotate text or graphics files created with other software programs. For example, to create a special effect, you can place the masthead of your newsletter vertically on the page.

Anchoring Graphics to Text

With WordPerfect, you can anchor charts, graphs, illustrations, scanned photographs or selected text to either a page position, an adjoining paragraph or a character.

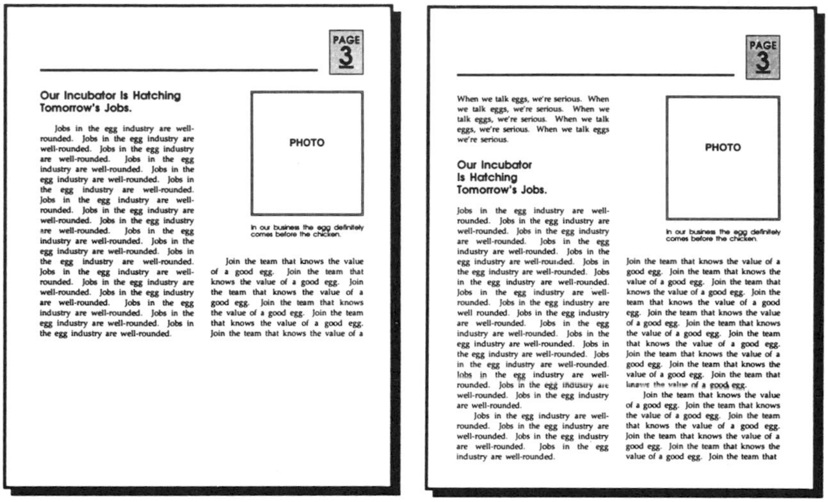

An illustration, for example, can be anchored to the upper right-hand corner of a page and will remain there, regardless of how much adjoining text is added, deleted or edited.

Alternately, the illustration can be anchored to a specific paragraph. The illustration then "floats" with the paragraph. If preceding text is deleted, the illustration is pulled toward the beginning of the publication. If text is added, the illustration is "pushed along" with the paragraph. By anchoring a graphic to a specific paragraph, the graphic is always located next to the body copy it illustrates.

Locking Captions with Graphics

Just as you can anchor graphics with text, WordPerfect lets you permanently link captions with the charts, graphs, illustrations or scanned photographs they describe. This technique speeds up your work and makes it difficult for an illustration and its caption to become "lost." All captions automatically are placed in the same position relative to the graphic. You can put captions above or below the illustrations and align them with either the left- or right-hand borders, etc.

In addition, WordPerfect helps you create good-looking documents by automatically maintaining consistent spacing between captions and the charts, graphs, illustrations or photographs they describe. Readers are extremely sensitive to slight differences in spacing. Consistent spacing helps your publication look better and boosts readers' confidence in your message or product.

Furthermore, whenever you move a chart, graph, illustration or scanned photograph, its caption automatically moves to the new location.

Manipulating Text Around Graphics

Text can be wrapped around or placed on top of charts, graphs, illustrations and scanned photographs. This technique further enhances your ability to create a distinct visual identity for your advertisement, brochure, newsletter, proposal or report.

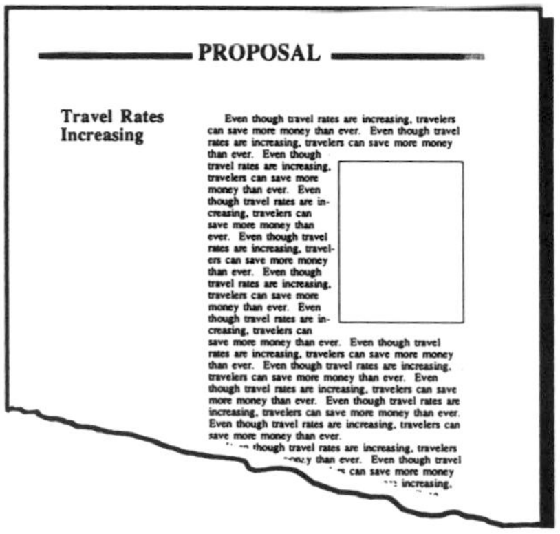

Automatic text wrap means that the lines of type become shorter if they encounter a chart, graph or illustration. These lines are readjusted if you add or delete preceding text.

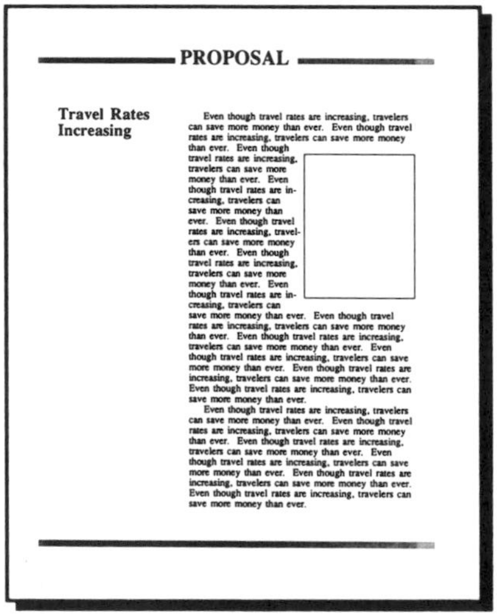

However, WordPerfect also gives you the option of superimposing text on top of an illustration or scanned photograph. This technique is useful when you're creating the cover of a brochure or adding explanations to illustrations in a training manual.

Borders and White Space

You can frame charts, graphs, illustrations, scanned photographs and text boxes with borders and white space.

Borders can be used to give your publication a distinct identity—appropriate for its overall purpose, as well as its design. Charts, graphs, illustrations and photographs can be surrounded by a wide choice of thick or thin lines, 100 percent black or screened to various shades of gray. You can even create dashed lines—useful for coupons.

Enhanced Laser Printer Support

WordPerfect was one of the first word processing programs to take full advantage of the flexibility offered by laser printers. Laser printers form the basis of desktop publishing, allowing you to attain a quality of document previously associated only with expensive professional typesetting.

In the past, you could create truly professional-looking documents only by using a daisywheel printer. Daisywheel printers use a technology similar to that of an IBM Selectric typewriter. Each typeface comes on its own daisywheel. When you want to change typeface or type size, you physically have to remove the daisywheel and insert another, just as you would a type element in a Selectric.

Laser printers operate on an entirely different principle. Instead of using a mechanical (and often noisy) process of hitting the outline of each letter or number and having it create an image through a ribbon onto the paper, laser printers quietly create letters, numbers and symbols using a technology similar to that of office copiers. Letters, numbers and graphic images are created using dots so small that it takes 300 of them to make an inch.

Each laser printer has various type and graphics capabilities. Accessing them, however, often has been a time-consuming and tedious experience.

With WordPerfect 5.0 and 5.1, all available typeface, type size and type style alternatives are shown (in English) on your computer screen as you prepare your project.

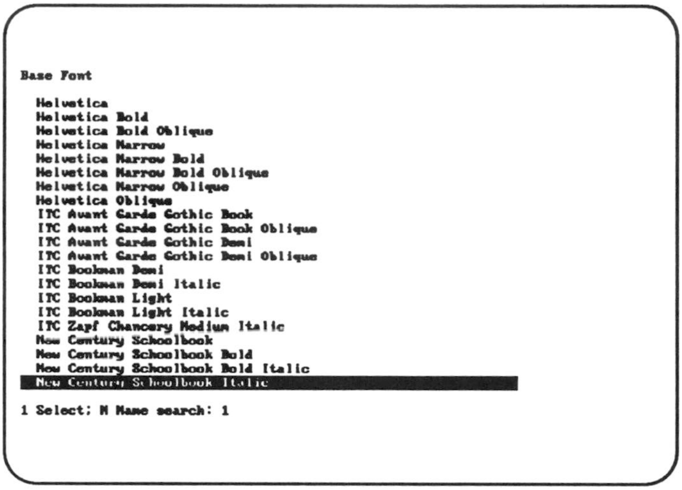

No longer must you deal with arcane codes or strange abbreviations. You can choose the particular characteristics by scrolling down the screen until the selection you want is highlighted. WordPerfect thus makes it easy to incorporate a variety of typefaces, type sizes and type styles into your document.

Typographic Refinements

WordPerfect offers precise control of letter and word spacing—both necessary tools for creating good-looking advertisements, brochures and newsletters.

A special ADVANCED PRINTER FUNCTIONS command allows you to kern (adjust spacing between individual pairs of letters), thus creating words out of isolated letters. Particularly important in designing headlines, kerning improves the appearance of large type and makes it easier to read.

AWAY
AWAY

With WordPerfect, you can expand or contract word and letter spacing throughout a document to influence the color of your page. Adding extra letter and word spacing opens up a document, making it easier to read.

Reducing letter and word spacing tightens a publication, increasing word density.

WordPerfect also lets you adjust line spacing, called leading, giving you more control over the vertical placement of type.

Leading is extremely important in creating high-impact headlines. If leading isn't modified, the lines of a headline often are spaced unnaturally. With reduced line spacing, the headlines appear as strong, bold units, surrounded and emphasized by plenty of white space.

Type Alignment Alternatives

With WordPerfect, type can be placed on a page in four ways.

Flush-left/ragged-right text (in which the left-hand margin of type is aligned) often is used to create contemporary, open documents. Words are spaced equally on each line, creating a ragged right-hand margin. Flush-left/ragged-right type is used for both headlines and body copy.

LIFESTYLE

Home Delivery Goes to the Dogs

Keep your dog happy with a constant supply of dog food, delivered to his door. Keep your dog happy with a constant supply of dog food, delivered to his door. Keep your dog happy with a constant supply of dog food, delivered to his door. Keep your dog happy with a constant supply of dog food, delivered to his door. Keep your dog happy with a constant supply of dog food, delivered to his door. Keep your dog happy with a constant supply of dog food, delivered to his door.

Keep your dog happy with a constant supply of dog food, delivered to his door. Keep your dog happy with a constant supply of dog food, delivered to his door. Keep your dog happy with a constant supply of dog food, delivered to his door. Keep your dog happy with a constant supply of dog food, delivered to his door. Keep your dog happy with a constant supply of dog food, delivered to his door. Keep your dog happy with a constant supply of dog food, delivered to his door. Keep your dog happy with a constant supply of dog food, delivered to his door. Keep your dog happy

Pet Food at Your Doorstep

with a constant supply of dog food, delivered to his door. Keep your dog happy with a constant supply of dog food, delivered to his door. Keep your dog happy with a constant supply of dog food, delivered to his door. Keep your dog happy with a constant supply of dog food, delivered to his door. Keep your dog happy with a constant supply of dog food, delivered to his door. Keep your dog happy with a constant supply of dog food, delivered to his door. Keep your dog happy

Centered type often is used for headlines. Equal amounts of white space appear before and after each line.

Flush-right type (in which only the right-hand margin of type is aligned) often is used in multicolumn documents to align subheads next to the body copy they introduce.

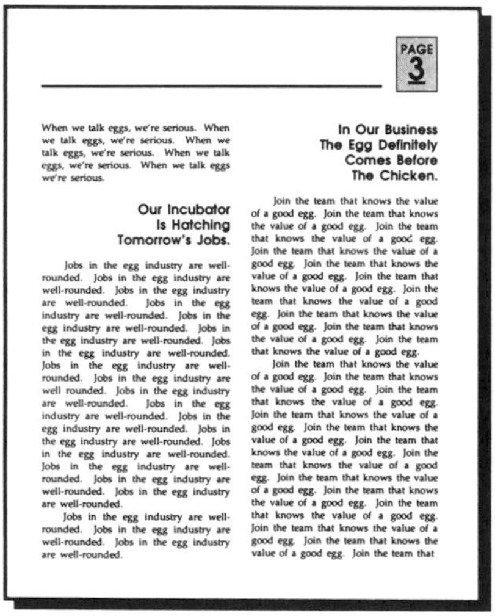

Flush-right type also is used in lists. In the example below, flush-right type makes it easy for readers to relate a job title to an individual's name.

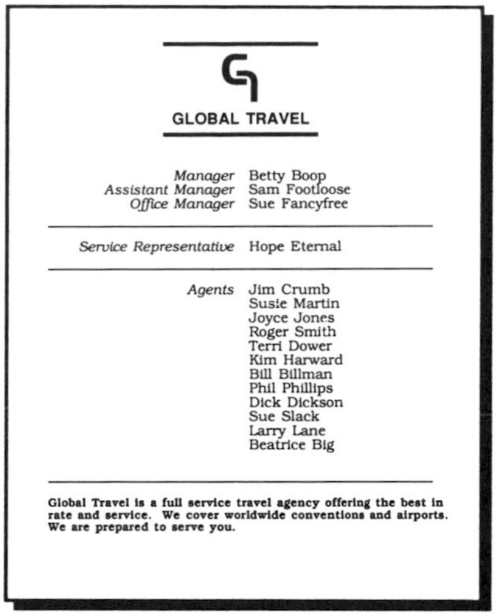

GLOBAL TRAVEL

Manager Betty Boop
Assistant Manager Sam Footloose
Office Manager Sue Fancyfree

Service Representative Hope Eternal

Agents Jim Crumb
Susie Martin
Joyce Jones
Roger Smith
Terri Dower
Kim Harward
Bill Billman
Phil Phillips
Dick Dickson
Sue Slack
Larry Lane
Beatrice Big

Global Travel is a full service travel agency offering the best in rate and service. We cover worldwide conventions and airports. We are prepared to serve you.

Justified text is WordPerfect's default setting. It occurs when all lines of text are the same length, with both the right and left margins aligned. In order to create lines of equal length, WordPerfect subtly adds or reduces word spacing within the line.

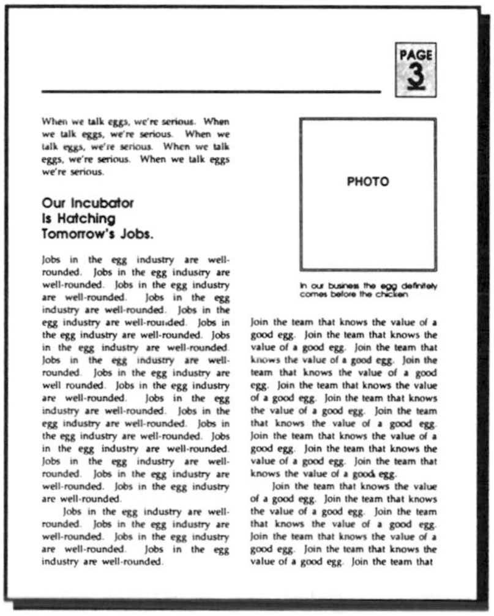

PAGE 3

When we talk eggs, we're serious. When we talk eggs, we're serious. When we talk eggs, we're serious. When we talk eggs, we're serious. When we talk eggs we're serious.

Our Incubator Is Hatching Tomorrow's Jobs.

Jobs in the egg industry are well-rounded. Jobs in the egg industry are well-rounded. Jobs in the egg industry are well-rounded. Jobs in the egg industry are well-rounded. Jobs in the egg industry are well-rounded. Jobs in the egg industry are well-rounded. Jobs in the egg industry are well-rounded. Jobs in the egg industry are well-rounded. Jobs in the egg industry are well rounded. Jobs in the egg industry are well-rounded. Jobs in the egg industry are well-rounded. Jobs in the egg industry are well-rounded. Jobs in the egg industry are well-rounded. Jobs in the egg industry are well-rounded. Jobs in the egg industry are well-rounded. Jobs in the egg industry are well-rounded. Jobs in the egg industry are well-rounded.

Jobs in the egg industry are well-rounded. Jobs in the egg industry are well-rounded. Jobs in the egg industry are well-rounded. Jobs in the egg industry are well-rounded.

PHOTO

In our business the egg definitely comes before the chicken

Join the team that knows the value of a good egg. Join the team that knows the value of a good egg. Join the team that knows the value of a good egg. Join the team that knows the value of a good egg. Join the team that knows the value of a good egg. Join the team that knows the value of a good egg. Join the team that knows the value of a good egg. Join the team that knows the value of a good egg. Join the team that knows the value of a good egg.

Join the team that knows the value of a good egg. Join the team that knows the value of a good egg. Join the team that knows the value of a good egg. Join the team that knows the value of a good egg. Join the team that knows the value of a good egg. Join the team that

Shading and Reversing Type

Text can be reversed, screened or—depending upon your printer—printed in color.

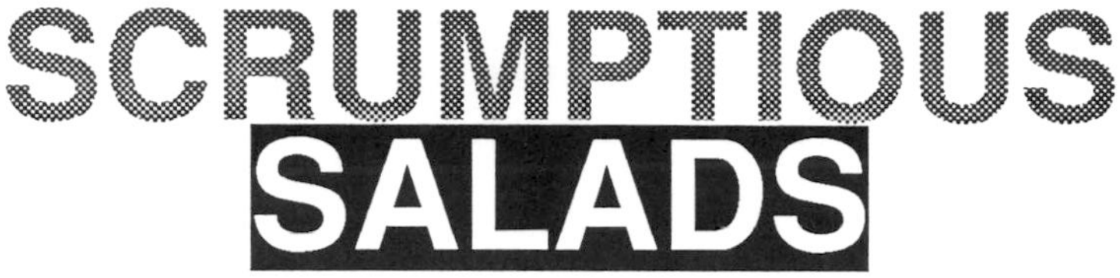

With an appropriate printer, WordPerfect lets you reverse headlines or departmental dividers, setting words in white against a black background.

WordPerfect's text-shading feature lets you achieve two-color effects at a one-color printing price. Brochure headlines, newsletter mastheads or departmental dividers within a book or training manual can be printed in various shades of gray, instead of 100 percent black.

In addition, WordPerfect is ready for the next generation of printers, now beginning to appear on the market. When these become competitively priced, you'll be able to precisely mix the ink colors used for text, rules and boxes.

Formatting with Macros and Styles

WordPerfect's advanced macros and styles simplify formatting and reformatting documents.

For instance, WordPerfect's STYLE feature lets you assign in a single keystroke a specified typeface, type size, style and alignment for headlines and text.

When you access the STYLE command, all available styles are displayed, accompanied by a brief description of their intended application. You scroll down the list and select a style.

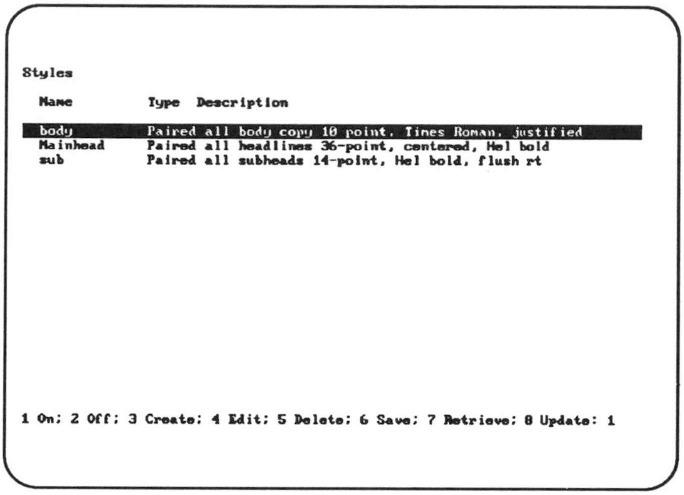
Styles
Name Type Description
body Paired all body copy 10 point, Times Roman, justified
Mainhead Paired all headlines 36-point, centered, Hel bold
sub Paired all subheads 14-point, Hel bold, flush rt
1 On; 2 Off; 3 Create; 4 Edit; 5 Delete; 6 Save; 7 Retrieve; 8 Update: 1

For example, you might want all headlines set in 36-point, centered, boldface Helvetica type, with reduced leading. You could store this setup as a STYLE called MAINHEAD.

ATTENTION!

For subheads, however, you might choose 14-point, Helvetica Bold Italics, flush-right, with slightly reduced line spacing. Those decisions could be stored as a STYLE called SUB.

CREATING GREAT HEADLINES HAS NEVER BEEN EASIER

Body copy, however, might be set in 10-point Times Roman type, with lines of equal length (justified). That could be saved as a STYLE identified simply as BODY.

WordPerfect styles can be applied at any point—while you write or edit, or later, after content has been finalized during the formatting stage.

WordPerfect's macros go even further, letting you repeat page layouts, including column alignments and graphic accents, such as rules, boxes and screens. Newsletter publishers, in particular, frequently use Word-Perfect's macro capability.

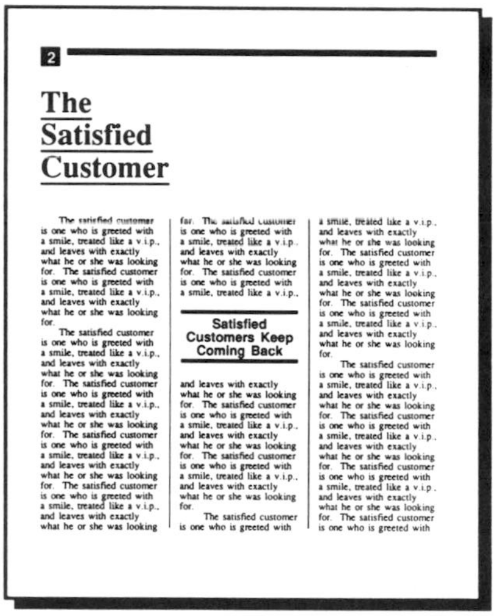

WordPerfect's MACRO feature lets you quickly switch between a two- and three-column format, or turn off the column feature entirely to create headlines that span two or more columns. Macros also allow you to force white space between the top and bottom borders of a page, and add borders or publication information (e.g., page numbers and dates).

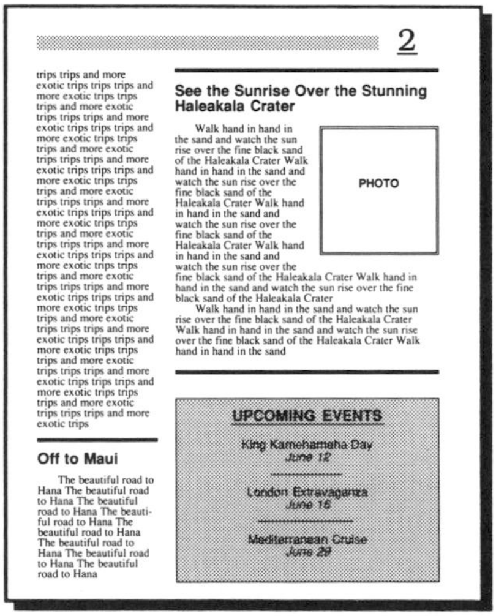

Macros simplify the process of creating screened boxes for sidebars or features, such as a table of contents or a calendar of upcoming events.

UPCOMING EVENTS

King Kamehameha Day
June 12

London Extravaganza
June 16

Mediterranean Cruise
June 29

Organizing Your Documents

WordPerfect goes far beyond most desktop publishing programs by offering highly sophisticated document organizing abilities. It automatically generates a table of contents, index and as many as ten different categories of lists.

You'll appreciate this power if you produce long documents, such as books, software documentation or training manuals.

WordPerfect can perform in seconds, and with great accuracy, organizational functions that normally would involve hours (if not days) of tedious work.

Eliminating Spelling Errors

WordPerfect's built-in spelling checker gives it a strong advantage as a desktop publishing program. Most dedicated page layout programs assume you're working with error-free text. They don't allow you to check the spelling of headlines, captions or text revisions that might have escaped a proofreader's scrutiny. As a result, typographic errors can show up in your published document.

WordPerfect's spelling checker eliminates that risk, giving you the capability of checking the spelling in your document at any point before you print it out.

Selecting Commands

Each WordPerfect command listed in a menu is paired with a number. To select an option like 1 (SIZE) from the FORMAT menu, you could type 1. But each command also has one letter that's highlighted, and you can select the command by typing that letter. So to select 1 (SIZE), you could type S. The highlighted letter is usually the initial letter of the command.

WordPerfect 5.1 provides yet another way to select commands. In addition to the usual command menus, the newest version of the program also features pull-down menus. Using your mouse, you can select a command simply by pointing and clicking. Although most useful when you're using a mouse, pull-down menus can also be accessed by pressing the [ALT] and [=] (equal) keys together.

Creating a Nonsense File

Before you begin to explore WordPerfect's desktop publishing power, you may want to create a simple, unformatted file to call up when you want to experiment with various page layout and text manipulation capabilities.

To create this multi-page "nonsense" file,

Type: The quick brown fox jumped over the lazy dog. The quick brown fox jumped over the lazy dog. The quick brown fox jumped over the lazy dog. The quick brown fox jumped over the lazy dog. The quick brown fox jumped over the lazy dog. The quick brown fox jumped over the lazy dog. The quick brown fox jumped over the lazy dog.

Press: (ENTER)

Press: (HOME) (HOME) Up cursor control key

That brings you to the beginning of the document.

Press: (ALT-F4) (HIGHLIGHT)

Press: (HOME) (HOME) Down cursor control key

That brings you down to the end of the document.

Press: (CTRL-F4) (MOVE)

Select: 1 (BLOCK)

Select: 2 (COPY)

Press: (ENTER)

That adds another copy of the text to your cursor location.

Repeat this process several times. Notice how you block and save twice as much text each time. Your file quickly grows. Continue until you've created two or three pages of text. Then, save the file.

Press: (F10) (SAVE)

Response: Document to be saved:

Type: AANONSEN

Press: (ENTER)

The "AA" prefix for the file name places the file at the top of your WordPerfect subdirectory when you use the LIST FILES command [F5]. That way you won't have to scroll through numerous files each time you want to load your "nonsense" file.

You now have a large, easy-to-find text file that you can use over and over again as you create different page layouts and explore WordPerfect's various typeface, type size and type style alternatives.

Moving On

In this chapter, you've been introduced to just a few of WordPerfect's new features that make it possible to create good-looking, easy-to-read documents. When you add those advantages to WordPerfect's already highly advanced and fast word-processing capabilities, you have a powerful work tool that will improve both the quality and speed with which you generate your print communications.

In the chapters that follow, you'll learn how to put WordPerfect's desktop publishing features to work, creating professional-looking advertisements, books, brochures, newsletters and training materials.

CHAPTER 2

BASIC DESKTOP PUBLISHING FEATURES

To begin your investigation of WordPerfect's desktop publishing capabilities, it's important to learn how easy it is to enhance the appearance of your documents by adding rules and boxes. Two of the most fundamental building blocks of graphic design, rules and boxes are likely to be often-repeated elements in your page layout, regardless of whether you're working on an advertisement, brochure, newsletter, book or training manual.

You'll also learn how WordPerfect's macro capabilities can expedite the placement of those graphics in your documents.

You can preview how those design elements look on the printed page by using WordPerfect's VIEW DOCUMENT feature. Let's start by exploring VIEW DOCUMENT. You'll then be able to see the fruits of your efforts as you create rules and boxes later in this chapter.

Previewing Finished Pages Before Printing

One of WordPerfect's virtues has always been its "clean" screen, which lets you concentrate on writing and editing. However, as you begin working with page layouts, you may want to preview how your finished page—complete with rules, boxes and imported graphics—will look when it's printed.

To do that, open an existing file that contains two or more pages. (When experimenting with WordPerfect, you may want to use the "nonsense" file described in Chapter 1.) Then,

Press: (SHIFT-F7) (PRINT)

Select: 6 (VIEW DOCUMENT)

Response: You'll see a reduced-size version of the finished page. Image detail is determined by the type of monitor you use. High-resolution monitors with VGA cards provide the most accurate displays.

WordPerfect lets you view your document at three different levels of magnification, as outlined below.

Select: 1 (100%)

This offers a view that's nearly the actual size of a portion of the page. Because the entire page is too large to be reproduced on your computer screen, you can move around the page by using the left/right/up/down cursor control keys. In addition, you can advance vertically through the document one screen at a time using the - or + cursor control keys.

Select: 2 (200%)

This provides a more detailed, close-up view of a smaller portion of the page. Again, you can move around, focusing on different parts of the page by using the left/right, up/down and - and + cursor control keys.

Select: 3 (FULL PAGE)

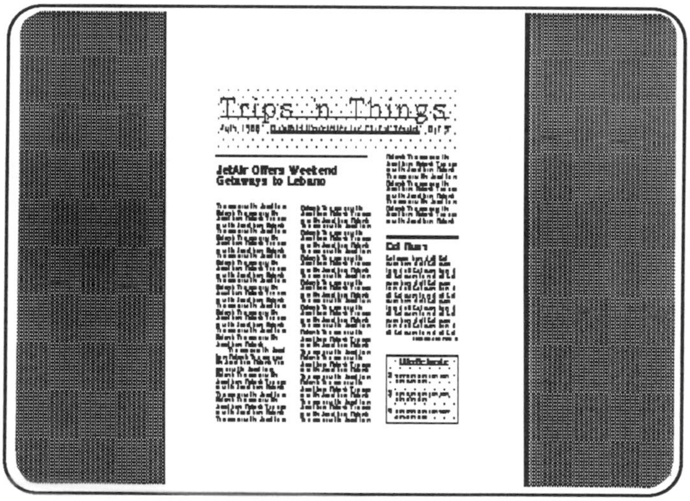

This provides a reduced, overall view of the full page, letting you review not only the placement of text and graphics, but the positioning of headers, footers and page numbers.

One of the most important rules in graphic design is to work in terms of two-page *spreads*. By doing so, you can avoid accidentally creating facing pages that "fight" each other. It's easy to design pages that look good by themselves, but look horrible when viewed side by side. WordPerfect's FACING PAGES feature helps you avoid that problem.

To move from Page 1 of your document to Pages 2 and 3 that face one another,

Press: (PAGE DOWN)

Select: 4 (FACING PAGES)

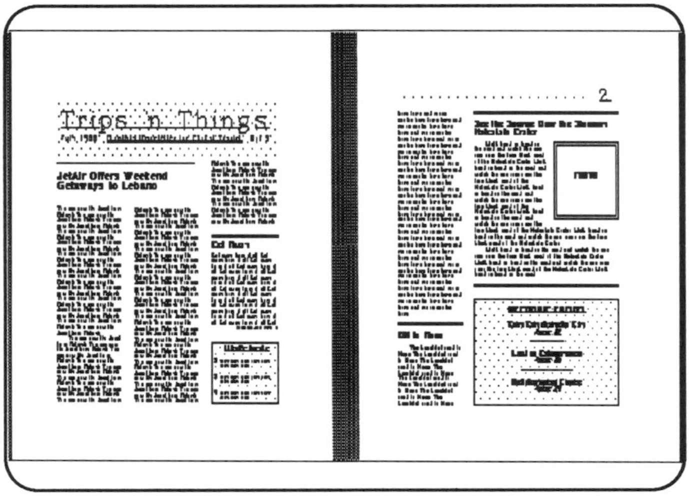

You now can view left- and right-hand pages side by side.

Moving Around a Page

When viewing your document at 100 or 200 percent magnification, you'll be able to see only a portion of the page, unless you're using a big-screen monitor. As previously explained, the up/down/ left/right cursor control keys, and the gray + and - keys let you view a different portion of the page.

A Few Shortcuts

You also can use WordPerfect's [HOME] key in conjunction with the cursor control keys to quickly change your view of different parts of a page. These keyboard sequences are useful when working at large screen magnifications (100 and 200 percent). For example, [HOME] [HOME] left cursor control key advances your screen view to the left-hand side of a page. In a similar fashion, [HOME] [HOME] right cursor control key advances your screen view to the right-hand side.

To quickly move toward the top of the page you're previewing, use [HOME] [HOME] -. Likewise, to advance to the bottom of the page, press [HOME] [HOME] +.

Viewing Different Pages

WordPerfect's VIEW DOCUMENT command offers two ways to scroll through multi-page documents, allowing you to see the progressive unfolding of your book, brochure, newsletter or training manual.

Press: (PAGE UP)

Response: This moves you to the previous page.

Press: (PAGE DOWN)

Response: This moves you to the next page.

You also can use WordPerfect's GO TO [CTRL-HOME] command, followed by entering the page number you want to view.

Press: (CTRL-HOME) (GO TO)

Response: Go To

Type: The page number you want to preview.

Press: (ENTER)

Note that WordPerfect's status line in the lower right corner of the screen always indicates the page number, or numbers, you're viewing.

You also can use WordPerfect's HOME command and cursor control keys to move quickly to the beginning or end of a document. To move to the end of a document,

Press: (HOME) (HOME) Down cursor control key

Response: You're moved to the end of your document.

Alternately, to move to the beginning of a document,

Press: (HOME) (HOME) Up cursor control key

Response: You're moved to the beginning of your document.

TIP: Remember that you cannot edit your document while in VIEW DOCUMENT; nor can you have both the REVEAL CODES and VIEW DOCUMENT functions operating simultaneously.

Exiting View Document

After previewing your work, press [F1] (CANCEL) to return to the PRINT menu. At that point, you'll probably choose one of the following three options:

1 (FULL DOCUMENT), if you want to print the entire document.

2 (PAGE), if you want to print just the page where your cursor is located.

5 (MULTIPLE PAGES), if you want to print several pages (available in Version 5.1).

[F1] (CANCEL) or [ENTER] to return to your document for continued text entry, editing or formatting.

Rules as Design Elements

Rules are lines of varying lengths, thicknesses and shading that serve many functions. They're used both to highlight important information as well as separate information. For example, the horizontal line under the headline on the next page strengthens and adds authority to the headline.

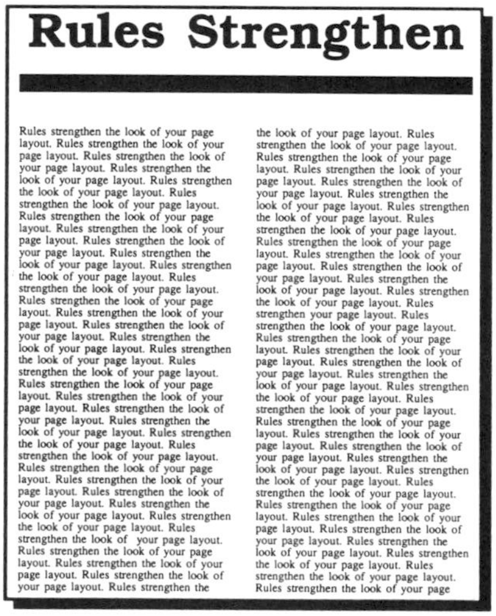

But, in the "Upcoming Events/Calendar" section of the following newsletter example, horizontal rules separate short topics from each other.

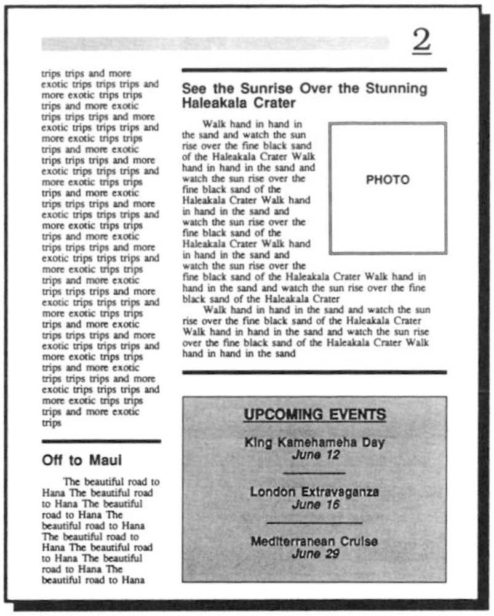

In newsletters and long documents, vertical rules often are used to separate columns.

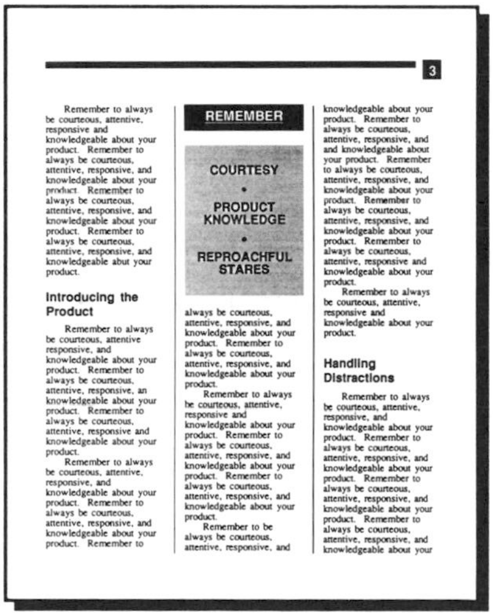

Horizontal and vertical rules of various lengths can also frame a page or an advertisement with attractive top, bottom and side borders.

WordPerfect makes it easy to add rules of varying lengths, thicknesses and shading to your documents. You can control where your rules are placed by using interactive menus that appear when you select the GRAPHICS command [ALT-F9]. By responding to the alternatives presented—for example, choosing 5 (LINE), followed by 1 (CREATE LINE: HORIZONTAL) or 2 (CREATE LINE: VERTICAL)—you easily can place a rule exactly where you want it.

Vertical Rules

WordPerfect makes it easy to add vertical lines to your documents. You can specify the placement, length, width and shading of these lines by simply choosing among the options presented to you after you select GRAPHICS LINE [ALT-F9, 5], followed by CREATE LINE: VERTICAL (Option 2).

Vertical lines easily can be drawn at any horizontal position on the page. Four options allow you to place the lines in the following locations:

1 LEFT (margin)

2 RIGHT (margin)

3 BETWEEN COLUMNS

4 SET POSITION

Option 4 (SET POSITION) lets you place lines by defining their position in inches from the left edge of the page (see Exercise One below).

Exercise One: Adding Rules to Your Documents

Let's assume you want to add a rule in the left-hand margin of a document. To do that,

Press: (ALT-F9) (GRAPHICS)

Select: 5 (LINE)

Select: 2 (CREATE LINE: VERTICAL)

Response: WordPerfect then displays the VERTICAL LINE menu.

Select: 1 (HORIZONTAL POSITION)

Response: HORIZONTAL POSITION options are:

1 (LEFT)

2 (RIGHT)

3 (BETWEEN COLUMNS)

4 (SET POSITION)

Select: 1 (LEFT)

Press: (F7) (EXIT)

Use WordPerfect's VIEW DOCUMENT command [SHIFT-F7, 6] to preview your work. You'll see that the vertical rule has been placed along the left-hand margin of the page.

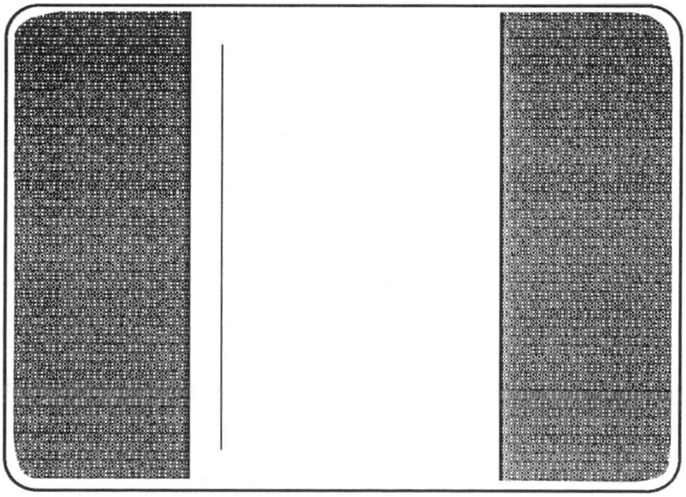

WordPerfect gives you total control over line placement. For example, you can describe the exact vertical position and line length.

Press: (ALT-F9) (GRAPHICS)

Select: 5 (LINE)

Select: 4 (EDIT LINE: VERTICAL)

Select: 2 (VERTICAL POSITION)

Response: 1 (FULL PAGE) The line will extend from top to bottom of the page.

2 (TOP) The line will extend down from the top of the page.

3 (CENTER) The line will extend an equal length toward the top and bottom of the page from the center of the page.

4 (BOTTOM) The line will extend up from the bottom of the page.

5 (SET POSITION) You can define a specific starting point from the top of the page.

If you select an option other than the default, FULL PAGE (Option 1), you have to define the line length. For example, to center the 4-inch-high line vertically along the left border of a page,

Select: 3 (CENTER)

Response: 9"

This default extends a line the full height of the page.

Select: 3 (LENGTH OF LINE)

Type: 4

Press: (ENTER)

This replaces the 9-inch default with a 4-inch line.

To make the line thicker,

Select: 4 (WIDTH OF LINE)

Response: 0.013"

Type: .25

This replaces the thin hairline with a .25-inch-wide line.

Press: (ENTER)

Press: (F7) (EXIT)

Response: The result is a centered, .25-inch-wide, 4-inch vertical line along the left-hand margin of the page. You can see the line by using WordPerfect's PRINT [SHIFT-F7, 2] or VIEW DOCUMENT [SHIFT-F7, 6] commands.

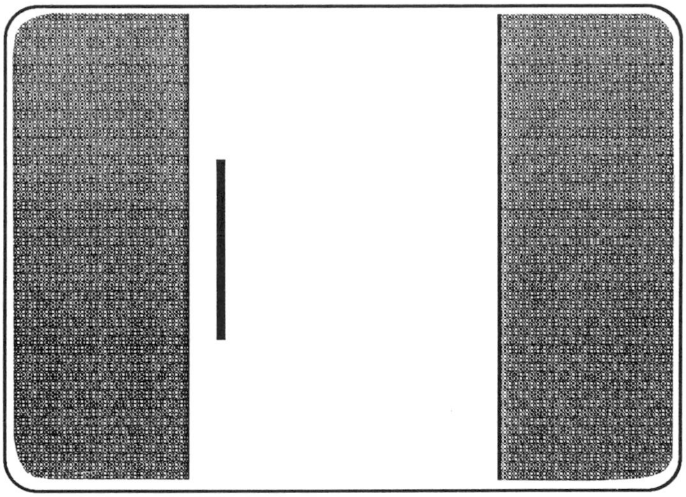

As the above example illustrates, trial and error may play an important role as you learn desktop publishing. Rather than resisting such efforts, welcome them. Only through experimentation will you become comfortable enough with WordPerfect to allow your talents to blossom. However, WordPerfect's REVEAL CODES [ALT-F3] command can save a lot of time.

Using Reveal Codes

When you print your first desktop publishing exercise, the importance of WordPerfect's REVEAL CODES command becomes apparent. After previewing and printing your work, you might decide you want lines thicker or thinner, or longer or shorter. WordPerfect's REVEAL CODES command [ALT-F3] makes that simple to adjust.

Press: (ALT-F3) (REVEAL CODES)

Response: The screen now is divided horizontally. (The top portion contains only your text. The bottom, however, contains a definition that specifies the length and placement of the rule you've just created.)

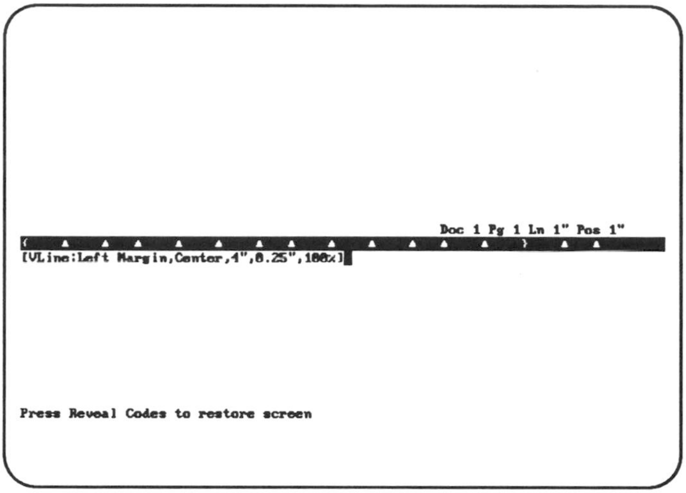

Note that when you use your cursor control keys, the cursor moves in both the "clean text" and coded areas of the screen.

To change the rule's appearance on the page, move the cursor until it highlights the definition code specifying the length and placement of the rule you created in the REVEAL CODES screen. Delete the line definition code with either the [DELETE] or backspace key. Then repeat the line creation process, changing line length or width specifications as desired.

Delete Versus Backspace

While in REVEAL CODES note the difference between "delete" and "backspace." Use the [DELETE] key while the cursor is on the line definition. Use the backspace key when the cursor highlights the space immediately following the definition.

Leaving Reveal Codes

To return to the normal editing screen,

Press: (ALT-F3) (REVEAL CODES)

Response: You'll be returned to the original editing screen.

Shaded Rules Add Document Color

As a design alternative, you might want to create rules in different shades of gray. Let's replace the vertical line drawn above with a line of the same length and thickness, but shaded to 60 percent of full black.

The first step is to use WordPerfect's REVEAL CODES command to locate the original line definition and delete it. Then, draw a new line in its place.

Press: (ALT-F3) (REVEAL CODES)

Now press the up/down/left/right cursor control keys to locate the line definition code in the REVEAL CODES screen.

Notice how the entire line definition is highlighted when the cursor touches it from either the left or right.

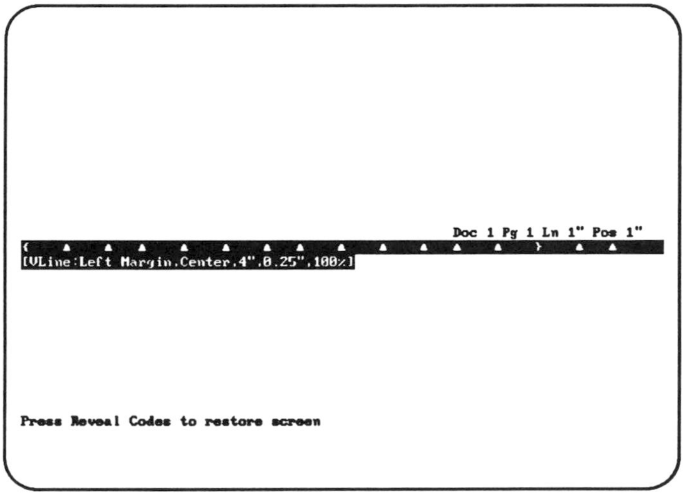

Press: (DELETE)

Response: This erases the entire line definition.

Now repeat the steps you went through above, but add one more step to the process. After you've created the line as described above, but before leaving the VERTICAL LINE menu,

Select: 5 (GRAY SHADING (% OF BLACK))

Response: 100 %

Type: 60

Press: (ENTER)

Press: (F7) (EXIT) (This ends the line creation sequence.)

To return to a full editing screen,

Press: (ALT-F3) (REVEAL CODES)

To preview your shaded line, enter [SHIFT-F7, 6] (VIEW DOCUMENT).

The difference should be quite noticeable. Gray rules add "color" in very apparent ways—yielding a two-color effect at a one-color cost. Compare the two following illustrations:

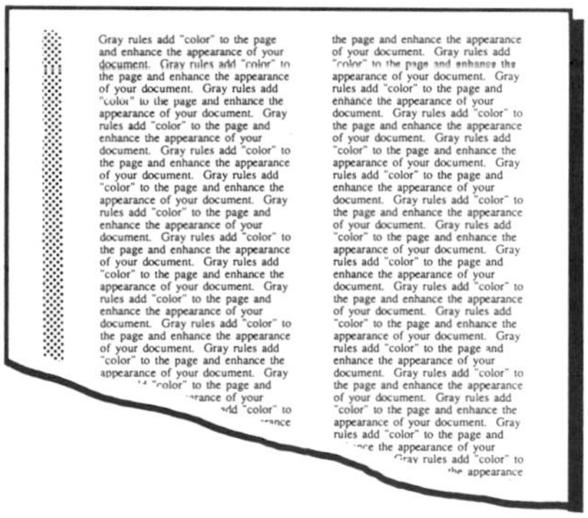

Macros and Line Creation

The more you use WordPerfect's many sophisticated options (line length, width, placement and shading options), the more you'll appreciate WordPerfect's macro capabilities. You can save a lot of time by turning on WordPerfect's MACRO command [ALT-F10] and naming and defining a macro for each type of line before you create and place lines.

Simplifying Things with Macros

WordPerfect's macros further simplify the placement of rules. Consisting of command files, macros let you execute a complicated sequence of keystrokes by simply activating a one-word file.

Let's assume, for example, that the page layout you've designed for your employee training manual contains a .25-inch-wide rule extending across the top of each page. Without WordPerfect's macro capability, you'd have to create this line from scratch on each page, or BLOCK [ALT-F4] and COPY [CTRL-F4, 1, 2], repeating the same keyboard commands each time. By simply creating a TOPBORD macro, as described below, you can add the border to the top of each page, eliminating the monotony of recreating it for each page of a document.

Exercise Two: Creating a Border Macro

Let's begin by creating a macro that adds a .25-inch horizontal border along the top of each page.

Start by defining the TOPBORD macro. First, move the cursor to the top of the document by pressing [HOME] [HOME] up cursor control key. To activate the MACRO DEFINE command,

Press: (CTRL-F10) (MACRO DEFINE)

Response: Define macro:

Type: TOPBORD

Press: (ENTER)

Response: Description:

(Note: your description is limited to 39 characters.)

Type: Add a 1/4-inch top border to each page

Press: (ENTER)

The flashing MACRO DEF prompt reminds you that all the keystrokes that follow will be memorized as part of the TOPBORD macro.

Now, place the cursor at the top of the page—or as far down from the top as you want the border to appear.

Press: (ALT-F9) (GRAPHICS)

Select: 5 (LINE)

Select: 1 (CREATE LINE: HORIZONTAL)

Response: The WordPerfect HORIZONTAL LINE menu appears.

```
Graphics: Horizontal Line

     1 - Horizontal Position       Full

     2 - Vertical Position         Baseline

     3 - Length of Line

     4 - Width of Line             0.01"

     5 - Gray Shading (% of black) 100%






Selection: 0
```

This menu allows you to define the line length, its alignment (left, right or centered), thickness and shading.

For the horizontal position, if you accept the default FULL (LEFT & RIGHT in version 5.0), the line will extend from column to column over the entire page. If you select 1 (HORIZONTAL POSITION), you'll be able to center the line, align it against either the left- or right-hand borders of the page or position it exactly where you want it from the left-hand margin of the page.

Select: 4 (3 in 5.0) (WIDTH OF LINE)

Then change the 0.013 default to 0.25:

Type: 0.25

Press: (ENTER)

Press: (F7) (EXIT) to close the file.

Press: (CTRL-F10) (to end the creation of your TOPBORD macro.)

Response: The MACRO DEF prompt disappears and you return to your document.

Previewing Your Work

Depending upon your monitor, the top border may or may not be visible on the screen. To make sure your rule has been placed in the correct position, use WordPerfect's VIEW DOCUMENT feature.

Press: (SHIFT-F7) (PRINT)

Select: 6 (VIEW DOCUMENT)

Select: 3 (FULL PAGE)

The page now appears in reduced size on your screen with the .25-inch border visible across the top of the page.

Adding the Border to the Following Pages

To add the border to the following pages, return to your document by pressing [F7] (EXIT), then advance to the next page with the down cursor control key. At the top of each new page (indicated by the changing page number at the bottom right of your screen),

Press: (ALT-F10) (MACRO)

Response: Macro:

Type: TOPBORD

Press: (ENTER)

Response: The top border automatically is placed in the cursor's position.

Note: If you'll be using multiple columns, you'll want to add the top and bottom borders *before* you create the columns (discussed in Chapter 3). Otherwise, borders will not extend across the entire page. (This can work to your advantage, however, when horizontal rules are used to separate items within a column.)

Another Way to Draw Lines

WordPerfect also offers a LINE DRAW command, accessed through the SCREEN command [CTRL-F3]. Lines drawn using the LINE DRAW command differ from lines created using WordPerfect's GRAPHICS command [ALT-F9]. LINE DRAW lines are drawn on the screen using the up/down/left/right cursor control keys. Although fewer thickness and shading options are available, you can draw lines with special characters (such as asterisks).

Lines created with LINE DRAW usually are visible immediately on the screen, whereas rules created with WordPerfect's GRAPHICS command often are made visible only by using WordPerfect's VIEW DOCUMENT feature. In addition, lines created with the LINE DRAW command can be edited with the [DELETE] and cursor control keys.

Printer limitations also are involved. Both lines and rules can be used in documents printed on Hewlett-Packard LaserJet Series II printers. However, lines created with WordPerfect's LINE DRAW command won't print on PostScript printers, such as the Apple LaserWriter Plus or the LaserWriter NT.

Other printer-to-printer and monitor-to-monitor variations involve creating a line out of special characters. However, you'll have to experiment with your particular monitor and printer to see just how much you can accomplish with the LINE DRAW feature.

Drawing Lines with Line Draw

To draw lines with your cursor control keys, place your cursor at the starting point of the line you want to draw. Then,

Press: (CTRL-F3) (SCREEN)

Select: 2 (LINE DRAW)

Select: 1 (SINGLE LINE)

Press: The left/right/up/down cursor control keys to draw either horizontal or vertical lines.

Note that corners automatically are created when you switch from horizontal to vertical cursor control keys. Small arrows appear at the beginning and end of each line you're drawing. (These arrows disappear when you PRINT.)

Note: WordPerfect's LINE DRAW [CTRL-F3, 2] command must be used very carefully, because it types over or deletes any text it encounters.

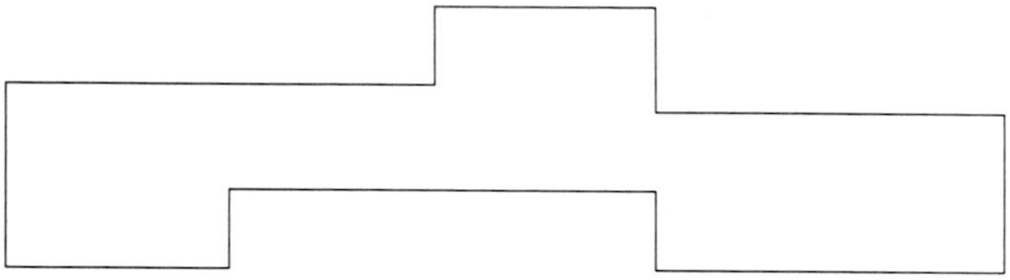

When you're finished,

Press: (F7) (EXIT)

A similar procedure is used to draw double lines:

Press: (CTRL-F3) (SCREEN)

Select: 2 (LINE DRAW)

Select: 2 (DOUBLE LINE)

Press: The left/right/up/down cursor control keys to draw either horizontal or vertical lines.

Press: (F7) (EXIT)

Choose 3 (*) instead of 1 (SINGLE LINE) or 2 (DOUBLE LINE), if you want to highlight important information with rows of asterisks. (The asterisk is a default that can be replaced by any other character, as described below.)

Changing Line Thickness or Shading

WordPerfect's LINE DRAW command offers a limited number of variations on line thickness and shading.

Press: (CTRL-F3) (SCREEN)

Select: 2 (LINE DRAW)

Select: 4 (CHANGE)

Response: You're presented with nine options:

1 Approximately 20 percent shaded, quarter-inch, horizontal, solid, one-eighth-inch vertical line.

2 Approximately 50 percent shaded, one-quarter-inch, horizontal, solid, one-eighth-inch vertical line.

3 Approximately 80 percent shaded, one-quarter-inch, horizontal, solid, one-eighth-inch vertical line.

4 Full black, one-quarter-inch, solid, horizontal line with thin divisions every inch.

5 Approximately one-eighth-inch, solid, horizontal line with broken three-sixteenths-inch vertical line.

6 Approximately one-quarter-inch, broken, horizontal line with solid, one-sixteenth-inch vertical line.

7 Approximately one-quarter-inch, shaded, broken, horizontal line with solid, one-sixteenth-inch vertical line.

8 Solid, approximately one-eighth-inch, horizontal line with three-sixteenths-inch, broken vertical line.

9 Allows you to use any letter or number or punctuation mark. WordPerfect responds with a SOLID CHARACTER: prompt, and allows you to type the character you want to use.

Below are samples of Options 5 and 9.

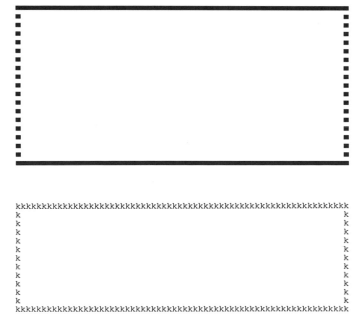

```
kkkkkkkkkkkkkkkkkkkkkkkkkkkkkkkkkkkkkkkkkkkkkkkkkkkkkkkkkkkkkkkkkkkkkkkkk
k                                                                       k
k                                                                       k
k                                                                       k
k                                                                       k
k                                                                       k
k                                                                       k
k                                                                       k
k                                                                       k
k                                                                       k
k                                                                       k
k                                                                       k
kkkkkkkkkkkkkkkkkkkkkkkkkkkkkkkkkkkkkkkkkkkkkkkkkkkkkkkkkkkkkkkkkkkkkkkkk
```

Erasing Lines and Moving the Cursor

When using the LINE DRAW feature, you can erase portions of the line you're working on by using the up/down/left/right cursor control keys from the current cursor position.

Press: (CTRL-F3) (SCREEN)

Select: 2 (LINE DRAW)

Select: 5 (ERASE)

After choosing ERASE, press [F7] (EXIT) to return to the editing screen.

When using the LINE DRAW command, there may be times when you'd like to move the cursor with the cursor control keys without drawing a line. 6 (MOVE) makes that possible. At any point, while drawing lines,

Press: (CTRL-F3) (SCREEN)

Select: 2 (LINE DRAW)

Select: 6 (MOVE)

This lets you reposition the cursor control keys without drawing lines. To resume drawing lines,

Select: 1, 2, 3 or 4 (Single, Double, * or Change)

When you're finished,

Press: (F7) (EXIT)

Line Limitations

Remember that lines created with WordPerfect's LINE DRAW command [CTRL-F3, 2] can be easily displaced. Words or spaces inserted in front of a vertical line, for example, push the line to the right.

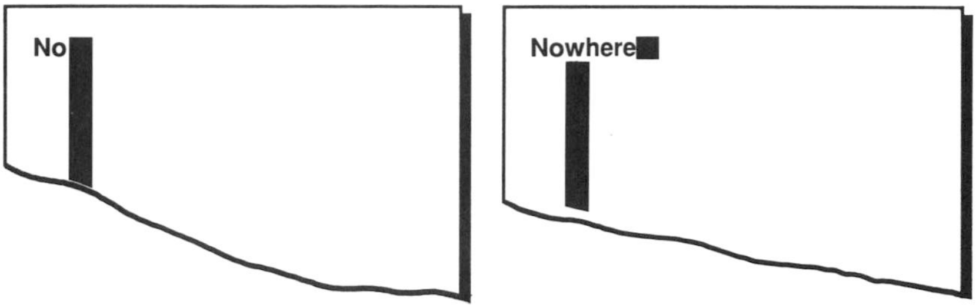

Likewise, backspaces or word deletions pull a vertical line to the left.

These limitations become even more apparent when you work with large documents. If text is deleted or inserted in a document above lines created with the LINE DRAW command [CTRL-F3, 2], the lines will move up or down to compensate for the editing.

Boxes as Design and Layout Tools

Another fundamental building block of design is the box, which creates powerful, good-looking print communications. However, boxes can be somewhat confusing, because they are among the most commonly encountered graphic design tools, as well as being one of WordPerfect's most important page layout tools.

Boxes as Design Elements

As graphic design tools, boxes are four-sided objects that can be used either to separate or draw attention to different categories of words.

For example, sidebars—short articles that accompany and support longer articles—are usually set in boxes to distinguish them from related text.

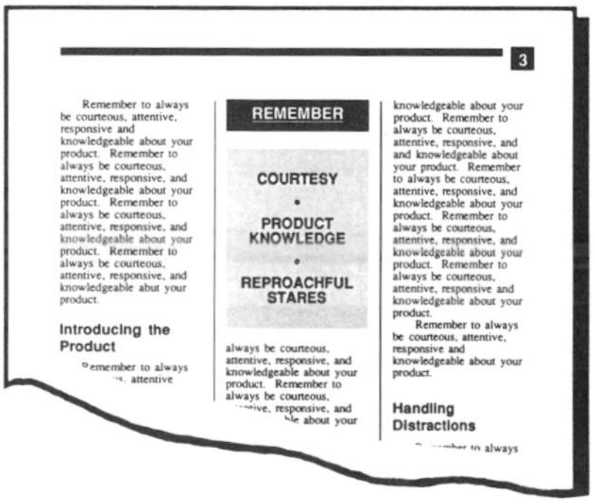

Pull-quotes—short sentences that summarize surrounding material—are another frequent application of boxes. Set in large type in a box within a page of text, pull-quotes provide visual contrast to long articles, as well as highlight important information. They're particularly useful in adding visual relief to a "gray" page when photos or illustrations aren't available.

Boxes can be used to draw attention to headlines, particularly reversed boxes that contain white type against a black background.

As a design tool, boxes can be used to isolate different categories of information. Many publications emphasize mailing and advertising information by setting it in a box.

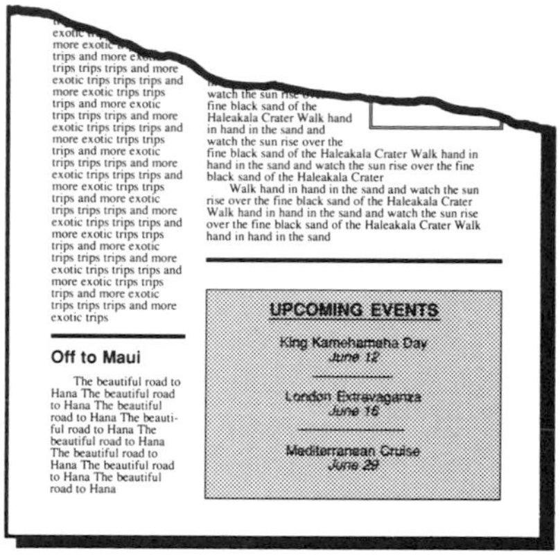

Boxes can add impact to graphs, charts, illustrations and photographs.

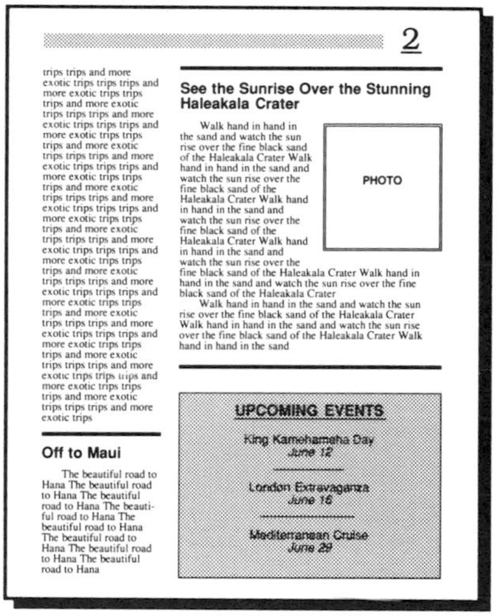

Boxes also can be used as a design element to enclose page numbers.

You can use boxes to create coupons in advertisements.

Boxes as Layout Tools

In addition to their design function, boxes play an important role in WordPerfect's advanced page layout and document organization capabilities. WordPerfect uses boxes as "containers" for text, charts, graphs, drawings and scanned photographs. WordPerfect also uses boxes for placing mastheads and logos created with separate draw-type programs.

Boxes not only provide a framework for words and graphic images, they help WordPerfect organize documents, such as books with a lot of photographs and illustrations, proposals and reports containing charts and graphs, or training manuals with technical drawings. After you've finished editing your document, WordPerfect automatically can generate lists of graphics and indicate the pages on which they appear, an important organizational tool to help readers locate information quickly.

WordPerfect gives you four ways to identify your boxes: FIGURE, TABLE, TEXT and USER-DEFINED. Note that words or graphic images can be entered into any type of box. The categories relate to the way WordPerfect numbers boxes when it generates lists of graphics at the conclusion of your project.

By providing both a structure for text and graphics, as well as organizing the contents of a document, boxes are crucial to WordPerfect's ability to smoothly integrate text and graphics into professional-looking, compelling documents.

Using Macros with Boxes

Just as macros expedite the placement of page borders, they also can be used to create and place boxes on a page. This can save time when you have to insert numerous boxes of the same size into a document.

Exercise Three: Creating a Text Box

Let's start by creating a small box for a pull-quote, contained within a newsletter or magazine column. (For multicolumn formatting, see Chapter 3.)

To start, place the cursor in the column where you want to insert the pull-quote. (If you're already familiar with WordPerfect, you'll know that to move horizontally from column to column you use a combination of the GO TO command [CTRL-HOME] and the left and right cursor control keys.) You then vertically position the cursor with the up/down cursor control keys.

When the cursor is correctly positioned,

Press: (ALT-F9) (GRAPHICS)

Select: 3 (TEXT BOX)
1 (CREATE)

At this point, you have a decision to make. If you're creating a simple pull-quote, you need not assign it a file name. If you don't specify a file name, WordPerfect won't include this TEXT BOX in the list—or index—of TEXT BOXes that it compiles at the end of your project. However, to fill the box with text from another file—for example, if you're creating a sidebar and want its text to come from another file—you must assign the box a file name, if you want WordPerfect to keep track of its location. Next,

Select: 6 (5 in 5.0) (HORIZONTAL POSITION)

You then are presented with various ways to place the TEXT BOX in or around the column. You'll probably choose either to center the TEXT BOX or have it extend from one column border to the other.

Select: 4 (FULL)

This creates a box that extends the width of the column.

Select: 7 (6 in 5.0) (SIZE)

Select: 2 (SET HEIGHT/AUTO WIDTH)

Response: 0.7"

(This figure may vary slightly, depending upon the dimensions of your page and the monitor you're using.)

Type: 1.5

Press: (ENTER)

That replaces the default with a box 1.5 inches high. Finally,

Select: 9 (8 in 5.0) (EDIT)

Enter the text of your pull-quote:

Type: The quick brown fox jumped over the lazy dog.

Remember that you can change typeface, type size and type style attributes as you enter these words. Usually the type in a pull-quote is larger than the surrounding body copy. As you'll learn in Chapter 5, you can change typeface, type size and style by executing WordPerfect's FONT command [CTRL-F8].

After you've entered and formatted your words,

Press: (F7) (EXIT) twice to return to your editing screen.

Preview your work [SHIFT-F7, 6] or print out the page [SHIFT-F7, 2]. It should be similar to the example below.

The quick brown fox jumped over the lazy dog.

Notice that WordPerfect's TEXT BOX defaults include thick top and bottom bars, no side borders and a 10 percent screened background. To change these defaults, return to your editing screen and place the cursor in a position that precedes the box. Then,

Press: (ALT-F9) (GRAPHICS)

Select: 3 (TEXT BOX)

Select: 4 (OPTIONS)

Response: You're presented with the TEXT BOX option screen.

```
Options:    Text Box

     1 - Border Style
              Left                          None
              Right                         None
              Top                           Thick
              Bottom                        Thick
     2 - Outside Border Space
              Left                          0.16"
              Right                         0.16"
              Top                           0.16"
              Bottom                        0.16"
     3 - Inside Border Space
              Left                          0.16"
              Right                         0.16"
              Top                           0.16"
              Bottom                        0.16"
     4 - First Level Numbering Method       Numbers
     5 - Second Level Numbering Method      Off
     6 - Caption Number Style               [BOLD]1[bold]
     7 - Position of Caption                Below box, Outside borders
     8 - Minimum Offset from Paragraph      0"
     9 - Gray Shading (% of black)          10%

Selection: 0
```

It includes a variety of TEXT BOX border treatments. Let's change the right- and left-hand borders to a single line.

Select: 1 (BORDER STYLE)

Response: You're offered a variety of options for the side border:

1 (NONE)—default

2 (SINGLE)

3 (DOUBLE)

4 (DASHED)

5 (DOTTED)

6 (THICK)

7 (EXTRA THICK)

Select: 7 (EXTRA THICK)

Response: The highlight automatically jumps down to the right-hand border of the next line.

Select: 7 (EXTRA THICK)

Press: (ENTER) (ENTER) to accept the default's thick borders for the top and bottom borders.

Adding a Screen to a Box

Before you leave the TEXT BOX OPTIONS definition screen, notice that the default shading for TEXT BOXes is 10 percent. You can add impact to your pull-quote by choosing a darker screen.

Select: 9 (GRAY SHADING (% OF BLACK))

Response: The cursor now appears under the 10 percent default.

Type: 40

Press: (ENTER)

Press: (F7) (EXIT)

The resulting pull-quote should resemble the example below.

Remember, these changes do not have to be repeated: They will remain in effect for each of the TEXT BOXes that follows.

Creating Sidebars

As previously mentioned, larger TEXT BOXes can be created to accommodate separate articles in a newsletter, cautionary tips in a training manual or a calendar of upcoming events in a newspaper. The principles are the same as those you just used to create a pull-quote. However, the dimensions of the TEXT BOX are larger.

Sidebars often are used as containers for integrating existing text files into a document. Let's assume you previously created a text file saved under the file name, JOURNAL. To place it in the publication you're currently working on,

Press: (ALT-F9) (GRAPHICS)

Select: 3 (TEXT BOX)

Select: 1 (CREATE)

Select: 1 (FILENAME)

Type: JOURNAL (or another file name for an existing text file.)

Press: (ENTER)

Press: (F7) (EXIT) (to return to editing your document.)

Preview your work on the screen [SHIFT-F7, 6] or print out the page [SHIFT-F7, 2].

Exercise Four: Resizing Text Boxes

In some cases, you might find that the TEXT BOX either isn't large enough to accommodate your text file or is too large. WordPerfect makes it easy to modify the dimensions of TEXT BOXes after they've been created. Start by executing the GRAPHICS command:

Press: (ALT-F9) (GRAPHICS)

Select: 3 (TEXT BOX)

Select: 2 (EDIT)

Response: Text box number? 1

Press: (ENTER)

Select: 7 (6 in 5.0) (SIZE)

Response: You'll be offered the following options:

1 (SET WIDTH/AUTO HEIGHT)

2 (SET HEIGHT/AUTO WIDTH)

3 (SET BOTH)

4 (AUTO BOTH) (Available in Version 5.1)

Select: 2 (SET HEIGHT/AUTO WIDTH)

Type: 8 (This replaces the default with the estimated 8-inch height of your sidebar.)

Press: (ENTER)

Press: (F7) (EXIT)

Preview your work on screen [SHIFT-F7, 6] or print the page [SHIFT-F7, 2] to check the accuracy of your space estimate. Repeat the above process, lengthening or shortening the height of the box, until it's just large enough to contain the text file you're importing.

Graphics Boxes

Graphics boxes are used when you want to place a previously created image file into your document. This file can be an illustration, a scanned photograph, or a masthead or logo created with a drawing program.

The principles of creating a graphics box are the same as those used to create TEXT BOXes, although more options are available for adjusting the placement of the graphic image in the box. Captions also are more important with FIGURE or TABLE BOXes.

Modifying imported text and graphics files is such an important issue that an entire chapter is devoted to the subject. (See Chapter 4.) For purposes of illustration, however, let's simply review the process.

Exercise Five: Creating a Figure Box

Let's place the previously drawn clock illustration into a box. (CLOCK is stored in a file named CLOCK.WPG, included with WordPerfect.) Start by moving the cursor to the column and vertical location where you want to insert a graphic image.

Press: (ALT-F9) (GRAPHICS)

Select: 1 (FIGURE)

Response: FIGURE menu appears

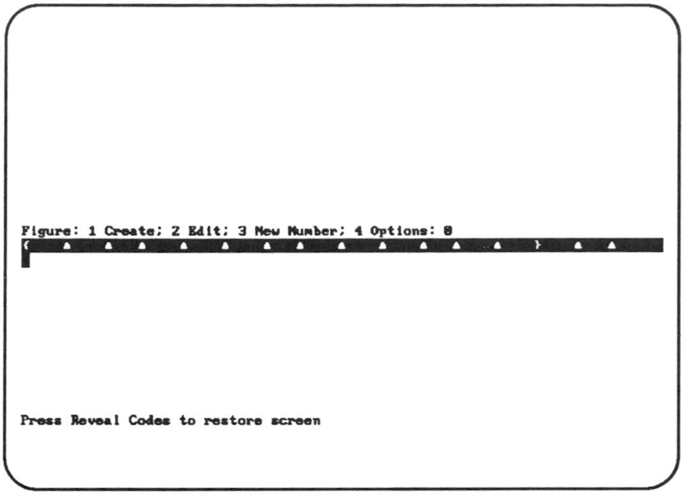

When the FIGURE menu appears,

Select: 1 (CREATE)

Select: 1 (FILENAME)

Type: The file name—in this case, CLOCK.WPG.

Press: (ENTER)

Select: 3 (2 in 5.0) (CAPTION)

Next, enter the caption for the illustration:

Type: "An example of a frequently used means of telling time." (Be sure to put one or more spaces before the caption to separate it from Figure 1. Otherwise, there will be no space between the figure number and the beginning of the caption. Longer captions will print automatically on the line beneath the figure number.)

In Chapter 4, you'll learn how to choose a particular typeface, type size, type style and alignment for your captions. In Chapter 7, you'll learn how to save these attributes as a STYLE which will simplify the process of achieving consistency throughout your document.

Press: (F7) (EXIT)

Now, to specify the illustration's position in the column,

Select: 6 (5 in 5.0) (HORIZONTAL POSITION)

Select: 4 (FULL)

Response: This centers the box in the column.

Press: (F7) (EXIT) (to exit to your document.)

To view the placement of the graphics box, return to the document and

Press: (SHIFT-F7) (PRINT)

Select: 6 (VIEW DOCUMENT)

If you'd like to print the document,

Press: (SHIFT-F7) (PRINT)

Select: 2 (PRINT PAGE)

Anchoring Box Location

WordPerfect offers you two ways to place boxes in your document. You can choose to anchor boxes to specific page locations or to the surrounding text.

When anchored to specific page locations, box positions remain unchanged, even if the text surrounding them changes during document editing. When a box is anchored to surrounding text, however, the box follows the text to which it's set, regardless of its column or page position. Boxes also can be anchored to specific sentences.

When there isn't space for a paragraph-anchored box to be printed in a column or on a page, the paragraph and accompanying box automatically move to the next column or page.

To anchor a box of any type—whether it contains words, illustrations or a numeric table—to a specific location on a page,

Press: (ALT-F9) (GRAPHICS)

Select: Either 1 (FIGURE), 2 (TABLE BOX), 3 (TEXT BOX) or 4 (USER BOX), depending upon the category of your box.

Select: 1 (CREATE)

Select: 4 (3 in 5.0) (ANCHOR TYPE)

Response: You're presented with the following choices:

Select 1 (PARAGRAPH) if you want to anchor the box and its caption to an adjacent paragraph.

Select 2 (PAGE) if you want the box and its caption to be anchored to a specific position on that particular page.

Select 3 (CHARACTER) if you want to anchor the box and its contents to a particular location in a sentence. This option often is used for page numbers or to create large initial caps.

The following examples show the difference between page-anchored, paragraph-anchored and character-anchored boxes.

This shows a graphics box placed on the page.

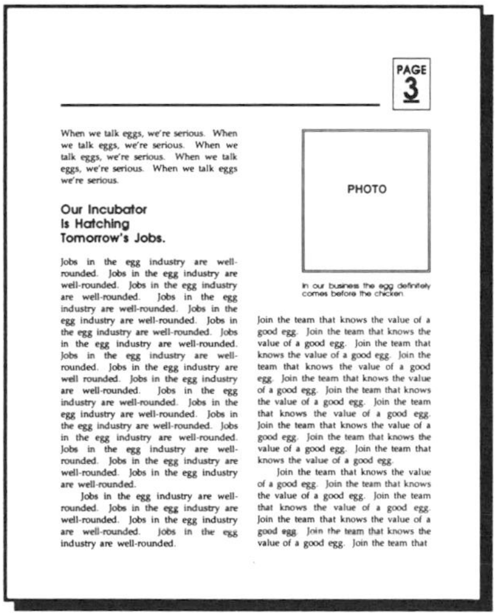

PAGE 3

When we talk eggs, we're serious. When we talk eggs, we're serious. When we talk eggs, we're serious. When we talk eggs, we're serious. When we talk eggs we're serious.

Our Incubator Is Hatching Tomorrow's Jobs.

Jobs in the egg industry are well-rounded. Jobs in the egg industry are well-rounded. Jobs in the egg industry are well-rounded. Jobs in the egg industry are well-rounded. Jobs in the egg industry are well-rounded. Jobs in the egg industry are well-rounded. Jobs in the egg industry are well-rounded. Jobs in the egg industry are well-rounded. Jobs in the egg industry are well rounded. Jobs in the egg industry are well-rounded. Jobs in the egg industry are well-rounded. Jobs in the egg industry are well-rounded. Jobs in the egg industry are well-rounded. Jobs in the egg industry are well-rounded. Jobs in the egg industry are well-rounded. Jobs in the egg industry are well-rounded. Jobs in the egg industry are well-rounded. Jobs in the egg industry are well-rounded.

Jobs in the egg industry are well-rounded. Jobs in the egg industry are well-rounded. Jobs in the egg industry are well-rounded. Jobs in the egg industry are well-rounded.

PHOTO

In our business the egg definitely comes before the chicken.

Join the team that knows the value of a good egg. Join the team that knows the value of a good egg. Join the team that knows the value of a good egg. Join the team that knows the value of a good egg. Join the team that knows the value of a good egg. Join the team that knows the value of a good egg. Join the team that knows the value of a good egg. Join the team that knows the value of a good egg. Join the team that knows the value of a good egg. Join the team that knows the value of a good egg.

Join the team that knows the value of a good egg. Join the team that knows the value of a good egg. Join the team that knows the value of a good egg. Join the team that knows the value of a good egg. Join the team that knows the value of a good egg. Join the team that

This is how the page appears after a paragraph has been deleted (Option 2).

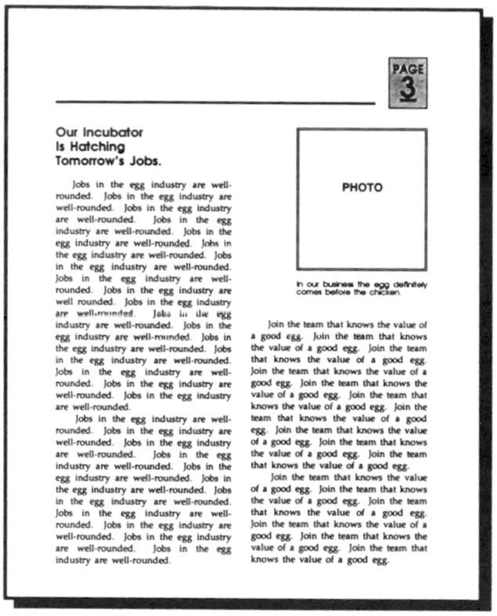

This is how the page appears when the box is character-locked (Option 3).

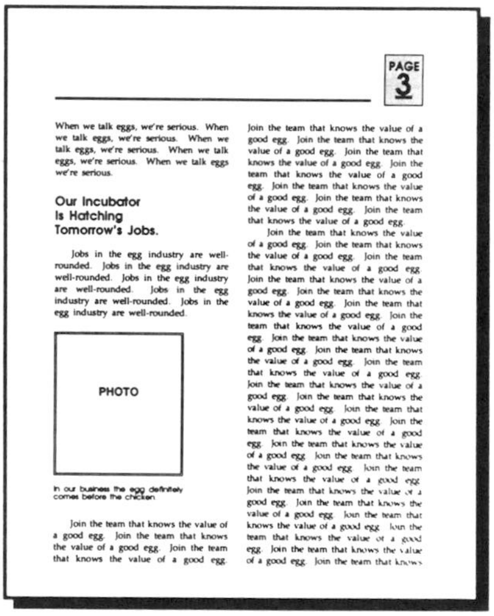

Deleting Boxes and Their Contents

Use WordPerfect's REVEAL CODES [ALT-F3] to delete a box from a page after it has been created. Simply advance the cursor until the box number, file name and caption are highlighted, then delete.

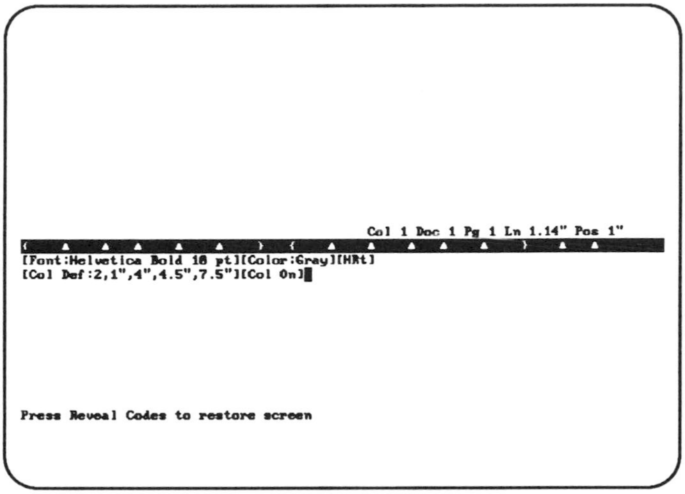

TIP: Exercise extreme care when removing boxes. After you've deleted a box using the [DELETE] key, it cannot be restored with WordPerfect's CANCEL command [F1].

Replacing the Contents of a Graphics Box

Instead of deleting the contents of a FIGURE BOX, leaving the box intact but empty, you can replace its contents with another previously created graphics image. Here's the sequence of steps to follow:

Press: (ALT-F9) (GRAPHICS)

Select: 1 (FIGURE)

Select: 2 (EDIT)

Response: Figure Number? 2 (or the number of the last TEXT BOX created on that page. If your cursor is on a following page, however, the default number will be one higher than the number of the last TEXT BOX created.)

Type: 1 (Replace the default number with the number of the FIGURE box you want to edit.)

Press: (ENTER)

Response: Again, you'll be presented with the FIGURE definition menu that contains the name of the previously placed file, CLOCK.WPG (GRAPHICS).

Select: 1 (FILENAME)

Type: ARROW1.WPG (It replaces CLOCK.WPG.)

Press: (ENTER)

Response: Replace contents with ARROW1.WPG? (Y/N) No

Type: Y

Again, the space bar returns you to your editing screen.

Deleting Box Contents

To delete the contents of a box, but leave its placement intact,

Press: (ALT-F9) (GRAPHICS)

Then, select the type of box you want to edit. You're presented with the following choices: 1 (FIGURE), 2 (TABLE BOX), 3 (TEXT BOX) or 4 (USER BOX). In this case, let's eliminate the clock figure from our first FIGURE box.

Select: 1 (FIGURE)

Select: 2 (EDIT)

Response: Figure Number? 2 (If the cursor is on the page containing a graphics box, WordPerfect defaults to the number of the last box created. If your cursor is on a following page, WordPerfect defaults to one number higher than the number of the last box created.)

To replace the default with the box number you want to modify,

Type: 1

Press: (ENTER)

Response: You're presented with the FIGURE definition menu that contains the name of the imported file, CLOCK.WPG.

Select: 1 (FILENAME)

Press: The (DELETE) key to erase the file name, CLOCK.WPG.

Press: (ENTER)

Response: Delete current contents of box? No (Yes)

Type: Y (This verifies your intention to delete the contents of FIGURE BOX 1, but leave the box in its present position.)

Press: (F7) (EXIT)

The space bar returns you to your editing screen.

Again, remember this is an irreversible step. You won't be able to restore the contents of the box with WordPerfect's CANCEL command [F1].

Editing Text Boxes

A similar procedure is used to edit, or replace, the contents of a TEXT BOX. Let's edit the TEXT BOX created above.

Press: (ALT-F9) (GRAPHICS)

Select: 3 (TEXT BOX)

Select: 2 (EDIT)

Response: Text Box number: 1

Again, the default is the number of the last TEXT BOX created on that page, or one number higher than the last box created if the cursor is on a following page.

Type: 1 (The number of the TEXT BOX you want to edit.)

Press: (ENTER)

Response: You'll be presented with the TEXT BOX definition menu that lets you modify its size, placement and contents.

Select: 9 (8 in 5.0) (EDIT)

Response: The original text of the pull-quote now appears on the screen.

Edit, delete or replace these words with other words. When you're finished,

Press: (F7) (EXIT)

Now press [F7] (EXIT) to return to the editing screen.

In Chapter 4, you'll learn ways of manipulating imported graphics, such as moving the image within the box, reducing or enlarging image size, rotating the image and changing background and frames, as well as ways of adjusting the distance between the contents of a box and its boundaries. You'll learn about the CLIPBOARD feature, found in the WordPerfect Library, which imports previously prepared graphic images.

Superimposing Boxes on Top of Each Other

Although you cannot create boxes within boxes, you can superimpose boxes, which means you can place text or graphics boxes in the white space of previously created boxes. You can add headline text within the white space defining the top of the page or place illustrations and captions within a band of white space to the left of your body copy.

Text or graphics boxes must be placed within other boxes by measurement, since you cannot create a box on top of a pre-existing one. To understand the process, let's import a graphic and place it in the left-hand white-space box created above.

Press:	(ALT-F9) (GRAPHICS)
Select:	1 (FIGURE)
Select:	1 (CREATE)
Select:	1 (FILENAME)
Type:	CLOCK.WPG
Press:	(ENTER)
Select:	3 (2 in 5.0) (CAPTION)
Type:	The preferred method of telling time when hourglasses aren't available.
Press:	(F7) (EXIT)
Select:	4 (3 in 5.0) (ANCHOR TYPE)
Select:	2 (PAGE)
Response:	Number of pages to skip: 0
Press:	(ENTER)
Select:	5 (4 in 5.0) (VERTICAL POSITION)
Select:	5 (SET POSITION)
Response:	Offset from top of page: 1"
Press:	3.25
Press:	(ENTER)
Select:	6 (5 in 5.0) (HORIZONTAL POSITION)
Select:	1 (MARGINS)
Select:	1 (LEFT)

Select: 7 (6 in 5.0) (SIZE)

Select: 1 (SET WIDTH/AUTO HEIGHT)

Response: Width = 2.16"

Type: 1.75

Press: (ENTER)

Reducing the size of the FIGURE BOX adds white space between the illustration and adjacent body copy.

Press: (F7) (EXIT)

This returns you to the editing screen.

Press: (SHIFT-F7) (PRINT)

Select: 6 (VIEW PAGE)

The result should appear as follows:

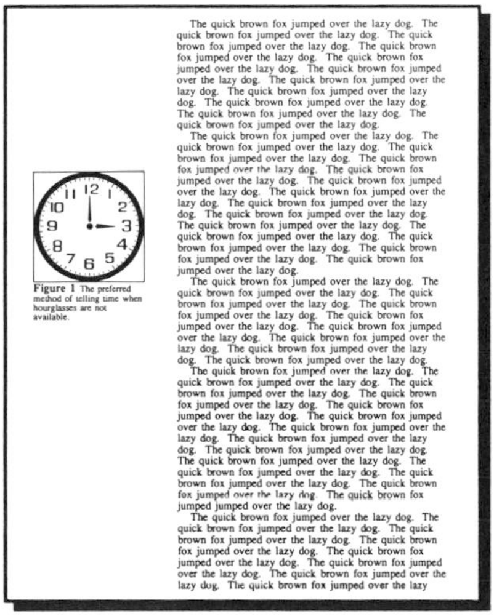

As you'll see in Chapter 4, rules and boxes also can be superimposed over existing white-space boxes, letting you create a variety of good-looking borders for your pages. You also can use this technique to add TEXT BOXes within white-space boxes, allowing you to place headlines and subheads adjacent to body copy.

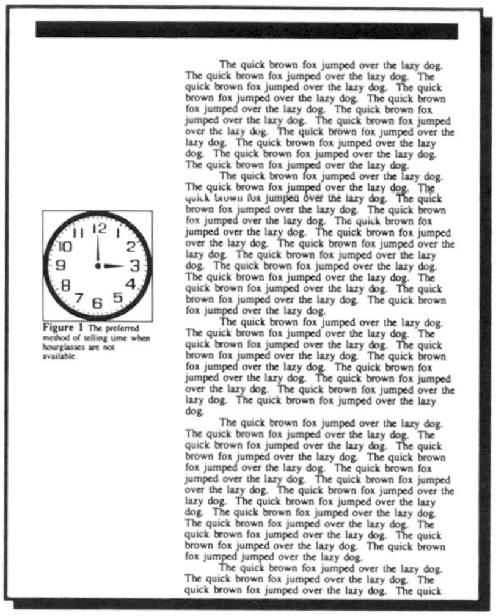

White-space boxes can be used to ensure accurate spacing between titles or headlines and the body copy they introduce, or between articles within newsletter columns. White-space boxes can also be used to create the first pages of chapters in a book.

In each case, WordPerfect's macro capability lets you store your white-space boxes as files, so that you easily can repeat these valuable graphics tools on each page.

Positioning Text

The location of text on a page is another important concern in desktop publishing. The way blocks of text are positioned affects the appearance, readability and "feeling" of a page. WordPerfect lets you determine precise locations for text blocks. Using the ADVANCE feature, you can locate text either at an absolute distance from the page edges or at a relative distance from the cursor. To use ADVANCE,

Press: (SHIFT-F8) (FORMAT)

Select: 4 (OTHER)

Select: 1 (ADVANCE)

3 (LINE) and 6 (POSITION) are used to set absolute vertical and horizontal distances, respectively. 1 (UP), 2 (DOWN), 4 (LEFT) and 5 (RIGHT) are used to set distances relative to the cursor's position.

Moving On

As you become increasingly involved with desktop publishing, you'll probably use WordPerfect's extensive line and box creation and editing capabilities frequently.

Next, let's take a closer look at WordPerfect's formatting capabilities—such as its ability to create multicolumn documents—and the polished image and flexibility columns can add to your design.

CHAPTER 3

WORKING WITH MULTICOLUMN LAYOUTS

In this chapter, you'll be introduced to a major WordPerfect enhancement: the ability to create multicolumn documents. Perhaps no design element is as important to producing professional-looking advertisements, booklets, brochures and newsletters as the ability to combine multicolumn formats with rules of different lengths, widths and shades of gray. These features make it easy to construct documents that are attractive, readable and have a great deal of design flexibility.

Using Column Display

When editing multicolumn documents, you can work more efficiently if you take advantage of WordPerfect's COLUMN DISPLAY feature. It gives you the option of seeing the columns on-screen, either side by side or on separate pages.

To activate, or deactivate, WordPerfect's COLUMN DISPLAY feature,

Press: (SHIFT-F1) (SETUP)

Select: 2 (3 in 5.0) (DISPLAY)

Select: 6 (EDIT-SCREEN OPTIONS) (not used in Version 5.0)

Select: 7 (8 in 5.0) (SIDE-BY-SIDE COLUMNS DISPLAY)

Response: Yes (No)

Accept the YES default if you want your screen to display columns side-by-side, as they're printed. Otherwise,

Type: N (NO)

Press: (F7) (EXIT)

That temporarily deactivates the side-by-side feature. Then you can concentrate on the contents of just one column at a time and enjoy faster editing and screen rewriting.

To verify your column setup, use REVEAL CODES [ALT-F3], which provides a visual review of the width and placement of each column, the type of column you've selected and whether the columns feature has been activated.

Creating Multiple Columns

It's a rare newsletter or manual that extends type from one page margin to another in a single, unbroken line. Effective, good-looking print communications usually are characterized by multiple columns of type—typically formatted in two or more columns.

WordPerfect makes it easy to create page layouts with columns. You can place as many as 24 columns on each page. Columns can be of the same or differing widths. You may apply column formatting to both new and existing documents.

To create a multicolumn document,

Press: (ALT-F7) (COLUMNS/TABLES)

Select: 1 (COLUMNS) (not used in Version 5.0)

Select: 3 (4 in 5.0) (DEFINE)

Response: WordPerfect's TEXT COLUMN definition screen appears.

```
Text Column Definition

     1 - Type                                          Newspaper

     2 - Number of Columns                             2

     3 - Distance Between Columns

     4 - Margins

     Column     Left       Right      Column     Left       Right
       1:       1"         4"          13:
       2:       4.5"       7.5"        14:
       3:                              15:
       4:                              16:
       5:                              17:
       6:                              18:
       7:                              19:
       8:                              20:
       9:                              21:
      10:                              22:
      11:                              23:
      12:                              24:

Selection: 0
```

At this point, define the type of columns you want to create.

Select: 1 (TYPE)

Response: You're presented with the three types of columns. Make your selection and press [ENTER].

If you choose Option 1 (NEWSPAPER), text will flow from the bottom of one column to the top of the next, filling each column in sequence until the page is filled. Type then continues to the top of the first column on the following page. Newspaper columns frequently are used for newsletters, books and magazines.

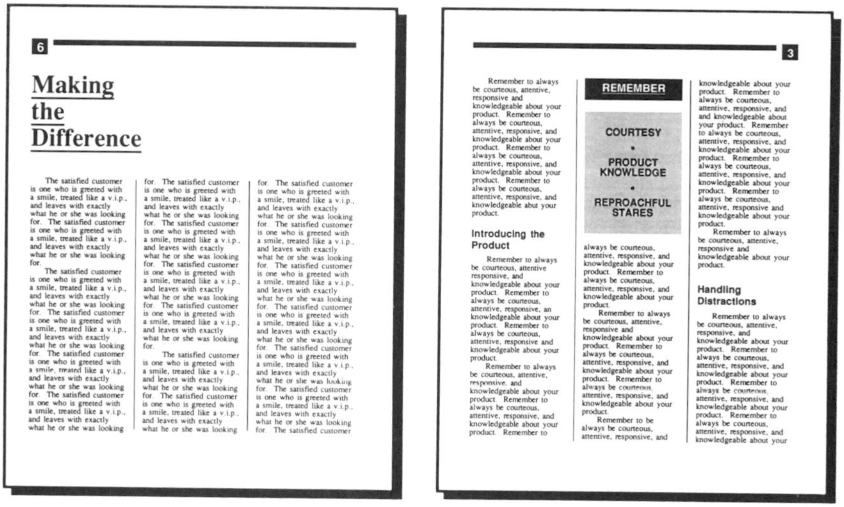

Choose Option 2 (PARALLEL) if you're creating documents in which information must be organized horizontally and the amount of copy in each column is likely to be different. If there's too much text to fit in a column on one page, the text will continue in the same column on the next page.

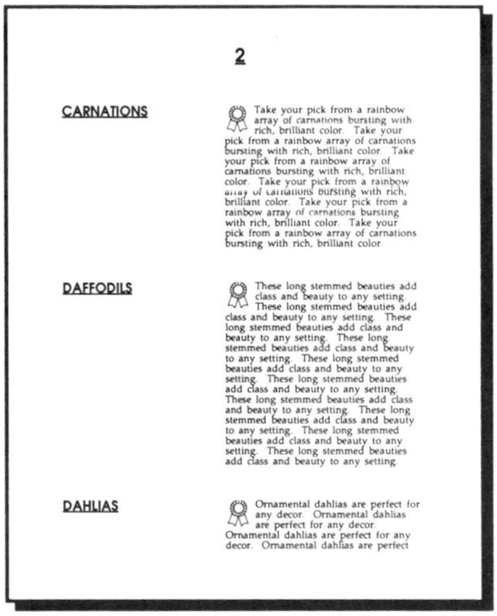

2

CARNATIONS	Take your pick from a rainbow array of carnations bursting with rich, brilliant color. Take your pick from a rainbow array of carnations bursting with rich, brilliant color. Take your pick from a rainbow array of carnations bursting with rich, brilliant color. Take your pick from a rainbow array of carnations bursting with rich, brilliant color. Take your pick from a rainbow array of carnations bursting with rich, brilliant color. Take your pick from a rainbow array of carnations bursting with rich, brilliant color.
DAFFODILS	These long stemmed beauties add class and beauty to any setting. These long stemmed beauties add class and beauty to any setting. These long stemmed beauties add class and beauty to any setting. These long stemmed beauties add class and beauty to any setting. These long stemmed beauties add class and beauty to any setting. These long stemmed beauties add class and beauty to any setting. These long stemmed beauties add class and beauty to any setting. These long stemmed beauties add class and beauty to any setting. These long stemmed beauties add class and beauty to any setting. These long stemmed beauties add class and beauty to any setting.
DAHLIAS	Ornamental dahlias are perfect for any decor. Ornamental dahlias are perfect for any decor. Ornamental dahlias are perfect for any decor. Ornamental dahlias are perfect

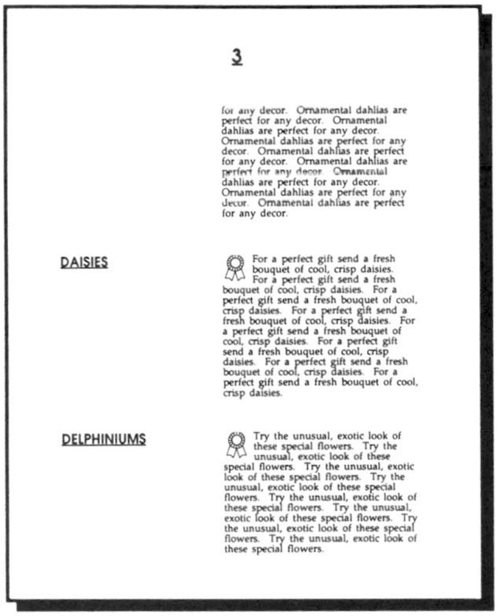

3

	for any decor. Ornamental dahlias are perfect for any decor. Ornamental dahlias are perfect for any decor. Ornamental dahlias are perfect for any decor. Ornamental dahlias are perfect for any decor. Ornamental dahlias are perfect for any decor. Ornamental dahlias are perfect for any decor. Ornamental dahlias are perfect for any decor.
DAISIES	For a perfect gift send a fresh bouquet of cool, crisp daisies. For a perfect gift send a fresh bouquet of cool, crisp daisies. For a perfect gift send a fresh bouquet of cool, crisp daisies. For a perfect gift send a fresh bouquet of cool, crisp daisies. For a perfect gift send a fresh bouquet of cool, crisp daisies. For a perfect gift send a fresh bouquet of cool, crisp daisies. For a perfect gift send a fresh bouquet of cool, crisp daisies. For a perfect gift send a fresh bouquet of cool, crisp daisies.
DELPHINIUMS	Try the unusual, exotic look of these special flowers. Try the unusual, exotic look of these special flowers. Try the unusual, exotic look of these special flowers. Try the unusual, exotic look of these special flowers. Try the unusual, exotic look of these special flowers. Try the unusual, exotic look of these special flowers. Try the unusual, exotic look of these special flowers. Try the unusual, exotic look of these special flowers.

Choose Option 3 (PARALLEL WITH BLOCK PROTECT) if you don't want paragraphs to be split at a page break. If your text is too long to fit on a page, the entire paragraph will move automatically to the next page. These columns often are used for price lists or inventory lists, in which text blocks or item descriptions must be kept together.

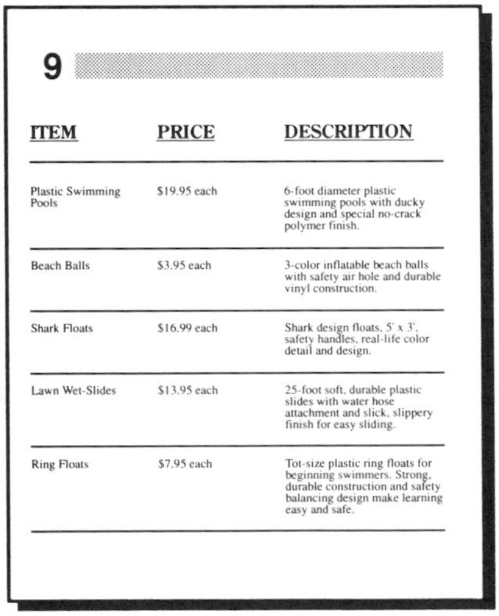

9

ITEM	PRICE	DESCRIPTION
Plastic Swimming Pools	$19.95 each	6-foot diameter plastic swimming pools with ducky design and special no-crack polymer finish.
Beach Balls	$3.95 each	3-color inflatable beach balls with safety air hole and durable vinyl construction.
Shark Floats	$16.99 each	Shark design floats, 5' x 3', safety handles, real-life color detail and design.
Lawn Wet-Slides	$13.95 each	25-foot soft, durable plastic slides with water hose attachment and slick, slippery finish for easy sliding.
Ring Floats	$7.95 each	Tot-size plastic ring floats for beginning swimmers. Strong, durable construction and safety balancing design make learning easy and safe.

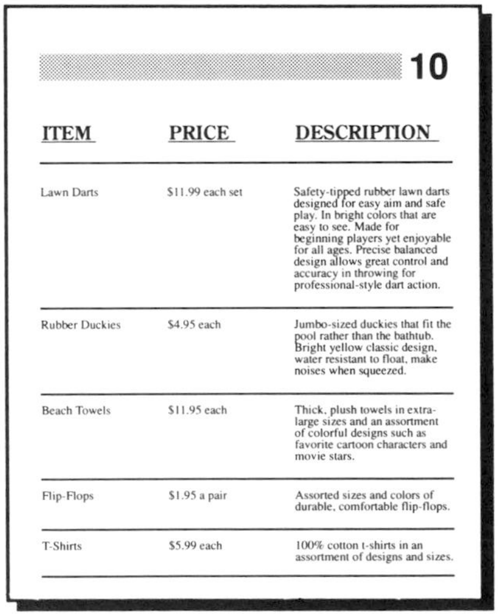

10

ITEM	PRICE	DESCRIPTION
Lawn Darts	$11.99 each set	Safety-tipped rubber lawn darts designed for easy aim and safe play. In bright colors that are easy to see. Made for beginning players yet enjoyable for all ages. Precise balanced design allows great control and accuracy in throwing for professional-style dart action.
Rubber Duckies	$4.95 each	Jumbo-sized duckies that fit the pool rather than the bathtub. Bright yellow classic design, water resistant to float, make noises when squeezed.
Beach Towels	$11.95 each	Thick, plush towels in extra-large sizes and an assortment of colorful designs such as favorite cartoon characters and movie stars.
Flip-Flops	$1.95 a pair	Assorted sizes and colors of durable, comfortable flip-flops.
T-Shirts	$5.99 each	100% cotton t-shirts in an assortment of designs and sizes.

Column Placement and Spacing

After you've selected the type of columns you want, you must determine their placement and spacing.

Column width, placement and spacing greatly influence the appearance and readability of your publications. As you'll learn in Chapter 9, "Planning and Producing Your Documents," column width should relate to the type size you're planning to use. In general, narrow columns work well with small type sizes, and wider columns work well with larger type sizes.

Small type placed in wide columns is difficult to read because the reader gets lost between the end of one line and the beginning of the next.

> 7-point text placed on a 24-pica column is very difficult to read. 7-point text placed on a 24-pica column is very difficult to read. 7-point text placed on a 24-pica column is very difficult to read. 7-point text placed on a 24-pica column is very difficult to read. 7-point text placed on a 24-pica column is very difficult to read. 7-point text placed on a 24-pica column is very difficult to read. 7-point text placed on a 24-pica column is very difficult to read. 7-point text placed on a 24-pica column is very difficult to read. 7-point text placed on a 24-pica column is very difficult to read. 7-point text placed on a

Large type in narrow columns leads to excessive hyphenation and gaps between words.

Your choice of justified or flush-left/ragged-right type also should influence column width.

> 16-point text placed on a 12 pica column is also very difficult to read.

Justified type occurs when the final letters of the text lines are aligned, making each line of type the same length.

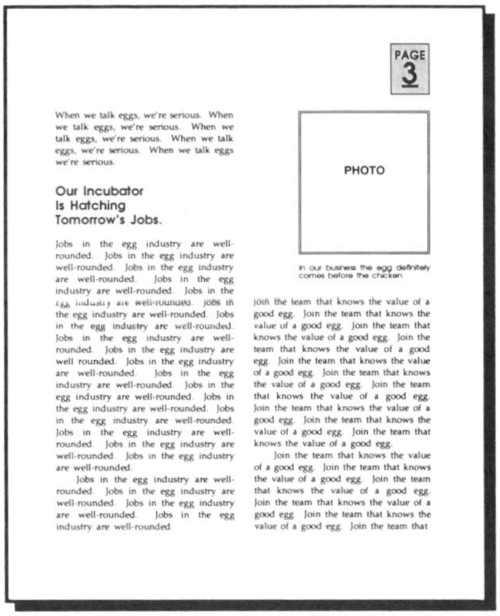

Flush-left/ragged-right type is characterized by lines of irregular length.

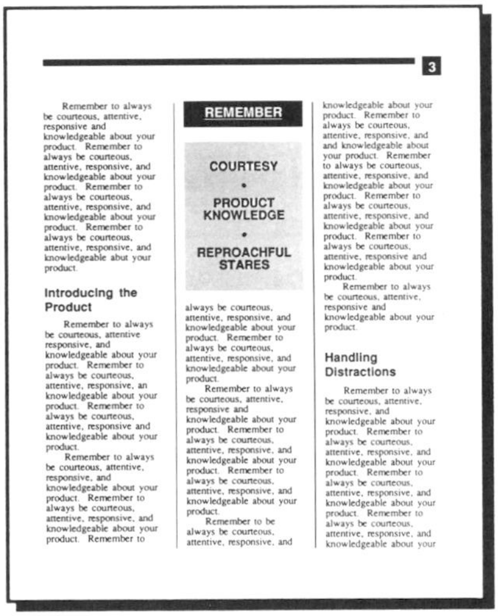

Because justified columns form more distinct visual elements, less space is needed between them than with flush-left/ragged-right columns.

Another design consideration concerns rules. If you plan to add vertical rules between the columns, extra space must be added.

Creating Multicolumn Documents

To create a publication with three columns, start at the Text Column Definition screen.

Select: 2 (NUMBER OF COLUMNS)

Response: 2

Type: 3

Press: (ENTER)

By entering a different number, you've replaced WordPerfect's default with the number of columns you want. Notice that when you replace the two-column default with a different number, column spacing automatically changes.

Next, define the distance between columns.

Select: 3 (DISTANCE BETWEEN COLUMNS)

Response: 0.5"

Type: .75

Press: (ENTER)

This replaces the .5-inch column spacing with a .75-inch gutter (space between columns). Notice that the column widths automatically change to compensate for increased or decreased column spacing.

Setting Individual Column Widths

One of the most important column definition functions is Option 4 (MARGINS), which lets you create columns of different widths. It also lets you determine where each column will be placed in relation to page boundaries.

Select: 4 (MARGINS)

Notice how the cursor immediately jumps to the left dimension of the first column. To accept the default dimension, which WordPerfect computes on the assumption that all columns are of equal width,

Press: (ENTER)

Response: This accepts the default and advances the cursor to the right-hand margin of the first column.

To create a narrow left-hand column for subheads,

Press: 2 (This replaces the 2.67-inch, right-hand default with a narrower column.)

Press: (ENTER) (This advances the screen to let you adjust the left-hand margin of the second column.)

Type: 2.75

Press: (ENTER)

Response: This advances the screen to let you adjust the right-hand margin of the second column.

Type: 4.25

Press: (ENTER)

Response: This advances the screen to let you adjust the left-hand margin of the third column.

Type: 4.5

Press: (ENTER)

This changes the default setting to the setting needed for the second wide column. It also moves the screen to the position where you can adjust the right-hand margin of the right-hand column. To accept this default,

Press: (ENTER)

Working with Multiple Columns

After you've defined the size and placement of each column, accept your column definitions by pressing [F7] (EXIT) or [ENTER].

You're then brought back to the initial COLUMNS/TABLES menu.

Once you've defined the column format you want, turn on WordPerfect's multicolumn feature. Otherwise, the text you enter will continue to extend in an unbroken line from the left-hand margin of the page to the right-hand margin. You may find yourself frequently switching back and forth between single- and multicolumn formats as you add graphic accents or previously created charts, graphs, illustrations or scanned photographs.

For example, you must be in a single-column mode if you want to add horizontal bars as borders at the top and bottom of each page. You also must be in a single-column format if you want to add a large headline that will span all the columns on a page.

To activate the multicolumn format,

Select: 1 (3 in 5.0) (ON)

In WordPerfect 5.0, Option 3 (COLUMN ON/OFF) toggles, or switches, your page format back and forth between single-column and multicolumn format. If you enter new text after WordPerfect's COLUMN feature has been activated, the text automatically will be placed in the correct column. If, however, you define and activate a column layout after text has been entered, you must execute WordPerfect's SCREEN REWRITE command [CTRL-F3, 3] (in WordPerfect 5.0, the commands are [CTRL-F3, 0]). Otherwise, the text will remain unformatted, extending from side to side on your screen until you advance the cursor through the text. To execute this command,

Press: (CTRL-F3) (SCREEN)

Select: 3 (0 in 5.0) (REWRITE)

If you're working in a multicolumn setting and want to return to a single-column format, you would press [ALT-F7] and then select 2 (OFF). In Version 5.0, you would press [ALT-F7] and then select 3 (COLUMNS ON/OFF).

Moving Between Columns

With WordPerfect, it's easy to advance from one column to the next during text entry or editing. When entering text with NEWSPAPER columns, your cursor automatically advances to the top of the next column when you reach the bottom of a column.

HARD PAGE [CTRL-ENTER] advances you from one column to another when you enter text with PARALLEL columns.

When editing text, you can move the cursor back and forth between columns by using WordPerfect's GO TO command [CTRL-HOME], followed by either the right or left cursor control key. For example, to move to the next column on the right,

Press: (CTRL-HOME)

Press: Right cursor control key

To move to the column on the left,

Press: (CTRL-HOME)

Press: Left cursor control key

When editing multicolumn documents, the up and down cursor control and [DELETE] keys are active only within each column. Thus, if you're in the first column, WordPerfect's DELETE TO END OF PAGE command [CTRL-PG DN] will erase text only in that column.

When working in multicolumn text, the status line at the lower right of your screen indicates the column in which you're working. For example, Col 1 shows that the cursor is located in the first column on the page.

Next Column Command

When working with newspaper-type columns, WordPerfect's HARD PAGE command [CTRL-ENTER] makes it easy to end one column and begin the next. Use HARD PAGE when you want subsequent text placed in the next column. This is particularly useful if you want to make the first column shorter than the others. For example, you can use this feature to isolate subheads in the first column of training manuals.

Creating Justified Columns

Before entering text in a column, you may want to switch from flush-left/ragged-right text to justified text. To reactivate text justification (if you've previously turned it off),

Press: (SHIFT-F8) (FORMAT)

Select: 1 (LINE)

Select: 3 (JUSTIFICATION)

In WordPerfect 5.0, you have only two choices: YES for full justification or NO for flush-left/ragged-right. But in Version 5.1, you'll see four choices:

1 Left
2 Center
3 Right
4 Full

Select: 4 (Full) (or type Y in Version 5.0)

Response: Full

Any text you place in the column now will be justified. Extra spaces will be inserted between each word in order to achieve lines of equal length.

If, however, you've been working with justified type, and want to create flush-left/ragged-right columns,

Press: (SHIFT-F8) (FORMAT)

Select: 1 (LINE)

Select: 3 (JUSTIFICATION)

Response: In Version 5.1, you'll again see the four alignment options.

Select: 1 (Left) (or type N in Version 5.0)

Press: (F7) (EXIT)

Words are separated by equal amounts of white space. As a result, each line will be a slightly different length. (As you'll see in Chapter 6, you can regulate the amount of white space in the right-hand margin of each line by using WordPerfect's HYPHENATION [SHIFT-F8, 1, Y]—in WordPerfect 5.0, the command is [SHIFT-F8, 1, 1, 3]—and HYPHENATION ZONE [SHIFT-F8, 1, 2] commands.)

Adding Vertical Rules Between Columns

WordPerfect makes it easy to add vertical rules between columns. As described in Chapter 2, rules can be as thick or thin as you want and—depending upon your printer—you can add "color" to your document by shading rules to various gradations of gray.

Vertical rules between columns can extend the full height of the page or can be shortened to accommodate headlines or illustrations that span more than one column.

Let's say you're working with a three-column document. To add full-length rules between the columns of the document,

Press: (ALT-F9) (GRAPHICS)

Select: 5 (LINE)

Select: 2 (CREATE LINE: VERTICAL)

Response: WordPerfect then displays the VERTICAL LINE menu.

Select: 1 (HORIZONTAL POSITION)

Select: 3 (BETWEEN COLUMNS)

Response: Place line to the Right of Column: 1. Accept this by pressing [ENTER] and then [F7] (EXIT).

Press: (ALT-F9) (GRAPHICS)

Select: 5 (LINE)

Select: 2 (VERTICAL LINE)

Response: WordPerfect then displays the VERTICAL LINE menu.

Select: 1 (HORIZONTAL POSITION)

Select: 3 (BETWEEN COLUMNS)

Response: Place line to the Right of Column: 1

Type: 2

Press: (ENTER)

Press: (F7) (EXIT)

Use WordPerfect's VIEW DOCUMENT command [SHIFT-F7, 6] to preview your work. You'll see that vertical rules extending the full height of each page have been accurately placed between the columns.

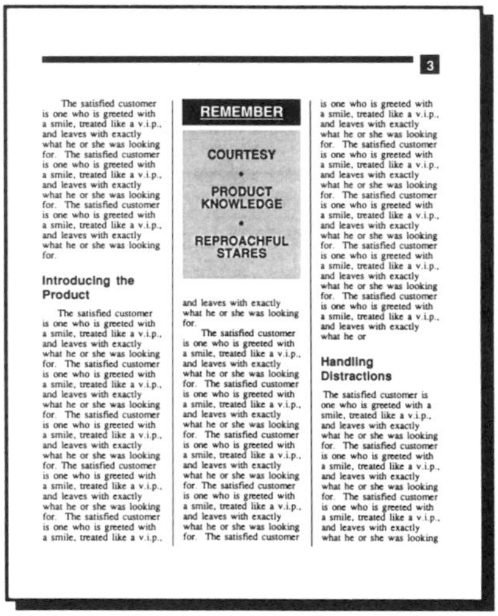

Creating Shorter Rules

WordPerfect also lets you create shorter lines that won't interfere with a headline or illustration spanning more than one column. Let's assume you're working on a three-column document with a headline.

Press: (ALT-F9) (GRAPHICS)

Select: 5 (LINE)

Select: 2 (CREATE LINE: VERTICAL)

Response: WordPerfect then displays the VERTICAL LINE menu.

Select: 1 (HORIZONTAL POSITION)

Select: 3 (BETWEEN COLUMNS)

Response: Place line to the Right of Column: 1. Accept this by pressing [ENTER].

Select: 2 (VERTICAL POSITION)

Select: 4 (BOTTOM)

The line will extend up from the bottom of the page. To determine how high you want the line to extend,

Select: 3 (LENGTH OF LINE)

Response: 9".

This is the normal default for a line that would extend the full height of the page. (Note that this number may be different, depending upon the particular page layout and your printer and monitor.)

Type: 6

Press: (ENTER)

That replaces the 9-inch default with a 6-inch line. To place a 6-inch vertical rule between columns two and three, press [F7] (EXIT). Then,

Press: (ALT-F9) (GRAPHICS)

Select: 5 (LINE)

Select: 2 (CREATE LINE: VERTICAL)

Response: WordPerfect then displays the VERTICAL LINE menu.

Select: 1 (HORIZONTAL POSITION)

Select: 3 (BETWEEN COLUMNS)

Response: Place line to the Right of Column: 1.

Type: 2

Press: (ENTER)

Press: (F7) (EXIT)

That places the line between the second and third columns.

Again, the 9-inch default is replaced with a 6-inch line.

When you PRINT [SHIFT-F7, 2] or VIEW DOCUMENT [SHIFT-F7, 6], you'll see that the 6-inch vertical rules now extend between each of the columns of the page, leaving space for a large headline, horizontal illustration or scanned photograph.

Similar steps are used to place the rule between columns and extend it from the *top* of a page. Let's say you're working on a three-column document that contains a 3-inch high photo at the bottom of the second and third columns. You'll want the rule between columns one and two to be full length. But you'll want columns two and three to be separated by a shorter rule.

Press: (ALT-F9) (GRAPHICS)

Select: 5 (LINE)

Select: 2 (CREATE LINE: VERTICAL)

Response: WordPerfect then displays the VERTICAL LINE menu.

Select: 1 (HORIZONTAL POSITION)

Select: 3 (BETWEEN COLUMNS)

Response: Place line to the Right of Column:1

Press: Accept this by pressing [ENTER] and then [F7] (EXIT). Notice that Option 2 (VERTICAL POSITION) default is FULL PAGE.

Press: (ALT-F9) (GRAPHICS)

Select: 5 (LINE)

Select:	2 (CREATE LINE: VERTICAL)
Response:	WordPerfect then displays the VERTICAL LINE menu.
Select:	1 (HORIZONTAL POSITION)
Select:	3 (BETWEEN COLUMNS)
Response:	Place line to right of Column: 1
Type:	2
Press:	(ENTER)

WordPerfect now knows that you're defining the attributes of the rule between the second and third columns.

Select:	2 (VERTICAL POSITION)
Select:	2 (TOP)

The line now extends down from the top of the page.

To determine how far down you want the line to extend,

Select:	3 (LENGTH OF LINE)
Response:	0.167".

This is the normal default for a line extending down from the top of a page.

Type:	6
Press:	(ENTER)
Press:	(F7) (EXIT)

That replaces the 0.167-inch default with a 6-inch line.

When you PRINT [SHIFT-F7, 2] or VIEW DOCUMENT [SHIFT-F7, 6], your page should resemble the following illustration. There is now room for a two-column chart, graph, illustration or scanned photograph.

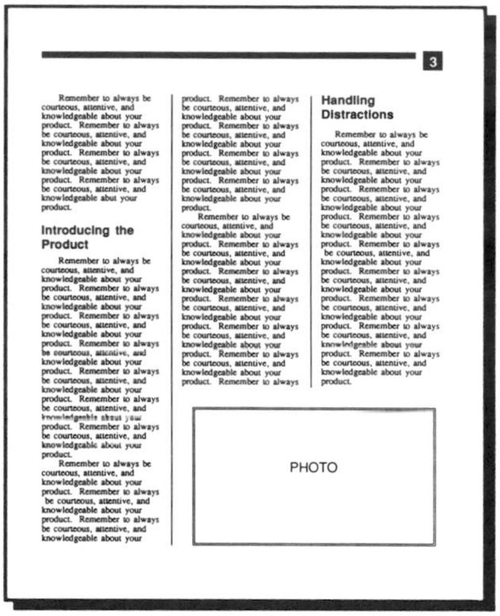

Using Macros to Speed Page Layout

It's entirely possible that you'll want to use more than one page layout structure for your projects. For example, you might want to have one column format for the introduction of your book, another format for the copy that follows and a third format for the index.

WordPerfect's macros make it easy to change from one column format to another. Assign a name to each column format (e.g., CHAPHDS, INTRO, TWOCOL, THREECOL, FOURCOL, etc.) and create a macro file (as described in Chapter 2) for each page format. (In Chapter 8, you'll learn how to edit these macro files.)

Planning Your Documents

You can expedite the process of creating multicolumn documents if you first make actual-size layouts of your pages using traditional design tools: a pencil, paper and ruler. Sketch the page layout you want to create, measure the placement and width of each column, and enter the correct numbers on WordPerfect's TEXT COLUMN definition screen.

Remember that without a large-screen monitor and enhanced graphics capabilities, you'll be able to see your page layouts only by using WordPerfect's VIEW DOCUMENT command [SHIFT-F7, 6]—or when you print your project. So, the more planning you do, the faster your projects will proceed. You'll learn more about this in Section Two.

Placing Headlines in Multicolumn Documents

WordPerfect offers two ways to create headlines or nameplates that span one or more columns when you're working in a multicolumn format. The method you choose depends upon the kind of printer you use and the typeface, type size and style options available. Your choice also will be influenced by whether you intend to use other drawing programs.

There probably will be times when you want to use a sophisticated drawing program to create a publication nameplate that will be repeated from issue to issue. A nameplate might include sophisticated text and graphics that are more efficiently created with a specialized drawing program than with WordPerfect. You might want to create your publication's masthead with a program such as PC Paintbrush, Windows Draw or Dr. Halo. They give you more power to adjust the precise location and shading of the various letters and integrate letters with illustrations (such as scanned images of your logo or corporate seal).

One way to create a headline that spans more than one column is to turn off WordPerfect's COLUMN feature. Let's assume you're working on a two-column document with a headline that extends across the full width of the page.

Press: (ALT-F7) (COLUMNS/TABLES)

Select: 2 (3 in 5.0) (OFF)

Headline text will stretch from the left-hand margin to the right-hand margin.

After you've entered the headline,

Press: (ALT-F7) (COLUMNS/TABLES)

Select: 1 (3 in 5.0) (ON)

You'll be returned again to a multicolumn format.

Headline Boxes

You also can use WordPerfect's USER BOX feature to create a headline box. First, if you're working in multicolumn format, use WordPerfect's COLUMNS/TABLES command [ALT-F7, 2]—or [ALT-F7, 3] in Version 5.0—to return to a single-column format.

Then, using WordPerfect's GRAPHICS command [ALT-F9], make a USER BOX (Option 4) that spans the column, or columns, in which the headline is to appear.

After creating the box, you either can enter the text or use the box as a container to import a headline or newsletter masthead file, previously created with a separate draw-type program. The advantage of using a USER BOX (Option 4) is that the headline won't be included in your document's list of tables, figures or text boxes when you use WordPerfect's LIST GENERATION command [ALT-F5, 6].

However, if you use TEXT BOXes (Option 3) as containers for sidebars, they automatically will be listed—along with short quotations or other text features placed inside TEXT BOXes—when you use the LIST GENERATION command.

To use that feature, let's assume you've created a short five-paragraph sidebar that elaborates upon a point raised in a major article. The index will be based on the caption you use to introduce the TEXT BOX containing the sidebar. Let's say that file has been saved under the file name, GOVERNOR, with the caption, "Governor endorses increased federal spending."

To place the sidebar in your document,

Press: (ALT-F9) (GRAPHICS)

Select: 3 (TEXT BOX)

Select: 1 (CREATE)

Select: 1 (FILENAME)

Type: GOVERNOR (The name of the previously saved text file.)

Response: Replace content with GOVERNOR? No (Yes)

Type: Y (Yes)

Response: GOVERNOR now appears next to the file name prompt.

Select: 3 (2 in 5.0) (CAPTION)

Type: Governor endorses increased federal spending.

WordPerfect uses this caption when compiling a list of sidebars or other text features.

Note how the vertical dimension of the TEXT BOX has been stretched to accommodate the amount of text you've entered. That's particularly important, because if you're working in a multicolumn format, the width of the TEXT BOX is determined by the column within which it's placed.

Press [F7] (EXIT) to get back to your editing screen. You then can evaluate your work by using either the PRINT [SHIFT-F7, 2] or VIEW DOCUMENT [SHIFT-F7, 6] command.

TIP: When creating TEXT BOXes, be sure you don't include more copy than can fit inside the TEXT BOX. Remember that space must be left below the sidebar for the caption.

In later chapters, you'll see how WordPerfect lets you modify the appearance of TEXT BOXes and edit their contents.

Using Horizontal Rules Within Columns

When working in a multicolumn format, remember that lines and boxes are limited to the size of the column within which they're created. If you want to create a line or box that extends beyond the boundaries of the current column, turn off WordPerfect's COLUMNS/TABLES feature [ALT-F7, 2]—or [ALT-F7, 3] in Version 5.0—before you create the line or box.

This works to your benefit, however, if you're using horizontal rules to separate adjacent articles or topics within a column. These rules automatically will conform to the dimensions of your column.

Let's assume you're working in multicolumn format and have just finished one article and are about to begin another. To create a strong horizontal rule that will clearly separate the two topics,

Press: The [ENTER] key to add some white space between the end of one article and the location of the horizontal rule.

Press: (ALT-F9) (GRAPHICS)

Select: 5 (LINE)

Select:	1 (HORIZONTAL LINE)
Select:	1 (HORIZONTAL POSITION)
Select:	4 (FULL) (called BOTH LEFT AND RIGHT in Version 5.0)
Select:	4 (3 in 5.0) (WIDTH OF LINE)
Response:	0.013"
Type:	.05
Press:	(ENTER)

This changes the default to a wider rule.

Press [F7] (EXIT) to return to your screen for editing. Use WordPerfect's PRINT [SHIFT-F7, 2] or VIEW DOCUMENT [SHIFT-F7, 6] command to verify that the rule has been placed correctly.

Remember to add one, or more, carriage returns to add white space below the rule before beginning work on the next article in the column.

Moving On

Now that you've surveyed WordPerfect's major page layout features, it's time to learn how to manipulate graphics—the foundation of graphic design. In the following two chapters, you'll learn how WordPerfect lets you manipulate graphic images to improve the appearance and readability of your documents.

You'll learn how to expedite document assembly by creating macros and styles. And you'll be introduced to the WordPerfect Library software program, a feature that can further improve your productivity.

CHAPTER 4

THE GRAPHICS CONNECTION

As described in Chapter 2, charts, graphs, illustrations and scanned photographs created with other software programs are placed in WordPerfect documents by using boxes—TEXT, FIGURE, TABLE and USER BOXes. These boxes smoothly integrate text and graphics into good-looking, effective print communications.

Even after they've been created, boxes offer a lot of design flexibility. They can be enlarged or reduced in size or moved to different positions. Box borders can be changed, and backgrounds screened. In addition, caption placement can be adjusted, as can the amount of white space between a box and its text, or surrounding a box.

WordPerfect gives you total control over the content of boxes. You can move, resize, rotate or even create reversal effects with graphic images.

Imported graphics, for example, can be cropped by moving them within their boxes.

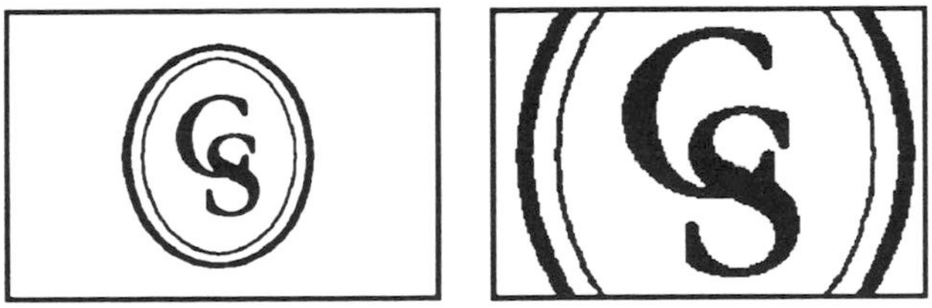

Likewise, imported graphic images can be increased or decreased in size:

What Are Graphics?

Illustrations and scanned photographs are the most frequently used types of graphics. Illustrations can be created with either draw-type or paint-type (bit-map) programs.

Images created with draw-type programs can be increased or decreased in size without losing quality.

Paint-type programs define the placement of individual dots—called pixels. They offer less latitude for image enlargement or reduction. When the images are reduced in size, the dots become too close to each other and detail is lost. Likewise, enlargement can cause an image to break up, because the dots defining the image are moved farther apart.

Photographs can be scanned. Some programs even allow you to hook up a home video camera to your computer and capture "live" images.

Software programs that create graphics files which can be directly placed in WordPerfect documents (partial list):

AutoCAD	Macintosh Paint
Dr. Halo II	PC Paint Plus
GEM Paint	PC Paintbrush
GEM SCAN	PFS: Professional Plan
Lotus 1-2-3	Microsoft Windows Paint
Lotus Symphony	

Software programs that create graphics files which can be placed in WordPerfect documents after conversion to a compatible file format (partial list):

Adobe Illustrator	HP Scanning Gallery
Boeing Graph	SuperCalc4
ChartMaster	VP Planner
Harvard Graphics	

Graphic images also include charts and graphs created with popular spreadsheet programs that convert the results of financial computation and analysis into strong visual statements. These programs include Lotus 1-2-3, Microsoft Excel, WordPerfect's PlanPerfect, Computer Associates' SuperCalc4 and others.

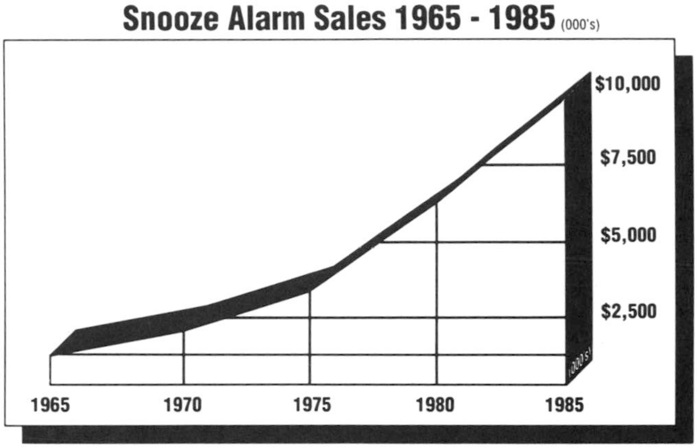

It's important to note, however, that there's more to graphics than illustrations, scanned photographs, graphs and charts. Words also can be "graphics."

For example, you can create a sophisticated masthead as a WordPerfect file, and import and resize it as needed. You might use a sophisticated drawing program to create a distinctive nameplate for a magazine or newsletter. You might even hire an outside graphic artist to create a nameplate file using a highly sophisticated drawing program you wouldn't normally need on a day-to-day basis.

Or, you might use a scanner to copy your firm's logo, so it easily can be placed in your advertisements, brochures and newsletters. Once your logo has been scanned, you can use it over and over again at various sizes in different documents.

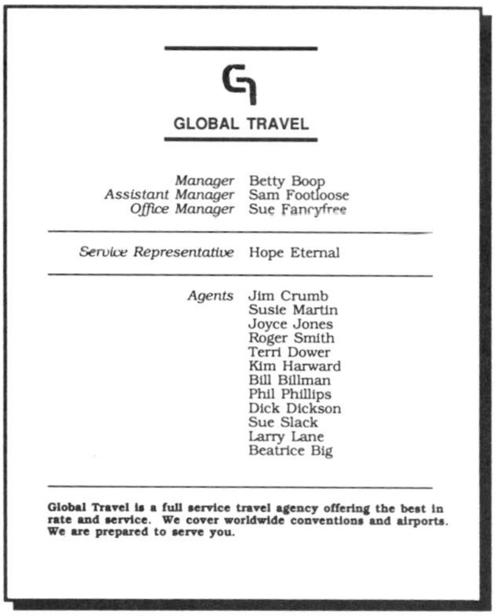
GLOBAL TRAVEL

Manager	Betty Boop
Assistant Manager	Sam Footloose
Office Manager	Sue Fancyfree
Service Representative	Hope Eternal
Agents	Jim Crumb Susie Martin Joyce Jones Roger Smith Terri Dower Kim Harward Bill Billman Phil Phillips Dick Dickson Sue Slack Larry Lane Beatrice Big

Global Travel is a full service travel agency offering the best in rate and service. We cover worldwide conventions and airports. We are prepared to serve you.

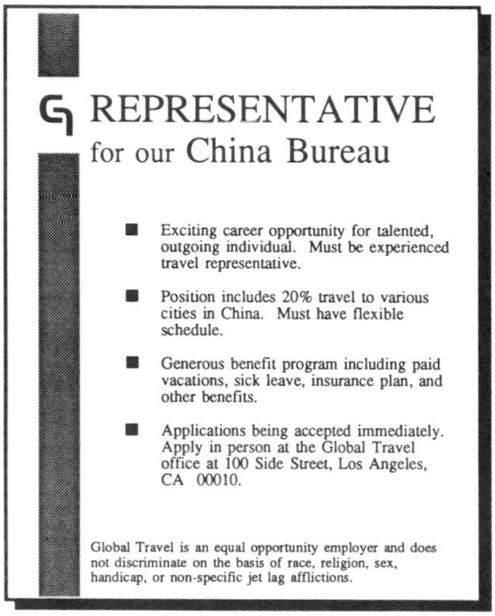
REPRESENTATIVE
for our China Bureau

- Exciting career opportunity for talented, outgoing individual. Must be experienced travel representative.
- Position includes 20% travel to various cities in China. Must have flexible schedule.
- Generous benefit program including paid vacations, sick leave, insurance plan, and other benefits.
- Applications being accepted immediately. Apply in person at the Global Travel office at 100 Side Street, Los Angeles, CA 00010.

Global Travel is an equal opportunity employer and does not discriminate on the basis of race, religion, sex, handicap, or non-specific jet lag afflictions.

Modifying Figure Boxes

After you've created a box, you may want to change its size or location. Your decision may be based on aesthetic considerations. A box might be so large that it overwhelms the page, or so small that it crowds the image it contains.

Another reason to change the size of a box relates to establishing a hierarchy of importance. Important graphics should be larger than supporting graphics. After laying out your publication, you might decide that certain charts, graphs, illustrations or scanned photographs deserve more emphasis. Therefore, they should be larger than the other images.

You might want to change the size and location of boxes when a page contains two or more charts, graphs or illustrations. Strong page design often features boxes of different sizes, adding contrast and increasing visual interest.

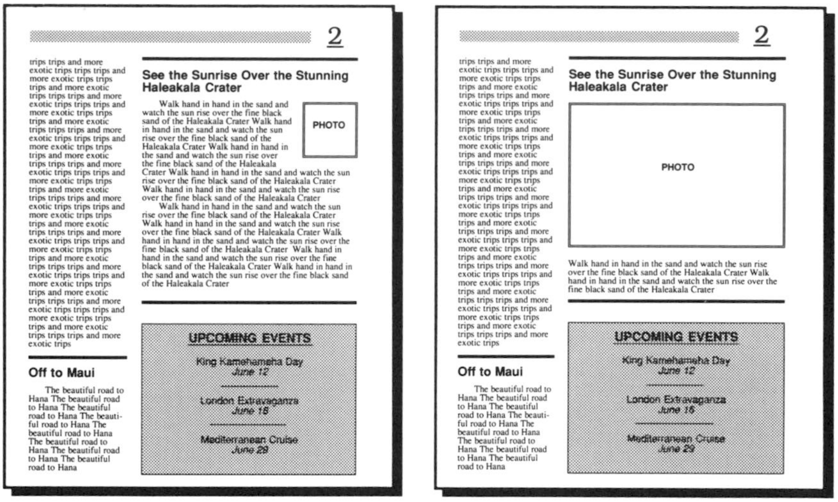

As an example of the ease with which you can change the location and dimensions of a box, start by creating a FIGURE BOX containing the CLOCK.WPG file (the same file used in Chapter 2).

TIP: Although you'll use FIGURE BOX in the following illustrations, remember that many of the same command options also work with TABLE, TEXT and USER BOXes. Remember that each type of box can contain text or graphics. The different box categories primarily exist so WordPerfect can generate different types of lists after your document has been completed. For example, it can compile a list of illustrations, if all illustrations have been placed in FIGURE BOXes. Or it can compile a list of charts, if all charts have been placed in TABLE BOXes.

Let's start by creating and modifying a FIGURE BOX containing the clock graphic used in Chapter 2. First, move the cursor to the top of the document.

Press: (ALT-F9) (GRAPHICS)

Select: 1 (FIGURE)

Select: 1 (CREATE)

Response: Figure Definition screen appears.

```
Definition: Figure

     1 - Filename

     2 - Contents              Empty

     3 - Caption

     4 - Anchor Type           Paragraph

     5 - Vertical Position     0"

     6 - Horizontal Position   Right

     7 - Size                  3.25" wide x 3.25" (high)

     8 - Wrap Text Around Box  Yes

     9 - Edit



Selection: 0
```

Select: 1 (FILENAME)

Type: CLOCK.WPG

Press: (ENTER)

Select: 4 (3 in 5.0) (ANCHOR TYPE)

Select: 2 (PAGE)

Response: Number of pages to skip: 0

Press: (ENTER)

Press: (F7) (EXIT)

This accepts all the defaults. The result is a 3.25-inch square FIGURE BOX. Since you accepted MARGIN, RIGHT as the HORIZONTAL POSITION, the box was placed against the right margin.

Use WordPerfect's VIEW DOCUMENT command [SHIFT-F7, 6] to preview the box; then PRINT [SHIFT-F7, 2], so that you can compare it with the example on the following page.

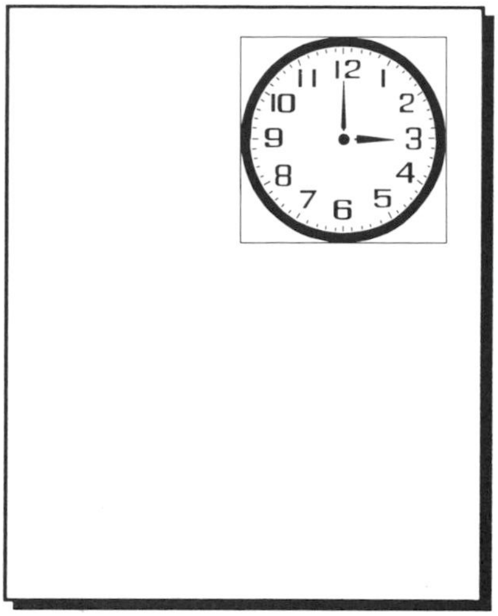

TIP: If the graphics file name has an extension (such as .WPG), be sure to include it when importing graphics. Otherwise, the file cannot be placed in your document. And remember to include the complete subdirectory path in the file name. Otherwise, WordPerfect won't know which subdirectory contains the file you want to import.

Graphics files are usually stored in the same subdirectories as the software programs used to create them, unless you specify otherwise. For example, Lotus 1-2-3 and PlanPerfect charts and graphs are created in their respective Lotus 1-2-3 and PlanPerfect subdirectories. Publisher's Paintbrush files are created in the subdirectory containing the Publisher's Paintbrush program, etc.

WordPerfect can't read your mind. It can't search for a specific file located somewhere in your hard disk. As a result, you must specify the subdirectory in which the graphics file you want to import is stored. Alternately, before assembling your document, copy the files containing graphics to the WordPerfect subdirectory.

Moving a Figure Box

To change the location of the clock on the page,

Press:	(ALT-F9) (GRAPHICS)
Select:	1 (FIGURE)
Select:	2 (EDIT)
Response:	Figure Number? 2 (Or one number higher than the last box created.)

Type: 1

Press: (ENTER)

Response: The original Figure Definition screen appears.

```
Definition: Figure

     1 - Filename               CLOCK.WPG (Graphic)

     2 - Contents               Empty

     3 - Caption

     4 - Anchor Type            Page

     5 - Vertical Position      Top

     6 - Horizontal Position    Margin, Right

     7 - Size                   3.25" wide x 3.25" (high)

     8 - Wrap Text Around Box   Yes

     9 - Edit



Selection: 0
```

To lower the box on the page,

Select: 5 (4 in 5.0) (VERTICAL POSITION)

Response: You'll be offered the following options:

1 (FULL PAGE)
2 (TOP)
3 (CENTER)
4 (BOTTOM)
5 (SET POSITION)

Select: 5 (SET POSITION)

Response: Offset from top of page 1.16"

Type: 3

Press: (ENTER)

Response: The graphics box is moved 3 inches down from the top of the page.

Press: (F7) (EXIT)

Response: This returns you to the editing screen and you can use VIEW DOCUMENT [SHIFT-F7, 6] to preview your page.

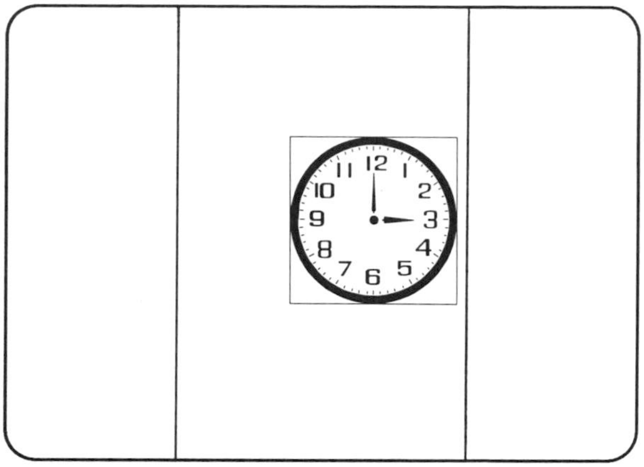

Now, let's move the box to the left.

Press: (ALT-F9) (GRAPHICS)

Select: 1 (FIGURE)

Select: 2 (EDIT)

Response: Figure 2

Again, replace the FIGURE 2 default with FIGURE 1.

Type: 1

Press: (ENTER)

When the original screen setup appears,

Select: 6 (5 in 5.0) (HORIZONTAL POSITION)

Response: You'll be offered the following choices:

1 (MARGINS)
2 (COLUMNS)
3 (SET POSITION)

Select: 3 (SET POSITION)

Response: Offset from left of page: 0"

Type: 3

Press: (ENTER)

Press: (F7) (EXIT)

The clock now is 3 inches from the left-hand border of the page in which it has been placed. Again, VIEW DOCUMENT [SHIFT-F7, 6] or PRINT [SHIFT-F7, 1].

By letting you align boxes with the borders of a page or column, WordPerfect makes it easy for you to control the appearance of your documents.

Other Placement Options

As described in Chapter 2, WordPerfect lets you define boxes as page-, paragraph- or character-anchored. A page-anchored box, such as the one used in the illustration above, is locked to a specific position on a page regardless of changes in the text surrounding it. Paragraph- and character-anchored boxes, however, are placed with specific text surrounding them and will change page position as the position of the text changes.

Remember that the original vertical and horizontal position of paragraph-anchored boxes is determined by cursor placement. By selecting Option 5 (4 in 5.0) (VERTICAL POSITION) and/or Option 6 (5 in 5.0) (HORIZONTAL POSITION), you can center the box on the page or within a column, or place it anywhere on the page. Choose from the following VERTICAL POSITION options:

1 (FULL PAGE)
2 (TOP)
3 (CENTER)
4 (BOTTOM)
5 (SET POSITION)

HORIZONTAL POSITION options are:

1 (MARGINS)
2 (COLUMNS)
3 (SET POSITION)

In both cases, SET POSITION lets you define the position of the box with mathematical accuracy. As you produce more sophisticated projects, you're likely to use the HORIZONTAL and VERTICAL POSITION options more and more.

TIP: You can change the measuring system at any point by executing WordPerfect's SETUP [SHIFT-F1] command. You can specify cursor location in inches, points, centimeters or the column/cursor position measuring system used in previous versions of WordPerfect.

Press: (SHIFT-F1) (SETUP)

Select: 3 (ENVIRONMENT) (This step is not used in Version 5.0.)

Select: 8 (UNITS OF MEASURE)

You can choose between the following options:

" for inches
i for inches
c for centimeters
p for points
w for 1200ths of an inch

You also can choose u (for lines and columns), which is similar to the way WordPerfect 4.2 kept track of cursor location.

Press: (F7) (EXIT) to return to the editing screen.

Resizing Figure Boxes

Not only is it easy to reposition boxes, it's also easy to enlarge or reduce them. Let's change the size of the FIGURE BOX:

Press: (ALT-F9) (GRAPHICS)

Select: 1 (FIGURE)

Select: 2 (EDIT)

Response: Figure 2 (or one number higher than the highest number created.)

Type: 1

Press: (ENTER)

This replaces the default FIGURE 2 with FIGURE 1. When the original screen setup appears,

Select: 7 (6 in 5.0) (SIZE)

Response: You're presented with four options (Version 5.0 offers only three options):

1 (SET WIDTH/AUTO HEIGHT)
2 (SET HEIGHT/AUTO WIDTH)
3 (SET BOTH)
4 (AUTO BOTH)

If you choose 1 (SET WIDTH/AUTO HEIGHT), the height of the box automatically will be made proportionate to the width of the graphics file being placed.

If you choose 2 (SET HEIGHT/AUTO WIDTH), the width of the box automatically will be made proportionate to the height of the graphics file being introduced.

Option 3 (SET BOTH) offers the most flexibility. You can arbitrarily determine the proportions of the box. You can distort the graphic by stretching or compressing it.

Option 4 (AUTO BOTH) resets the box's height and width to their original dimensions.

Proportionately Increasing Box Width

Let's make the box wider, but maintain correct proportions. Continuing from the three options presented above,

Select: 1 (SET WIDTH/AUTO HEIGHT)

Response: Width = 3.25"

Type: 5

Press: (ENTER)

Response: Notice that because CLOCK.WPG is a square graphic, the height also is made 5 inches. If the original graphic were a rectangle, the height would increase by an amount proportionate to the width.

Proportionately Increasing Box Height

Next, let's proportionately reduce box size.

Select: 7 (6 in 5.0) (SIZE)

Select: 2 (SET HEIGHT/AUTO WIDTH)

Response: Height = 3.25"

Type: 2

Press: (ENTER)

Response: Notice how the width is reduced to 2 inches, again maintaining the correct proportions of the square graphic.

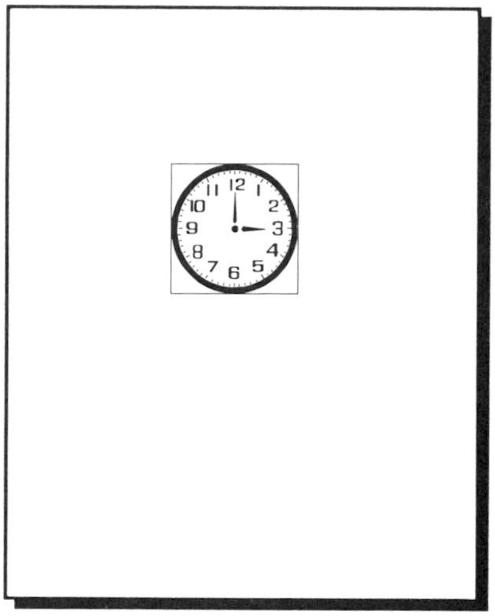

Now, change the FIGURE BOX to a rectangular box for the square graphic. Working with the same figure you just modified,

Select: 7 (6 in 5.0) (SIZE)

Select: 3 (SET BOTH)

Response: Width = 5"

Press: (ENTER)

Response: Height = 2"

Type: 4

Press: (ENTER)

Press: (F7) (EXIT)

When you use VIEW DOCUMENT [SHIFT-F7, 6] or PRINT [SHIFT-F7, 1], the clock will be centered in the rectangular box.

TIP: If you're using a Hewlett-Packard LaserJet II printer, remember that the maximum size of graphic images you can print is determined by the amount of printer memory. If you exceed memory limitations, graphic images will be printed on separate pieces of paper.

Creating Empty Figure Boxes

WordPerfect lets you create empty FIGURE BOXes before you create the files that will be placed in them. You can define their position and size, and place the graphics files in them later. To create empty FIGURE BOXes, leave 1 (FILENAME) blank.

Press: (ALT-F9) (GRAPHICS)

Select: 1 (FIGURE)

Select: 1 (CREATE)

Leave 1 (FILENAME) blank, and enter the TYPE, VERTICAL POSITION, HORIZONTAL POSITION and SIZE placement and dimensions desired. Press [ENTER] after you've defined the size and position.

Filling Empty Figure Boxes

Later you can return to the empty FIGURE BOX and place a graphics file.

Press: (ALT-F9) (GRAPHICS)

Select: 1 (FIGURE)

Select: 2 (EDIT)

Response: A new figure number (one higher than the number of the last FIGURE BOX you created) will be assigned.

Type: The number of the FIGURE BOX you want to fill.

Select: 1 (FILENAME)

Type: The name of the graphics file you want to insert. In this case, ARROW1.WPG.

Press: (ENTER)

Press: (F7) (EXIT)

Note that when you use VIEW DOCUMENT [SHIFT-F7, 6] or PRINT [SHIFT-F7, 1] the box automatically will be resized to accommodate the graphics file you've imported.

Moving Graphics Inside Boxes

You also can change the vertical or horizontal location of a graphic inside a box. This is similar to the way photographs are cropped, eliminating distracting details on the edges.

Press: (ALT-F9) (GRAPHICS)

Select: 1 (FIGURE)

Select: 2 (EDIT)

Response: Figure 2 (WordPerfect defaults to highest figure created.)

Type: 1

Press: (ENTER)

Select: 9 (8 in 5.0) (EDIT)

Response: Figure 1, with the clock graphic, now appears on the screen.

Press: Left cursor control key

Response: Each time you press the left cursor control key, the clock will move slightly to the left, shifting by the percentage indicated in the lower right-hand corner of the screen. The default is 10 percent.

Press: (INSERT) (This changes the amount of displacement. You can choose 1, 5, 10 or 25 percent displacement.)

You also can move the graphic a specific distance.

Select: 1 (MOVE)

Response: Horizontal: 1"

Type: 2

Press: (ENTER) (ENTER)

This moves the clock 2 inches to the right.

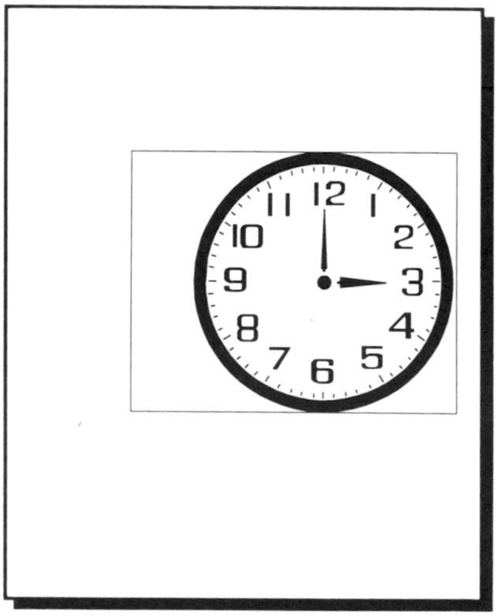

If you want to move the clock 2 inches to the left, enter a negative number (e.g., -2).

To move the graphic vertically,

Select: 1 (MOVE)

Press: (ENTER)

Response: Vertical: 1"

Type: 1.5

Press: (ENTER)

This moves the clock image 1.5 inches higher in the box.

If you want to lower the clock 1.5 inches, enter a negative number (e.g., -1.5).

Remember, positive numbers move the graphic image up and/or to the right. Negative numbers move the graphic down and/or to the left.

Resizing Graphic Images Within Boxes

While in the GRAPHICS EDIT mode, you also can increase or decrease the size of the graphic image without changing the size of the box. Graphic images can be enlarged or reduced to emphasize important parts or eliminate unnecessary details at the edges.

Press: [PAGE UP]

Response: The clock is increased in size proportionate to the percentage indicated in the lower right-hand corner of your screen.

To reduce the size of the clock,

Press: [PAGE DOWN]

Response: The clock is decreased in size proportionate to the percentage indicated in the lower right-hand corner of your screen.

To change the percentage of enlargement or reduction,

Press: [INSERT]

Again, you can increase or decrease image size 1, 5, 10 or 25 percent by pressing the [INSERT] key.

You'll find that WordPerfect's MOVE and SCALE capabilities greatly improve the appearance of your projects by letting you place the graphics exactly where you want them, scaled to the size you want.

Creating Special Effects with Distorted Images

WordPerfect allows you to create special effects by distorting a graphic—disproportionately modifying the height and width of the image. While in the EDIT mode,

Seloct: 2 (SCALE)

Response: Scale X: 100

Type: 150

Press: (ENTER)

Response: Scale Y: 100

Type: 300

Press: (ENTER)

The result is a seriously distorted clock!

Returning to Your Original Graphic Image

After experimenting with moving and resizing the clock graphic, you may wish there were an easy way to return to the original clock image. WordPerfect provides one.

Press: (CTRL-HOME) (GO TO)

Response: Instantly, the graphic returns to its original image.

Rotating Graphic Images

You also can rotate imported graphic images. To rotate the clock to the left,

Press: - (The gray minus key)

To rotate the clock to the right,

Press: + (The gray plus key)

Once again, you can control the degree of rotation by using the (INSERT) key to toggle between 1, 5, 10 and 25 percent image rotation.

Alternately, you can rotate the graphic image a specific number of degrees. To do this,

Select: 3 (ROTATE)

Response: Enter number of degrees (0-360): 0

Type: 90

Press: (ENTER)

Response: Mirror image? No (Yes)

Press: (ENTER)

Response: The clock is rotated 90 degrees to the left (or counter-clockwise).

TIP: You can rotate a graphic image only from its original position. For example, if you want to rotate an image 90 degrees, you must rotate it in one step, rather than in two separate 45-degree incremental steps.

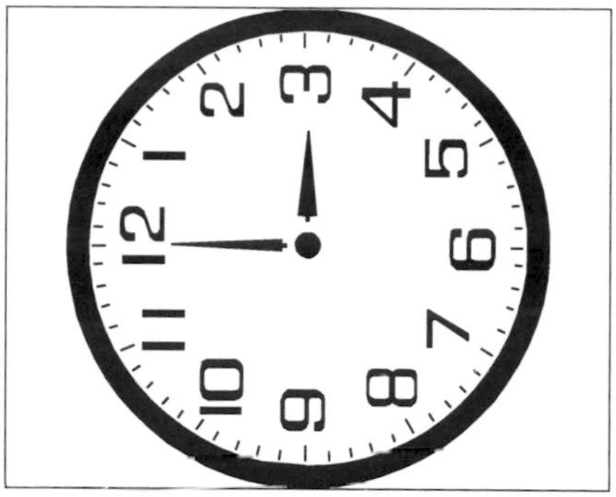

If, you want a mirror image, at the above prompt,

Type: Y

Response: The clock is rotated 90 degrees and appears in mirror image.

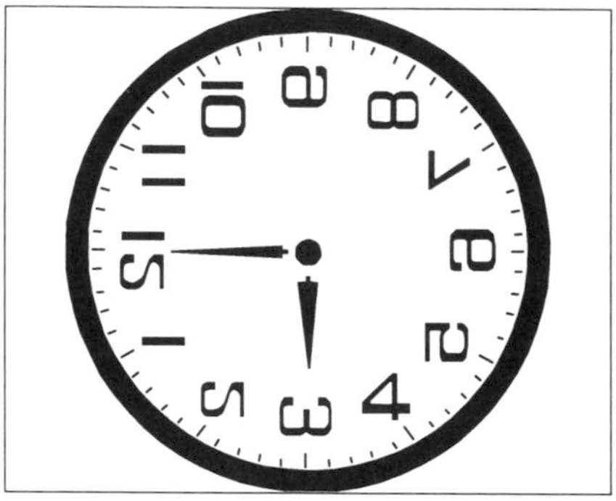

Again, you can restore the original graphic image by using WordPerfect's GO TO command [CTRL-HOME].

Reversed Images

While editing bit-mapped graphic images, you can create negative, or reversal, effects. Bit-mapped graphic images are created with paint-type drawing programs and certain image scanners which let you create illustrations with a lot of shadow effects and varying shades of gray.

Reversed images can be used to create artistic, impressionistic effects. When you reverse a bit-mapped image, the white areas become black, and the black areas become white. The shape of the original illustration or scanned image remains recognizable, but more abstract and stylized. To reverse the clock image,

Select: 4 (INVERT)

Note that this command has no effect upon draw-type images. It's primarily used with scanned photographs and illustrations.

In all of the above cases, WordPerfect's graphics power lets you manipulate boxes and graphic images until their proportions are exactly "right" for their environment.

Changing Borders and Backgrounds

With WordPerfect, you easily can change the borders of FIGURE, TABLE, TEXT and USER BOXes. These changes will affect all the boxes that follow in a document. So make sure the cursor is on the FIGURE BOX definition code before proceeding.

Press: (ALT-F9) (GRAPHICS)

Select: 1 (FIGURE)

Select: 4 (OPTIONS)

Response: You're presented with the FIGURE BOX options menu.

```
Options: Figure

     1 - Border Style
              Left                         Single
              Right                        Single
              Top                          Single
              Bottom                       Single
     2 - Outside Border Space
              Left                         0.167"
              Right                        0.167"
              Top                          0.167"
              Bottom                       0.167"
     3 - Inside Border Space
              Left                         0"
              Right                        0"
              Top                          0"
              Bottom                       0"
     4 - First Level Numbering Method      Numbers
     5 - Second Level Numbering Method     Off
     6 - Caption Number Style              [BOLD]Figure 1[bold]
     7 - Position of Caption               Below box, Outside borders
     8 - Minimum Offset from Paragraph     0"
     9 - Gray Shading (% of black)         0%

Selection: 0
```

Select: 1 (BORDER STYLE)

Note the options available for each of the four sides of the FIGURE BOX:

1 (NONE)
2 (SINGLE)
3 (DOUBLE)
4 (DASHED)
5 (DOTTED)
6 (THICK)
7 (EXTRA THICK)

For purposes of illustration, let's replace the SINGLE border default with an EXTRA THICK border.

Select: 7 (EXTRA THICK)

Response: This replaces the SINGLE left border default with the EXTRA THICK default. The cursor is advanced down to the right border setting. Again,

Select: 7 (EXTRA THICK)

Repeat this two more times, for the top and bottom borders, and preview your work.

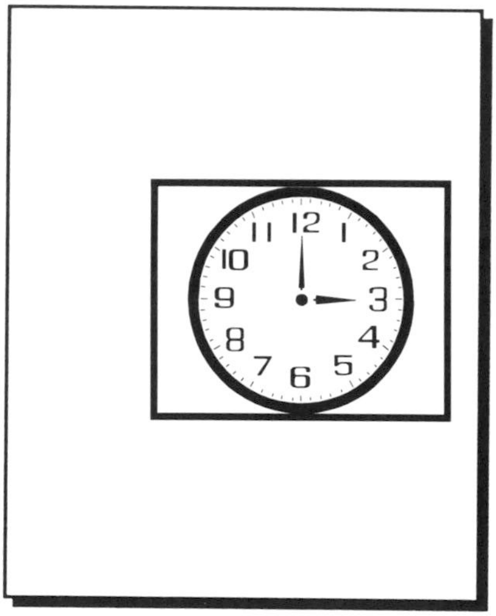

If you want the clock to "float" on the page, remove the borders. First, make sure the cursor is on the FIGURE BOX definition code. Then, for the BORDER STYLE option,

Select: 1 (NONE) (for each of the borders)

Press: (F7) (EXIT)

Adding Shaded Backgrounds to Figure Boxes

Return again to the FIGURE BOX options screen and replace the thin single line default borders. Be sure the cursor is on the FIGURE BOX definition code.

Select: 9 (GRAY SHADING (% OF BLACK))

Response: Note that the default is 0%, which means that the graphic image appears against a white background.

Type: 20 (This changes the original 0% default to 20%.)

Press: (ENTER)

Press: (F7) (EXIT)

Preview or print.

Notice how the appearance of the graphic image has changed. The light gray background behind the graphic image helps distinguish it from the surrounding body copy.

Adding White Space Around Boxes

Now you've seen how WordPerfect allows you to manipulate imported graphic images creatively—moving them, resizing them, distorting them and even in some cases reversing them. WordPerfect lets you orchestrate precisely the way the graphic images and their captions relate to surrounding headlines and body copy.

For example, you can adjust the amount of space between a box and adjacent body copy. Adjusting the white space surrounding FIGURE, TABLE, TEXT and USER BOXes greatly influences the "color" of your document. Start with the cursor on the FIGURE BOX definition code.

Press: (ALT-F9) (GRAPHICS)

Select: 1 (FIGURE)

Select: 4 (OPTIONS)

Select: 2 (OUTSIDE BORDER SPACE)

Response: The cursor advances to the 0.167 percent default for the left border.

Type: .5

Press: (ENTER)

Response: The cursor advances to the 0.167-inch default for the right border.

Type: .25

Press: (ENTER)

Response: The cursor advances to the 0.167-inch default for the top border.

Type: .5

Press: (ENTER)

Response: The cursor advances to the 0.167-inch default for the bottom border.

Type: 1

Press: (ENTER)

Press: (F7) (EXIT)

When you preview or print the page, the difference will be obvious.

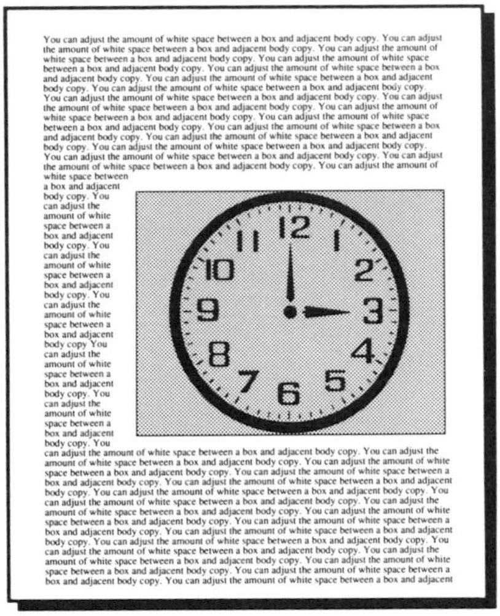

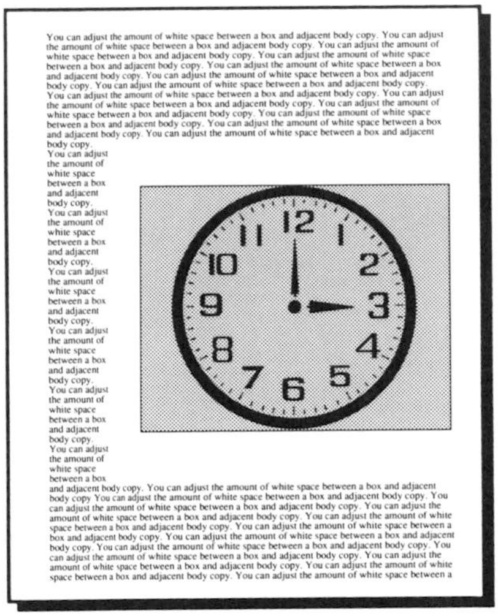

Adding White Space Within Boxes

Likewise, you can adjust the internal space between a box and its contents. Start with the cursor on the FIGURE BOX definition code.

Press: (ALT-F9) (GRAPHICS)

Select: 1 (FIGURE)

Select: 4 (OPTIONS)

Select: 3 (INSIDE BORDER SPACE)

Response: The cursor advances to the 0" default for the inside left border.

Replace the 0" defaults for the Left, Right, Top and Bottom spaces with new figures. That adds white space within boxes, again "opening up" the design of your document.

Compare this...

with this...

Captions

WordPerfect does most of the work involved in placing captions, which automatically extend the width of any FIGURE, TABLE, TEXT or USER BOX you create. If you change the dimensions of the box, the caption length automatically changes.

Compare this...

The time is 3:00 on the dot. Is it not?

with this...

The time is 3:00 on the dot. Is it not?

Placing Captions

WordPerfect lets you place captions either above or below FIGURE, TABLE, TEXT or USER BOXes. Make sure the cursor is on the FIGURE BOX definition code.

Press: (ALT-F9) (GRAPHICS)

Select: 1 (FIGURE)

Select: 4 (OPTIONS)

Select: 7 (POSITION OF CAPTION)

Select: 1 (BELOW BOX)
or
2 (ABOVE BOX)

Regardless of which option you choose, you then can decide whether you want to place the caption inside or next to the box.

Select: 1 (OUTSIDE OF BORDER)

or

2 (INSIDE OF BORDER)

Press: (F7) (EXIT)

WordPerfect thus gives you four ways captions can relate to FIGURE, TABLE, TEXT or USER BOXes. By carefully using these alternatives, you can provide your document with a distinctive look.

The time is 3:00 on the dot. Is it not?

The time is 3:00 on the dot. Is it not?

Other Caption Options

WordPerfect makes it easy to define other caption attributes. For example, you can choose a specific caption numbering style, as well as define a typeface and type size to be used in all captions. At the Options screen,

Select: 6 (CAPTION NUMBER STYLE)

Response: Replace with: (BOLD)Figure 1(bold)

At this point, you can eliminate the boldface type or, using WordPerfect's FONT command [CTRL-F8] described in Chapter 5, define the specific type characteristics you want for the captions. You can, for example, choose a small italic type and select either flush-left/ragged-right or jus-justified lines of type.

You also can define the caption numbering scheme. At the Options screen,

Select: 4 (FIRST LEVEL NUMBERING METHOD)

Response: 1 (OFF)
2 (NUMBERS)
3 (LETTERS)
4 (ROMAN NUMERALS)

Select: Choose the option that best fits the graphic identity of your project.

Likewise, if you're using two-level caption numbering (each caption is numbered according to the chapter in which it's located), you can repeat the process and select a number scheme for second-level captions. At the Options screen,

Select: 5 (SECOND LEVEL NUMBERING METHOD)

Response: 1 (OFF)
2 (NUMBERS)
3 (LETTERS)
4 (ROMAN NUMERALS)

Select: Again, choose the option that best fits in with the graphic identity of your project.

Adjusting Minimum Paragraph Offset

WordPerfect lets you determine the minimum amount of white space that separates a box from an adjacent paragraph. At the Options screen,

Select: 8 (MINIMUM OFFSET FROM PARAGRAPH)

Response: 0" (Default)

When placing a PARAGRAPH BOX, WordPerfect often reduces the white space between the paragraph and the box, in order to place both on the same page. This can lead to inconsistency, however, creating more space around some boxes than others. You can avoid this by specifying a minimum value.

Type: .25

Press: (ENTER)

At least .25 inch of white space will be maintained between the box and the top of the paragraph. If the paragraph is too long to allow for that on one page, the box will be shifted to the next page.

Overlapping Text and Graphics

There may be occasions when you would like words—particularly headlines—to be superimposed over graphic images. To place text over an existing FIGURE BOX,

Press:	(ALT-F9) (GRAPHICS)
Select:	1 (FIGURE)
Select:	2 (EDIT)
Response:	One number higher than the number of the last FIGURE BOX created.
Type:	The number of the box over which you want to superimpose type.
Press:	(ENTER)
Select:	8 (7 in 5.0) (WRAP TEXT AROUND BOX)
Response:	Yes (No)
Type:	N (NO)
Press:	(F7) (EXIT)

This replaces the YES default. Type will be superimposed over the imported graphic.

Moving On

As the examples in this chapter indicate, desktop publishing with WordPerfect is made possible by careful definition and placement of FIGURE, TABLE, TEXT and USER BOXes. These boxes allow you to integrate your words with previously created charts, drawings, graphs, scanned photographs and text units, such as logos and mastheads.

In the next chapter, you'll learn some of the ways WordPerfect lets you control the placement and appearance of words. You'll find its typographic features to be as exciting as its ability to place and manipulate graphics.

CHAPTER 5

WORKING WITH TYPE

What most distinguishes desktop-published materials from conventional typewritten documents? The answer is type—meaning the wealth of typefaces, type sizes and type styles that gives even the simplest document a professional look.

After all, which of the two resumes below would you prefer if you were an employer making a hiring decision or a job-seeker applying for a job?

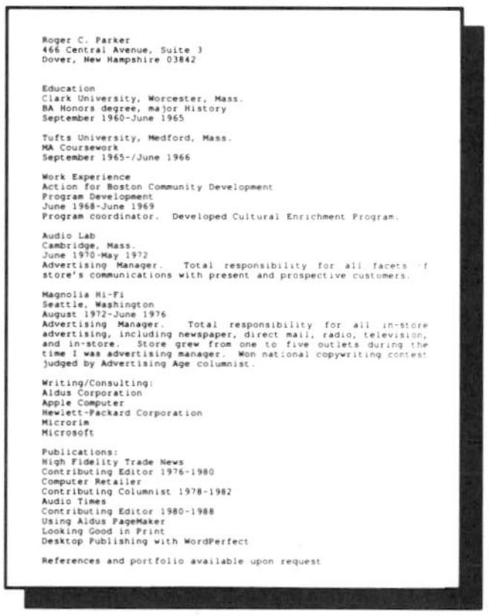

Roger C. Parker
466 Central Avenue, Suite 3
Dover, New Hampshire 03842

Education
Clark University, Worcester, Mass.
BA Honors degree, major History
September 1960-June 1965

Tufts University, Medford, Mass.
MA Coursework
September 1965-/June 1966

Work Experience
Action for Boston Community Development
Program Development
June 1968-June 1969
Program coordinator. Developed Cultural Enrichment Program.

Audio Lab
Cambridge, Mass.
June 1970-May 1972
Advertising Manager. Total responsibility for all facets of store's communications with present and prospective customers.

Magnolia Hi-Fi
Seattle, Washington
August 1972-June 1976
Advertising Manager. Total responsibility for all in-store advertising, including newspaper, direct mail, radio, television, and in-store. Store grew from one to five outlets during the time I was advertising manager. Won national copywriting contest judged by Advertising Age columnist.

Writing/Consulting:
Aldus Corporation
Apple Computer
Hewlett-Packard Corporation
Microrim
Microsoft

Publications:
High Fidelity Trade News
Contributing Editor 1976-1980
Computer Retailer
Contributing Columnist 1978-1982
Audio Times
Contributing Editor 1980-1988
Using Aldus PageMaker
Looking Good in Print
Desktop Publishing with WordPerfect

References and portfolio available upon request

ROGER C. PARKER

466 Central Avenue, Suite 3
Dover, New Hampshire 03842
603-742-9673

EDUCATION

Clark University, Worcester, Mass.
BA Honors degree, major History
September 1960-June 1965

Tufts University, Medford, Mass.
MA Coursework
September 1965-/June 1966

EMPLOYMENT

Action for Boston Community Development
Program Development
June 1968-June 1969
Program coordinator. Developed Cultural Enrichment Program.

Audio Lab
Cambridge, Mass.
June 1970-May 1972
Advertising Manager. Total responsibility for all facets of store's communications with present and prospective customers.

Magnolia Hi-Fi
Seattle, Washington
August 1972-June 1976
Advertising Manager. Total responsibility for all in store advertising, including newspaper, direct mail, radio, television, and in-store. Store grew from one to five outlets during the time I was advertising manager. Won national copywriting contest judged by Advertising Age columnist.

WRITING/CONSULTING

Aldus Corporation
Apple Computer
Hewlett-Packard Corporation
Microrim
Microsoft

PUBLICATIONS

High Fidelity Trade News
Contributing Editor 1976-1980
Computer Retailer
Contributing Columnist 1978-1982
Audio Times
Contributing Editor 1980-1988
Using Aldus PageMaker
Looking Good in Print
Desktop Publishing with WordPerfect

REFERENCES

Jeff Sandine
Ballard Computer, Inc.
206-782-8591

Len Twesen
Magnolia Hi-Fi and Video, Inc.
206-234-0987

Larry Daywitt
Analog and Digital Systems, Inc.
617-782-0987

Portfolio available upon request

WordPerfect makes it easy to incorporate a variety of typefaces, type sizes and type styles—bold, italics, etc.—into your projects, even while you're writing or editing them.

Type Influences Readership

"Font" is an all-encompassing term referring to a complete set of letters, numbers and symbols (asterisks, copyright symbols, etc.) which appear in a particular typeface, type size and type style.

By using WordPerfect's FONT command [CTRL-F8], you can select or change the typeface, type size or type style used in your document while you're writing it. All words entered after the FONT command is activated will appear in the newly selected type characteristics.

Or, you can use the FONT command while editing or formatting your document by highlighting the words or phrases you want to appear in a typeface, type size or type style different from that used for the unhighlighted text.

Typographical variations enhance the communicating power of your documents in several ways:

First, they help organize a hierarchy of information. Important words, such as headlines, can be made larger in order to attract more attention than supporting body copy.

Moreover, you can help readers quickly locate information by using subheads, which not only supplement headlines but highlight key sections throughout your document.

Finally, the use of different typefaces, type sizes and type styles provides visual contrast, keeping readers interested.

A Brief Review of Basic Typography

Five characteristics determine the way words and letters appear on the printed page: typeface, type size, attributes, alignment and spacing. Each characteristic is defined below.

Typeface

Each typeface has its own distinct appearance and personality, created by the shape of its letters. The thickness of the strokes of each letter and its decorative characteristics also affect the "look" of each typeface.

Typefaces have two primary distinguishing characteristics. First, they are either serif or sans-serif (without serif). Serifs are decorative strokes at the ends of the main stems of letters. Notice that in this book, the body copy is serif, while the section headings are sans-serif. Second, a typeface is either equally spaced or proportionally spaced. In a proportional typeface, letters like "i" and "l" take up less room than letters like "o" and "d."

Each typeface speaks to readers in a different tone of voice. Some typefaces are formal, some elegant, and some authoritative. Some typefaces create an old-fashioned feeling, others a contemporary atmosphere. Some typefaces—often referred to as decorative or "display" faces—are best for headlines. Other typefaces are better suited for body copy.

Park Avenue is an elegant typeface, ideally suited for formal invitations and menus for expensive restaurants.

You're Invited To The Grand Opening
Of Our New Salon

Avant Garde has a clean, contemporary look.

Vision and Intuition,
Architects and Planners, Inc.

Bookman has a decorative feel without being overdone.

Now You Can Enjoy
Country Living In The City

A typeface visually colors a publication, influencing readership. Some typefaces are dense, with closely packed letters. Others spread the letters out, increasing readability. Notice the difference in line length between the three samples below, all set in the same type size:

The quick brown fox jumped.

The quick brown fox jumped.

The quick brown fox jumped.

Times Roman, a popular choice for body copy, allows many words to fit within a given space. Helvetica type spaces the letters farther apart.

Type Size

Type size is measured in points. There are 72 points to the inch. The body copy of this book appears in 10-point Palatino type. The header at the top of each page is set in 8-point Avant Garde. Chapter titles on the first page of each chapter are set in 26-point Avant Garde type. Subheads introducing the major subdivisions of each chapter are set in 12.5-point

Avant Garde. Secondary subheads are set in 11-point type, while page numbers are set in 8-point Avant Garde.

Attributes

Within each typeface are several variations, or attributes, in addition to regular (roman) type. The most common include **boldface**, *italics* and underlined.

Alignment

Type can be placed flush-left, flush-right, centered or justified. Most type is set flush-left, which is easy to read because the reader's eyes can locate the beginning of each line quickly.

Flush-left/ragged-right type is characterized by irregular line endings. Most lines break at the ends of words. Some lines break with hyphenation—words split by syllables. The irregular amounts of white space at the end of each line create documents with an "open" or "contemporary" feeling that invites the eye.

The quick brown fox
jumped over the lazy
dog. The quick brown
fox jumped over the
lazy dog.

When type is justified, the first and last letters in each line are aligned with the first and last letters in the lines above and below it. WordPerfect subtly and automatically increases or decreases word spacing so that each line is of equal length. Justified type has a "formal" look to it and lets you increase the word density of your documents.

The quick brown fox
jumped over the lazy
dog. The quick brown
fox jumped over the
lazy dog.

Centered text is used primarily for headlines that contain no more than four lines of type. Centered text reduces readability, because readers have to make a conscious effort to find the beginning of each line.

The quick brown fox
jumped over the
lazy dog. The
quick brown fox
jumped over the
lazy dog.

Flush-right text also slows down reading and is best used for special applications. These include

- Relating subheads to body copy.
- Organizing lists so that related information in an adjacent column is as close as possible.
- Captions set to the left of a photograph or illustration.
- Short headlines.

The quick brown fox
jumped over the
lazy dog. The
quick brown fox
jumped over the
lazy dog.

Spacing

Letter, line, word and paragraph spacing have a great deal of influence on the appearance of the printed page.

As you'll see in Chapter 6, WordPerfect lets you adjust letter spacing throughout your document or limit it to the spacing between selected pairs of letters, which can improve the readability and appearance of your headlines.

Increasing word spacing can make a publication easier to read. Decreasing it allows you to include more words in your publication.

Likewise, you can visually "open up" a publication and make it more readable by increasing line spacing and adding extra space between paragraphs. Decreased line spacing creates stronger headlines, as does increasing the white space surrounding them.

Laser Printers

A serious discussion about typography is impossible without first taking a look at laser printers. Although millions of WordPerfect documents are printed every day on daisywheel or dot-matrix printers, serious desktop publishing requires access to a laser printer.

Because each laser printer is equipped with a set number of typefaces, the kind of printer you choose has a great deal of influence on the type options available to you.

The introduction of affordable laser printers made desktop publishing possible. These printers—which now cost between $1,500 and $6,000—offer nearly typeset quality at a fraction of the cost of phototypesetting machines or "first generation" laser printers (which used to cost nearly $100,000).

Laser printers fall into two primary families—PostScript and non-PostScript. Although Hewlett-Packard set the non-PostScript standard, dozens of printers made by other companies use those same standards. To easily identify them, let's refer to them as HP-compatible laser printers.

First, let's investigate the options available to owners of HP-compatible printers. Then we'll consider the options available to owners of PostScript printers, such as the Apple LaserWriter series. (If you already own a PostScript printer, skip to that section.)

With HP-compatible printers, multiple typefaces, type sizes and type styles are available in three forms: resident fonts, font cartridges and downloadable fonts.

Resident Fonts

HP-compatible printers contain resident fonts built into the electrical circuitry of the printers. The number of resident fonts depends upon the printer. Hewlett-Packard LaserJet Series II, for example, includes Courier—a typeface resembling a standard typewriter—Courier Bold and a Line Printer font with letters spaced extremely close together. These fonts are available in 12- and 8.5-point type.

Resident fonts can be placed on the page in either portrait or landscape orientation. Portrait orientation refers to lines of type that extend across the short dimension of an 8 1/2- by 11-inch sheet of paper, the format of a standard letter. With landscape orientation, type extends across the long, or 11-inch, dimension of paper.

The limitations of Hewlett-Packard LaserJet II's resident fonts are obvious. Printed pages resemble typewritten pages. Serious desktop publishing requires a wider variety of typefaces, type sizes and type styles, available as extra cost options.

Font Cartridges

The easiest and least expensive way to add typefaces to your HP-compatible printer is to plug in one or more font cartridges, each of which includes a limited selection of typeface, type size and type style choices.

The Microsoft "Z" cartridge, for example, offers four type size variations of two of the most widely used typefaces available—Helvetica and Times Roman. Two type sizes are available in three styles: medium, bold and italics. The Microsoft "Z" cartridge includes

14 point Helv bold	**14 point TmsRmn bold**
12 point Helv bold	**12 point TmsRmn bold**
12 point Helv medium	12 point TmsRmn medium
12 point Helv italic	*12 point TmsRmn italic*
10 point Helv bold	**10 point TmsRmn bold**
10 point Helv medium	10 point TmsRmn medium
10 point Helv italic	*10 point TmsRmn italic*
8 point Helv medium	8 point TmsRmn medium

Note that "Helv" and "TmsRmn" are variations on the original Helvetica and Times Roman typefaces, licensed from the International Typographic Corporation (ITC). If you were to make a letter-by-letter comparison of the samples above with the actual ITC fonts, you would probably notice slight variations in the design of individual letters.

Installing HP Font Cartridges

WordPerfect makes it easy to select typeface, type size and type style alternatives with font cartridges. As you read about font cartridge installation below, remember that the process can be speeded up by creating macros or stylesheets.

To install a new font cartridge in your laser printer,

Press: (SHIFT-F7) (PRINT)

Select: S (SELECT PRINTER)

Response: You're presented with the name of the currently chosen printer. (Several names can be listed. An asterisk appears next to the one currently selected.)

Select: 3 (EDIT)

Select: 4 (5 in 5.0) (CARTRIDGES AND FONTS)

Press: Up/down cursor control keys to scroll to CARTRIDGE FONTS.

Select: 1 (SELECT FONTS)

Response: Your screen now is filled with a list of all available font cartridges.

Use the up or down cursor control keys to scroll through the list until the font cartridge you want to install is highlighted. Then press [ENTER]. An asterisk will appear next to the cartridge you've selected, indicating that it's available for use. If you're installing more than one font cartridge, follow the same procedure to select the second.

To exit the font selection process, press WordPerfect's EXIT command [F7] twice. A prompt at the bottom of the screen will indicate that screen fonts are being updated.

When files have been updated, you'll be returned to the SELECT PRINTER: EDIT screen. To return to your document,

Press: (F7) (EXIT) three times

You're now ready to begin work.

Downloadable Fonts

Downloadable, or *soft*, fonts offer a wider, richer selection of typefaces and type sizes. However, they must be loaded into your printer's memory each time you turn on the printer. WordPerfect makes it easy to use downloadable fonts by letting you load them at the start of your work session. Because they take up a great deal of printer memory, WordPerfect's "font-swapping" feature conserves precious printer memory, at the same time giving you a wider choice of fonts.

Downloadable fonts are available from Hewlett-Packard, Adobe, Bitstream and others. Hewlett-Packard downloadable fonts are available in sizes up to 34 points, so you can include larger headlines in your documents. Downloadable fonts from other firms allow you to create even larger headlines.

Downloadable fonts also let you take advantage of typographic refinements described in the next chapter, such as kerning (the ability to adjust the spacing between individual pairs of letters). In addition, by combining downloadable fonts with software programs available from firms such as Softcraft, you can create reversed or shaded type effects that can't be achieved with resident fonts or font cartridges.

Reversed type appears as white type against a black background.

BIG HIT!

Shaded type appears in various shades of gray, instead of the standard 100 percent black.

BIGGER HIT!

The number of downloadable fonts that can be used in a single document is determined by your printer's memory. Additional printer memory allows you to include a wider variety of typefaces in your documents (as well as larger graphic images).

Installing Downloadable Fonts

To add downloadable fonts to your typeface alternatives,

Press: (SHIFT-F7) (PRINT)

Select: S (SELECT PRINTER)

Select: 3 (EDIT)

Select: 6 (7 in 5.0) (PATH FOR DOWNLOADABLE FONTS AND PRINTER COMMAND FILES)

Type: The name of the subdirectory where you've stored the font files, if you haven't included them with your WordPerfect files.

Select: 4 (5 in 5.0) (CARTRIDGES AND FONTS)

Press: Up/down cursor control keys to scroll to SOFT FONTS. (This only applies to LaserJet.)

Select: 1 (SELECT FONTS)

You'll then be presented with an alphabetical list of all font files in the selected subdirectory, sorted by type specifications (e.g., bold or italics).

Scroll down until you reach the first typeface, size and style alternative you want to include in your document. If you want the font always to be available when printing begins,

Type: * (asterisk)

Or, if you want to conserve printer memory, which will let you include larger graphic images on each page, and download the font only when it's needed,

Type: + (plus sign)

When you're finished,

Press: (F7) (EXIT) five times

To make these fonts available, you'll have to initialize your printer by selecting [SHIFT-F7] (Print), then 7 (INITIALIZE PRINTER), then Y (YES). This operation downloads the fonts you marked with *. Each time you turn on your printer, you'll need to initialize it to have access to your downloadable fonts.

Now let's consider the other major printer family, based on the PostScript Page Description Language.

PostScript Printers

PostScript-based printers, such as the Apple LaserWriter Plus and LaserWriter II NT, offer a richer choice of type characteristics than do HP-compatible printers. Without adding downloadable fonts, you immediately have access to a wide selection of built-in typefaces, each of which can be reproduced in any point size or style from small to large, from regular to bold—to even boldface italics.

PostScript's flexibility stems from its ability to define the shape—or outline—of letters, numbers and drawings as a series of coordinates, which are similar to latitude and longitude markings on a map. The shape of each letter, number and part of a drawing is defined by identifying the starting and ending points of the numerous lines that comprise its outline. After the letters and numbers have been outlined, the space between the outlines is shaded (filled in).

PostScript printers have virtually unlimited type size variations. Because you're not limited to the sizes built into font cartridges or downloadable files, you can specify each typeface in any size from one point to letters that are large enough to fill an entire page! You can even include half-point sizes (for example, 8.5-point type).

RRRRRR

In addition, you can achieve creative effects by rotating type or creating mirror graphic images.

For example, you can rotate type 90 degrees to create a vertical newsletter masthead. You also can place photo credits in a vertical position next to the photographs, where they won't interfere with the captions or body copy.

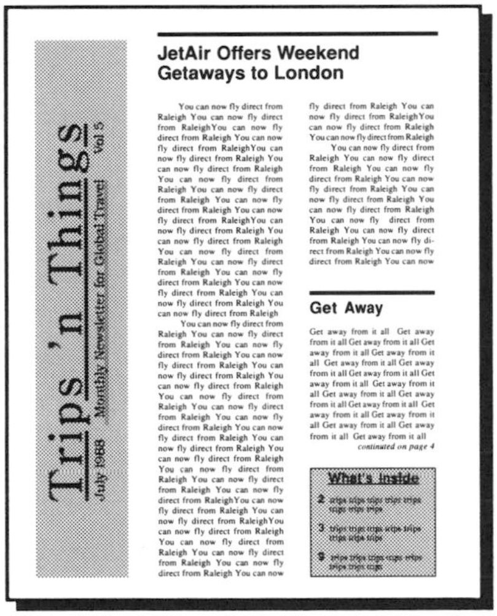

Routine illustrations or scanned photographs can be enhanced creatively by using mirror images.

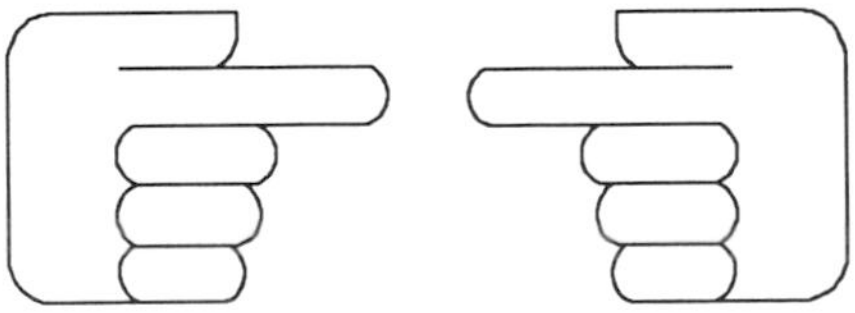

PostScript laser printers also offer typographic refinements, such as kerning (the ability to adjust the spacing between individual pairs of letters) and tracking (the ability to adjust letter spacing throughout a document) without purchasing additional downloadable fonts or font-manipulation programs. You also can create reversed headlines—white type against a black background—without additional purchases. (With HP-compatible printers, additional software programs are required to achieve these effects.)

The original Apple LaserWriter Plus has been augmented by PostScript printers from numerous other vendors, such as AST, QMS and a new generation of Apple laser printers, such as the Apple LaserWriter II NT.

One choice, the Apple LaserWriter II NT, easily can be connected to your computer through the standard printer RS-232 connection. Like the original LaserWriter Plus, it features several built-in typefaces. In addition to the basic "typewriter-style" Courier type, its type choices include the following:

Palatino	ITC Avant Garde Gothic Book
Palatino Bold	*ITC Avant Garde Gothic Book Oblique*
Palatino Bold Italic	**ITC Avant Garde Gothic Demi**
Palatino Italic	***ITC Avant Garde Gothic Demi Oblique***
Times Roman	**ITC Bookman Demi**
Times Roman Bold	***ITC Bookman Demi Italic***
Times Roman Bold Italic	ITC Bookman Light
Times Roman Italic	*ITC Bookman Light Italic*
Helvetica	*ITC Zapf Chancery Medium Italic*
Helvetica Bold	*ITC Zapf Dingbats*
Helvetica Bold Oblique	Symbol
Helvetica Narrow	New Century Schoolbook
Helvetica Narrow Bold	**New Century Schoolbook Bold**
Helvetica Narrow Bold Oblique	***New Century Schoolbook Bold Italic***
Helvetica Narrow Oblique	*New Century Schoolbook Italic*

Boldface, italic and boldface/italic variations of each typeface also are available.

The Apple LaserWriter II SC, primarily designed for use with the Macintosh, includes only four built-in typefaces (Courier, Symbol, Helvetica and Times). The LaserWriter II NTX offers the same typeface alternatives as the LaserWriter II NT, but operates faster and easily can be hooked up to more than one computer.

PostScript Font Options

Although PostScript font cartridges aren't available, a full range of downloadable fonts can be added to a PostScript printer. They're available from a variety of independent vendors, including Adobe and Bitstream.

The process of adding downloadable fonts to PostScript printers is similar to that of adding downloadable fonts to HP-compatible printers.

Press: (F7) (PRINT)

Select: S (SELECT PRINTER)

Select: 3 (EDIT)

Select: 4 (5 in 5.0) (CARTRIDGES AND FONTS)

Response: Downloadable Fonts

Select: 1 (SELECT FONTS)

You're presented with a list of all available downloadable fonts installed in your hard disk. Scroll through the list using your up or down cursor control keys. To make a font for downloading,

Type: * (asterisk)

If you want a font to be downloaded only when it's needed to print a particular part of your document,

Type: + (plus sign)

After you've finished selecting the fonts you want to use,

Press: (F7) (EXIT) five times

As explained earlier, downloadable fonts are available only after you've initialized your printer. So to download the fonts you've marked with *, select [SHIFT-F7] (PRINT), then 7 (INITIALIZE PRINTER), then Y (YES).

QMS JetScript

Owners of Hewlett-Packard Series II printers can upgrade to PostScript by adding the QMS JetScript, a hardware and software package that adds PostScript compatibility.

The QMS JetScript consists of software and two plug-in circuit boards (one of which is added to an expansion slot in your computer, the other to your printer). The QMS JetScript offers an easy migration path to

LaserJet printer owners who want the flexibility and additional resident fonts of a PostScript printer without having to buy a new printer.

The QMS JetScript is easily installed and doesn't affect the normal operation of the printer. Nor does it alter the LaserJet Series II's warranty.

Working with Fonts

The first step in creating a desktop-published document is to choose a particular typeface, type size or type style that will be used for the majority of your documents. These specifications will be referred to as the INITIAL FONT, which will be the default font. You can, of course, override the default font in a document.

WordPerfect gives you three ways to set an initial font. You can set it for the current document, for all documents, or for each printer.

To set the initial font for the current document only,

Press: (SHIFT-F8) (FORMAT)

Select: 3 (DOCUMENT)

Select: 3 (INITIAL BASE FONT)

Response: You're shown an alphabetical list of fonts.

Press: Up or down cursor control keys to highlight the font you want.

Select: 1 (SELECT)

In Version 5.1, you can set the initial font for all new documents at the SETUP menu.

Press: (SHIFT-F1) (SETUP)

Select: 4 (INITIAL SETTINGS)

Select: 5 (INITIAL CODES)

Press: (CTRL-F8) (FONT)

Select: 4 (BASE FONT)

Response: You're presented with a list of fonts.

Press: Up or down cursor control keys to highlight the font you want.

Select: 1 (SELECT)

If you have more than one printer connected to your system, WordPerfect lets you set a different initial font for each. To choose an initial font for a printer,

Press: (SHIFT-F7) (PRINT)

Select: S (SELECT PRINTER)

Response: You're presented with a list of printers you've previously chosen. The currently active printer will be highlighted and appear with an asterisk.

If you're working with more than one printer and wish to switch to a different printer, scroll down until the printer you want is highlighted and select 1 (SELECT). Then select S (SELECT PRINTER) again.

Select: 3 (EDIT)

Select: 5 (6 in 5.0) (INITIAL BASE FONT)

Response: Your printer's particular default resident font will be replaced by an alphabetical list of all typefaces and type styles available as resident fonts, downloadable fonts and, in the case of HP-compatible printers, font cartridges.

Press: The up or down cursor control keys to highlight the font you want.

Select: 1 (SELECT)

Response: If your printer is HP-compatible, your options include the specific type sizes available.

If, however, you're using a PostScript printer, you must select the default type size. Note that 10 appears at the lower left of your screen. If you want to use 10-point type as the default,

Press: (ENTER)

If, however, you want your INITIAL FONT to be larger or smaller, enter the particular type size you want. For example,

Type: 12

Press: (ENTER)

To return to your editing screen,

Press: (F7) (EXIT) three times

Choosing a Base Font

Often, you'll want to override the initial font and choose a different typeface, type size and type style to use for a particular document. WordPerfect offers a BASE FONT feature that makes it easy to choose a particular set of type specifications for a document, regardless of the type of printer you use.

To choose a BASE FONT,

Press: (CTRL-F8) (FONT)

Select: 4 (BASE FONT)

The screen then displays an alphabetical list of all available type alternatives, which includes your currently selected printer's resident fonts and any font cartridges or downloadable fonts you've installed.

```
Base Font

* Courier
  Courier Bold
  Courier Bold Oblique
  Courier Oblique
  Helvetica
  Helvetica Bold
  Helvetica Bold Oblique
  Helvetica Narrow
  Helvetica Narrow Bold
  Helvetica Narrow Bold Oblique
  Helvetica Narrow Oblique
  Helvetica Oblique
  ITC Avant Garde Gothic Book
  ITC Avant Garde Gothic Book Oblique
  ITC Avant Garde Gothic Demi
  ITC Avant Garde Gothic Demi Oblique
  ITC Bookman Demi
  ITC Bookman Demi Italic
  ITC Bookman Light
  ITC Bookman Light Italic
  ITC Zapf Chancery Medium Italic

1 Select; N Name search: 1
```

Scroll down until your typeface choice is highlighted. If you're using an HP-compatible printer, note that a type size accompanies each typeface and type style alternative. When you come to the font alternative you want to use throughout your document,

Select: 1 (SELECT)

or

Press: (ENTER)

If you're using an HP-compatible printer, your type size is chosen automatically when you choose the typeface and style.

If, however, you're using a PostScript printer, you'll be prompted to choose a type size.

Type: 12 (or the size you want.)

Press: (ENTER)

Response: This replaces the 10-point default with the type size you want for your BASE FONT.

You then will be returned to your document automatically. All the text that follows will appear in the type options you just chose, as will everything you type from that point forward. These type specifications will continue to be used until you either select a new BASE FONT or a new type size or style.

Screen Display

Note that unless you've installed the Hercules RamFont video card described in Appendix B, the size and appearance of the type on your screen will remain the same regardless of the font you've chosen. This important point reflects one area in which WordPerfect differs from dedicated page layout programs.

To double-check your BASE FONT, use WordPerfect's REVEAL CODES command [ALT-F3] or VIEW DOCUMENT [SHIFT-F7, 6].

Choosing Larger or Smaller Type

Regardless of the type of printer you're using, you easily can choose larger or smaller type sizes while you're writing or editing your document. This makes it easy to create a very visible hierarchy of information, ranging from large headlines and smaller subheads to even smaller body copy and captions.

WordPerfect offers a shortcut that automatically changes type size to the next available alternative, larger or smaller. You can use this valuable time-saving feature while entering new text or by blocking previously entered text.

To change the type size of new text,

Press: (CTRL-F8) (FONT)

Select: 1 (SIZE)

Response: You're presented with the following size options:

1 SUPRSCPT (Superscript—letters raised above their original baseline, or regular vertical position)

2 SUBSCPT (Subscript—letters placed below their original baseline, or normal vertical position)

3 FINE

4 SMALL

5 LARGE

6 VRY LARGE (Very Large)

7 EXT LARGE (Extra Large)

Select: The option that describes the type size you want.

For purposes of illustration,

Select: 5 (LARGE)

If you're using a color monitor, any words you type will appear on your screen in a different color. When printed, the words will be larger than the BASE FONT.

This base font is Times Roman 10 point.

Now you have selected LARGE type.

Remember that the type sizes chosen for FINE, SMALL, LARGE, etc., are determined both by the type sizes available on your computer, as well as the size of the BASE FONT you've chosen. As the illustrations below show, type sizes that relate to a PostScript, Times Roman, 10-point BASE FONT are different from those that relate to a Times Roman, 12-point BASE FONT.

10-point BASE FONT-FINE

10-point BASE FONT-LARGE

12-point BASE FONT-FINE

12-point BASE FONT-LARGE

Use VIEW DOCUMENT [SHIFT-F7, 6] or PRINT [SHIFT-F7, 2] to preview your work.

Returning to Base Font

To return to the BASE FONT in this document,

Press: (CTRL-F8) (FONT)

Select: 3 (NORMAL)

Text entered after this point will be set in the typeface and type size you've defined as your BASE FONT. These two steps are not necessary when you apply a size or appearance option to a block of existing text.

Choosing a Particular Type Size

Although WordPerfect's BASE FONT feature is used primarily to establish a default for the body copy in your document, you also can use it to choose a particular type size for a special purpose—such as a headline. Users of PostScript printers probably will make frequent use of this feature.

Let's assume you have a PostScript printer and want to create a headline set in 48-point Helvetica type.

Press: (CTRL-F8) (FONT)

Select: 4 (BASE FONT)

Response: A list of all available resident and downloadable fonts will appear.

Press: The up or down cursor control key to move the cursor to the particular typeface you want for your headline—in this case, Helvetica.

Response: Type size: 10 (or the previously chosen BASE FONT type size.)

Type: 48

Press: (ENTER)

Response: You'll be returned to the editing screen.

TIP: After you've modified the BASE FONT to select a specific headline typeface and type size, you must repeat the process to reselect the BASE FONT you were using for the majority of the text in your document.

Changing Type Size in Previously Entered Text

It's even easier to change the type size of previously entered text. First, select—or highlight—the text you want modified.

Press: (ALT-F4) (BLOCK)

Press: Right cursor control key

This highlights the letter to the right of the cursor. Use [CTRL] plus the right cursor control key to highlight one word at a time. Use [HOME] [HOME] and the right cursor control key to highlight the remainder of the line. Use the down cursor control key to advance blocking through the next line.

After you've highlighted all the words in the passage,

Press: (CTRL-F8) (FONT)

Response: You're presented with two alternatives:

1 (SIZE)

2 (APPEARANCE)

Select: 1 (SIZE)

Response: You're again presented with the type size alternatives.

Select: The size alternative you want.

Response: You immediately will return to your normal editing screen.

Changing Type Styles in New Text

In a similar way, you can change the appearance of previously entered text or new text as you enter it. You can emphasize certain words by underlining them or setting them in boldface or italic type.

To change the appearance of new text,

Press: (CTRL-F8) (FONT)

Select: 2 (APPEARANCE)

Response: The following choices appear on your screen:

1 BOLD

2 UNDRLN (underline)

3 DBL UND (double underline)

4 ITALC (italics)

5 OUTLN (outline)

6 SHADW (shadow)

7 SM CAP (small uppercase)

8 REDLN (redline. This highlights text or places dark text against a white background. It's a technique used to indicate that text has been added or modified, which is useful when two or more individuals are editing a document.)

9 STKOUT (strikeout—a favorite used to indicate changes in legal documents.)

For purposes of illustration,

Select: 1 (BOLD)

Response: You'll be returned to your normal editing screen. New text you type will now appear bold.

As a further illustration,

Press: (CTRL-F8) (FONT)

Select: 2 (APPEARANCE)

Select: 4 (ITALICS)

Response: You'll be returned to the editing screen and new text will appear in bold italics.

Returning to Normal Type Style with New Text

To return to normal (or roman) text after typing new text in bold, italics or any other option,

Press: (CTRL-F8) (FONT)

Select: 3 (NORMAL)

Response: You'll be returned to your document, and newly entered text will appear in the base font. These two steps are unnecessary if you apply an option to a block of existing text.

TIP: After completing the above exercise, use WordPerfect's VIEW DOCUMENT [SHIFT-F7, 6] to observe how the type styles have alternated between bold, italics and roman. PRINT [SHIFT-F7, 2] to see how these screen images translate to the printed page.

Changing Type Styles of Previously Entered Text

While editing your document, you can change the appearance of previously entered text.

Press: (ALT-F4) (BLOCK)

Press: The cursor control keys to highlight text to be changed.

Press: (CTRL-F8) (FONT)

Select: 2 (APPEARANCE)

Response: Again, the appearance options appear on your screen.

TIP: Remember that you can still use the regular WordPerfect BOLD [F6] and UNDERLINE [F8] commands. They can be used when entering new text or applied to highlighted text.

After you've changed the type style of previously entered text by highlighting it, you automatically are returned to your previously selected BASE FONT. You do not need to select NORMAL (Option 3).

Color Monitors

One of the advantages of using WordPerfect with a color monitor is that you can use different combinations of background and foreground colors to indicate which type size or style is currently being used.

To choose colors,

Press: (SHIFT-F1) (SETUP)

Select: 2 (3 in 5.0) (DISPLAY)

Select: 1 (2 in 5.0) (COLORS/FONTS/ATTRIBUTES)

Select: 1 (SCREEN COLORS)

Response: Depending upon which color monitor you use, you'll be able to assign different foreground and background colors for the various type sizes and styles you'll be using in your document.

Use your up/down/left/right cursor control keys to locate the size and style attributes you want to highlight. Move the cursor to FOREGROUND or BACKGROUND columns and type the letter corresponding to the colors you want. Notice that the "sample" column immediately shows you how the particular mixture of your foreground and background colors will appear on your screen.

When you're finished,

Press: (F7) (EXIT) twice

This returns you to your editing screen.

TIP: As with previous versions, WordPerfect 5.1 lets you write and edit two documents simultaneously, changing between them by using the SWITCH command [SHIFT-F3]. You can choose the same background colors for both Document 1 and Document 2 or different background colors for each document (which lets you know at a glance which document you're working on).

Moving On

In this chapter, you reviewed the basic WordPerfect commands for creating attractive, easy-to-read documents based on the use of multiple typefaces, sizes and styles.

In the next chapter, "Typographic Refinements," you'll explore WordPerfect's ability to manipulate the appearance and placement of text. You'll find that WordPerfect rivals dedicated desktop publishing programs—and even expensive phototypesetting systems—in its ability to let you precisely adjust letter, word, line and paragraph spacing as well as create special effects like reversed and shaded type.

With typographic refinements, you can create attention-getting publications that look like they were professionally designed and typeset.

CHAPTER 6

TYPOGRAPHIC REFINEMENTS

Creating attractive, readable documents involves many design considerations. Among the most important decisions is where to place type on a page, which also involves defining the spacing between letters, words, lines and paragraphs. WordPerfect makes it easy to set and adjust spacing, as well as hyphenation.

As with other type-related features, your printer and the kind of fonts you use determine the degree to which you can use WordPerfect's spacing and hyphenation features.

For example, users of HP-compatible printers must have downloadable fonts to take full advantage of WordPerfect's ability to manipulate letter, word and line spacing precisely. However, these refinements are immediately available to PostScript printer users, because WordPerfect can adjust the spacing of PostScript's resident fonts.

Finally, in this chapter, you'll learn the steps necessary to create and refine a high-impact reversed headline with a PostScript printer. Nothing attracts attention like white words appearing against a black background! You'll also look at WordPerfect's ability to create type in shades of gray.

(Owners of HP-compatible printers who want the same features should read Appendix B, which lists various SoftCraft programs that give those printers capabilities similar to those of a PostScript printer.)

Advanced Typographic Terms

Kerning

Kerning refers to adjusting the space between selected pairs, or groups, of letters. Decreased letter spacing creates words out of otherwise isolated letters. Increased letter spacing emphasizes otherwise "lost" letters—such as a lowercase "i" dwarfed between an "l" and a "t."

Tracking

Tracking refers to increasing or decreasing letter spacing throughout a document, as opposed to kerning, which applies only to the spacing of certain letters.

Leading

Leading is the term for line spacing. The appearance of headlines often can be improved by reducing line spacing, which creates a tighter grouping of words. Line spacing also can be increased. For example, if you want to give a headline more impact, you can increase line spacing and add horizontal lines beneath the headline.

Widows and Orphans

A widow is a single word or syllable isolated by itself at the end of a paragraph, column or page. An orphan occurs when the last line of a paragraph appears by itself at the top of a column or the beginning of the following page. Widows and orphans are unsightly, stranded words that occupy an entire line, distracting readers and playing havoc with an otherwise tight page layout.

WordPerfect has a special feature that protects copy from widows and orphans, thus improving the appearance of your document.

Kerning with WordPerfect

Kerning becomes increasingly important as type size increases. Normal letter spacing for some combinations of letters (e.g., an uppercase "W" next to a lowercase "a") becomes noticeably exaggerated when set in large type.

WordPerfect's kerning capability lets you reduce letter spacing to compensate for that. The result is a more pleasing headline for your brochure or newsletter. Compare these two examples.

W a v e

Wave

Based on the resident and downloadable fonts you use, WordPerfect offers both automatic and selective kerning.

The example below illustrates how kerning can improve the appearance of a headline, based on a resident font in a PostScript printer. To begin, turn off justification:

Press: (SHIFT-F8) (FORMAT)

Select: 1 (LINE)

Select: 3 (JUSTIFICATION)

Response: You'll see the four alignment options:
1 (LEFT)
2 (CENTER)
3 (RIGHT)
4 (FULL)
(In WordPerfect 5.0, your choices are YES and NO.)

Select: 1 (LEFT) (or type N (NO) in Version 5.0.)

Press: (F7) (EXIT)

You're returned to your editing screen and are ready to get down to business.

Press: (CTRL-F8) (FONT)

Select: 4 (BASE FONT)

Response: You're presented with an alphabetical list of all available resident and downloaded fonts.

Select: Helvetica

Response: Point size: 10

Type: 40

Press: (ENTER)

Type: World Kerning Conference

Now preview your work using WordPerfect's VIEW DOCUMENT command [SHIFT-F7, 6]. Select 100% or 200% magnification to get a closer look at the letter spacing.

Note the gaps between the uppercase W and the lowercase o, and between the uppercase K and the lowercase e, as well as the large space separating the uppercase C and the lowercase o.

To have a permanent record of a headline that hasn't been kerned, PRINT the page [SHIFT-F7, 2].

World Kerning
Conference

Automatic Kerning

To apply automatic kerning, place the cursor in front of the W and

Press: (SHIFT-F8) (FORMAT)

Select: 4 (OTHER)

Select: 6 (PRINTER FUNCTIONS)

Select: 1 (KERNING)

Response: The cursor will blink under the word No.

Type: Y (Yes)

Press: (F7) (EXIT)

Use WordPerfect's VIEW DOCUMENT command [SHIFT-F7, 6] at 100% or 200% to preview your work, or PRINT the page [SHIFT-F7, 2]. Compare it with the page you printed before you selected the KERNING feature. Notice the improvement in letter spacing. Certain pairs of letters have been pulled closer together.

Selective Kerning

You also can adjust letter spacing on a more selective basis. Instead of using WordPerfect's automatic kerning feature, you can choose to adjust individual letter pairs precisely. To illustrate, let's reduce the spacing between the W and the o in World.

Move: The cursor in front of the W.

Press: (SHIFT-F8) (FORMAT)

Select: 4 (OTHER)

Select: 6 (PRINTER FUNCTIONS)

Select: 3 (WORD SPACING)

Response: 1 (NORMAL) This setting looks best, according to the printer manufacturer.
2 (OPTIMAL) This setting looks best, according to the WordPerfect Corp. (often the same setting as 1).
3 (PERCENT OF OPTIMAL) Numbers less than 100 percent reduce space from the WordPerfect OPTIMAL; numbers greater than 100 percent increase space from OPTIMAL.
4 (SET PITCH) You can specify the exact number of characters per inch.

Press: (ENTER)

This accepts the 2 (OPTIMAL) default and advances you to the LETTER SPACING menu, which lists four options:

1 (NORMAL)
2 (OPTIMAL) This adjusts letter spacing on the basis of type size.
3 (PERCENT OF OPTIMAL)
4 (SET PITCH)

You now can adjust letter spacing from this point in your document forward. The setting you choose will remain in effect until you advance the cursor past the o and return letter spacing to optimal.

Select: 3 (PERCENT OF OPTIMAL)

Response: 100

Type: 85

Press: (ENTER)

Press: (F7) (EXIT)

This returns you to your editing screen. VIEW DOCUMENT [SHIFT-F7, 6] or PRINT [SHIFT-F7, 2]. Notice the difference in the letter spacing.

You can *expand* letter spacing in a similar way. Take for example the way a lowercase "i" is obscured when placed between an "l" and a "t." You easily can add a little air around the "i" by slightly increasing letter spacing. Again, it's a three-step process:

1. Start by positioning the cursor before the letter pairs you want to expand.
2. Using the LETTER SPACING feature found in the PRINTER FUNCTION menu, add space (e.g., replace the 100% default with 110% of optimal).
3. Position the cursor after the letter pairs you want to expand and return letter spacing to optimal.

lite
l i te

Returning to Normal Letter Spacing

To return to regular letter spacing, advance the cursor until it's between the o and the r. Then,

Press: (SHIFT-F8) (FORMAT)

Select: 4 (OTHER)

Select: 6 (PRINTER FUNCTIONS)

Select: 3 (WORD SPACING)

Select: 2 (OPTIMAL)

Response: This advances you to the LETTER SPACING menu.

Select: 2 (OPTIMAL)

Press: (F7) (EXIT)

VIEW DOCUMENT [SHIFT-F7, 6] or PRINT [SHIFT-F7, 2]. The difference will be apparent immediately. The letters which follow the o are now spaced farther apart.

Creative Applications

You can use WordPerfect's SET PITCH command [SHIFT-F8, 4, 6, 3] to create exaggerated letter spacing for special effects, such as departmental headers in a newsletter (e.g., "Upcoming Events"). The SET PITCH command allows you to specify the number of characters per inch, automatically choosing the correct spacing.

To illustrate this important feature, let's assume you want to create centered departmental headings using widely spaced, uppercase, 14-point, Times Roman type.

Press: (CTRL-F8) (FONT)

Select: 4 (BASE FONT)

Response: You're presented with a list of available resident and downloaded fonts.

Press: Up/down cursor control keys until TIMES ROMAN is highlighted.

Select: 1 (Select)

Response: Point size: 10 (or last chosen point size.)

Type: 14

Press: (ENTER)

Type: UPCOMING EVENTS

Press: (ENTER)

The above gives you a frame of reference for the effects of WordPerfect's powerful SET PITCH command. To continue,

Press: (SHIFT-F8) (FORMAT)

Select: 4 (OTHER)

Select: 6 (PRINTER FUNCTIONS)

Select: 3 (WORD SPACING)

Response: The various word-spacing options appear.

Press: (ENTER) (to accept 2 [OPTIMAL].)

Response: The various letter-spacing options appear.

Select: 4 (SET PITCH)

Response: 9.3 (The pitch that corresponds to the default's OPTIMAL setting.)

Type: 6

Press: (ENTER)

Press: (F7) (EXIT)

This indicates that you want six characters per inch. You then are returned to the editing screen.

Type: UPCOMING EVENTS

Press: (ENTER)

By using the VIEW DOCUMENT command [SHIFT-F7, 6] or PRINT [SHIFT-F7, 2], you will be able to see the difference immediately.

UPCOMING EVENTS

U P C O M I N G   E V E N T S

Adjusting Word Spacing

WordPerfect lets you adjust word spacing to fine-tune the appearance of your document, as well as adjust the word density. Adjusting space between words also lets you "lighten" or "darken" a publication.

To modify word spacing, advance your cursor to the beginning of your document. The quickest way to do that is to use WordPerfect's HOME command [HOME], [HOME], Up cursor control key. Then,

Press: (SHIFT-F8) (FORMAT)

Select: 4 (OTHER)

Select: 6 (PRINTER FUNCTIONS)

Select: 3 (WORD SPACING)

Response: You're presented with the following choices:
1 (NORMAL)
2 (OPTIMAL)
3 (PERCENT OF OPTIMAL)
4 (SET PITCH)

Select: 3 (PERCENT OF OPTIMAL)

If you want word spacing to be reduced and density increased, type in a figure less than 100. If you want to spread out word spacing, enter a figure greater than 100. Then press [F7] (EXIT). This command is useful when you're working with narrow columns and too many words are being hyphenated.

TIP: Just as SET PITCH was used as a creative tool in the letterspacing example above, you can use SET PITCH to force unnaturally wide or narrow spaces between words to create special, exaggerated effects.

Adjusting Line Spacing

With WordPerfect, you also can modify leading (line spacing). Again, this refinement becomes extremely important as type size increases. The appearance of headlines set on several lines, for example, is often greatly improved by reduced line spacing. Tighter spacing makes a headline look more like a unit, rather than a series of unrelated lines of type.

Start by creating a centered multi-line headline (be sure to select LEFT justification before typing):

Press: (CTRL-F8) (FONT)

Select: 4 (BASE FONT)

Response: A list of all available resident and downloadable fonts.

Scroll up or down until you reach HELVETICA BOLD.

Select: 1 (Select)

Response: Point size: 10 (or last chosen type size)

Type: 24

Press: (ENTER)

Type: AMAZING DISCOVERY

Press: (ENTER)

Type: No Need to Change

Press: (ENTER)

Type: Vacuum Cleaner Bags

Press: (ENTER)

Return to the beginning of the headline.

Press: (ALT-F4) (BLOCK)

Move the cursor to the end of the headline.

Press: (SHIFT-F6) (CENTER)

Response: (Center) No (Yes)

Type: Y

Response: This creates a centered, three-line headline.

To reduce line height, place your cursor at the beginning of the headline, and

Press: (SHIFT-F8) (FORMAT)

Select: 1 (LINE)

Response: You're presented with the FORMAT: LINE menu, which lists numerous options.

Select: 4 (LINE HEIGHT)

Response: You're presented with two alternatives:
1 (AUTO)
2 (FIXED)

Select: 2 (FIXED)

Response: 0.35"

Type: .30

Press: (ENTER)

Press: (F7) (EXIT)

When you VIEW DOCUMENT [SHIFT-F7, 6] or PRINT [SHIFT-F7, 2], the change will be readily apparent.

AMAZING DISCOVERY
No Need to Change
Vacuum Cleaner Bags.

There may be occasions when you want to increase line height—for instance, if you want to emphasize a headline by adding horizontal rules under the words. In that case, you might want to choose line height of .75 inch.

AMAZING DISCOVERY

No Need to Change

Vacuum Cleaner Bags.

WordPerfect 5.1 gives you even greater control over leading by letting you set paragraph spacing independent of line spacing. Thus, it's possible to add a little extra space between paragraphs so that each paragraph appears as a unit. To adjust line and paragraph leading,

Select: (SHIFT-F8) (Format)

Select: 4 (Other)

Select: 6 (Printer Functions)

Select: 6 (Leading)

Response: 1 Optimal; 2 Set Leading: 0

Select: 2 (Set Leading)

Response: The cursor moves to Primary.

Type: The within-paragraph leading

Press: (ENTER)

Note: If you've chosen points as your units of measure (under the [SHIFT-F1] (SET UP) menu), you may enter the leading in points; for example, 3p would mean 3 points.

Response: The cursor moves to Secondary.

Type: The between-paragraph leading

Press: (ENTER)

Press: (F7) (EXIT)

Adjusting White Space at the Beginning of Lines

One of the ways you can control the overall "color" of your document is to adjust tabs and indention, thereby adding or reducing white space at the beginning of each line.

Often, tabs and indents appropriate for word-processed manuscripts are too deep for narrower columns, particularly if a different typeface or type size has been chosen.

To adjust the amount of indention at the beginnings of paragraphs,

Press: (SHIFT-F8) (FORMAT)

Select: 1 (LINE)

Select: 8 (TAB SET)

Response: You'll see a ruler showing the half-inch default spacing for tabs.

Press: (HOME) (HOME) Left cursor control key

This moves your cursor to the left-hand edge of the page.

Press: (CTRL-END) (DELETE TO END OF LINE) (to eliminate all existing tabs.)

Press: The right/left cursor control keys to advance the cursor to the position where you want to place a tab.

Type: L (at each position where you want a left-align tab to appear.)

Press: (F7) (EXIT) twice (to return to the editing screen.)

Adjusting White Space Within and at the End of Lines

Your choice of hyphenation also influences the "color" of your documents. This is true whether you're placing text in flush-left/ragged-right or justified columns. With hyphenation, words that are too long to fit comfortably on one line are broken between syllables and set on two lines. Although most often used with justified text, hyphenation is an equally important tool for flush-left/ragged-right text.

Compare the examples below:

sleeping puppy. We observed the
brownish fox jumping happily
around the sleeping puppy. We
observed the brownish fox
jumping happily around the

around the sleeping puppy. We
observed the brownish fox jumping happily around the sleeping
puppy. We observed the brownish
fox jumping happily around the

We observed the brownish fox
jumping happily around the
sleeping puppy. We observed the
brownish fox jumping happily
around the sleeping puppy. We

observed the brownish fox jumping
happily around the sleeping puppy.
We observed the brownish fox
jumping happily around the sleep-

You can see that activating WordPerfect's HYPHENATION feature eliminates the large gaps of white space at the end of flush-left/ragged-right lines. Likewise, HYPHENATION eliminates unnatural word spacing that occurs within lines of justified type—especially short lines of text set in a large type size.

To activate HYPHENATION,

Press: (SHIFT-F8) (FORMAT)

Select: 1 (LINE)
1 (HYPHENATION)

Response: No (Yes). In Version 5.0, you'll see three options: 1 (Off), 2 (Manual) and 3 (Auto).

Type: Y (or select 3 (AUTO) in Version 5.0.)

WordPerfect automatically will hyphenate words that are too long to fit on one line.

Press: (F7) (EXIT)

This returns you to your editing screen.

Adjusting the Hyphenation Zone

By adjusting the HYPHENATION ZONE, you can increase or decrease the number of words that will be hyphenated. Words that begin before or after the HYPHENATION ZONE are automatically hyphenated (or manually hyphenated). Words that begin after the left side of the

HYPHENATION ZONE and extend past the right side are moved in their entirety to the next line.

By adjusting the width of the zone, you can control the number of words that will be hyphenated:

- A narrower zone increases the number of hyphenated words.
- A wider zone reduces hyphenation.

To adjust the HYPHENATION ZONE,

Press: (SHIFT-F8) (FORMAT)

Select: 1 (LINE)

Select: 2 (HYPHENATION ZONE)

Response: Left 10%
Right 4%

To reduce hyphenation, increase the HYPHENATION ZONE.

Type: 12

Press: (ENTER)

Response: This replaces the 10% default with a 12% setting and advances your cursor to the Right setting.

Type: 6

Press: (ENTER)

Response: This replaces the 4% default with a 6% figure.

The HYPHENATION ZONE is now wider. To return to your editing screen,

Press: (F7) (EXIT)

To create a narrower HYPHENATION ZONE, which often improves the appearance of flush-left/ragged-right columns,

Press: (SHIFT-F8) (FORMAT)

Select: 1 (LINE)

Select: 2 (HYPHENATION ZONE)

Response: Left 10%
Right 4%

To increase hyphenation, reduce the HYPHENATION ZONE.

Type: 8

Press: (ENTER)

Response: This replaces the 10% default with an 8% setting and advances your cursor to the Right setting.

Type: 3

Press: (ENTER)

Response: This replaces the 4% default with a 3% figure.

The HYPHENATION ZONE is now narrower, which means more words will be split between lines. To return to your editing screen,

Press: (F7) (EXIT)

Modifying Justification Limits

WordPerfect also allows you to modify justification limits—the minimum or maximum amount of space between words when lines are justified (or of equal length). Because this affects the density of words per line, it influences publication "color."

With WordPerfect, you can adjust justification limits in the following ways:

- Word spacing can be compressed from 0% to 100%. The default is 75%.
- Word spacing can be expanded from 100% to unlimited. The default is 400%.

To adjust word-spacing justification limits,

Press: (SHIFT-F8) (FORMAT)

Select: 4 (OTHER)

Select: 6 (PRINTER FUNCTIONS)

Select: 4 (WORD SPACING JUSTIFICATION LIMITS)

Response: Compressed to (0% - 100%) 60%
(This is the compression default. If you accept it, word spacing will never be less than 60 percent of ideal.)

Type: Any value between 0% and 100%.

Press: (ENTER)

Smaller numbers indicate that, when necessary, the spaces between words will be reduced to accommodate justification. The disadvantage of smaller numbers is that the spacing can be tightened to the point that the words run together to achieve justification, making your publication difficult to read. Larger numbers "open up" a document by forcing more space between words.

Response: Expanded to (100% - unlimited) 400%

Type: Any value between 100% and 400%.

Press: (ENTER)

Press: (F7) (EXIT)

The value for normal word spacing is 100 percent. As you enter larger numbers, more and more space between words is added when necessary to justify the lines. However, extra space can be visually distracting and create ugly "rivers" of white space running through your publication.

Eliminating Widows and Orphans

The appearance and credibility of your document can be enhanced by WordPerfect's ability to automatically eliminate widows and orphans, described earlier in this chapter. To activate WordPerfect's WIDOW/ORPHAN feature,

Press: (SHIFT-F8) (FORMAT)

Select: 1 (LINE)

Select: 9 (WIDOW/ORPHAN PROTECTION)

Response: The blinking cursor under the N in No indicates that WIDOW/ORPHAN PROTECTION has not been activated.

Type: Y

Press: (F7) (EXIT)

Response: You're returned to the editing screen. WIDOW/ORPHAN PROTECTION will be in effect from the cursor location forward.

Rotating Text

WordPerfect lets you rotate text for special effects. By taking a line of type and rotating it 90 degrees, for example, you can stand it on its head, so that it runs up the side of your page. Or, you can rotate the text 180 degrees so that the line appears upside down. This technique can come in handy when preparing a horizontal address panel for the back of a three-panel brochure.

Text rotation requires the use of graphics boxes. Let's start by creating a new graphics box for this example.

Press: (ALT-F9) (GRAPHICS)

Select: 4 (USER BOX)

Select: 1 (CREATE)

Select: 4 (3 in 5.0) (ANCHOR TYPE)

Select: 2 (PAGE)

Response: Number of pages to skip: 0

Press: (ENTER)

Select: 5 (4 in 5.0) (VERTICAL POSITION)

Select: 1 (FULL PAGE)

Select: 6 (5 in 5.0) (HORIZONTAL POSITION)

Select: 1 (MARGINS)

Select: 1 (LEFT)

Select: 7 (6 in 5.0) (SIZE)

Select: 3 (SET BOTH)

Response: Width = 6.5" (This figure depends both on the margins as well as the measuring system you've chosen.)

Type: 2

Press: (ENTER)

Response: Height = 9"

Press: (ENTER)

Select: 9 (8 in 5.0) (EDIT)

Now that the size and placement of the box have been determined, select a typeface, type size and type style for a headline and enter the words.

Press: (CTRL-F8) (FONT)

Select: 4 (BASE FONT)

Press: Up/down cursor control keys to advance the cursor to the position where HELVETICA is highlighted.

Select: 1 (Select)

Response: Point size: 10

Type: 36

Press: (ENTER)

Type: Graphic excellence can be yours!

Press: (ENTER)

To rotate the type and place it vertically on the page,

Press: (ALT-F9) (GRAPHICS)

Response: 1 (0°)
2 (90°)
3 (180°)
4 (270°)

Select: 2 (90°)

Press: (F7) (EXIT) twice

The result should be similar to the illustration below:

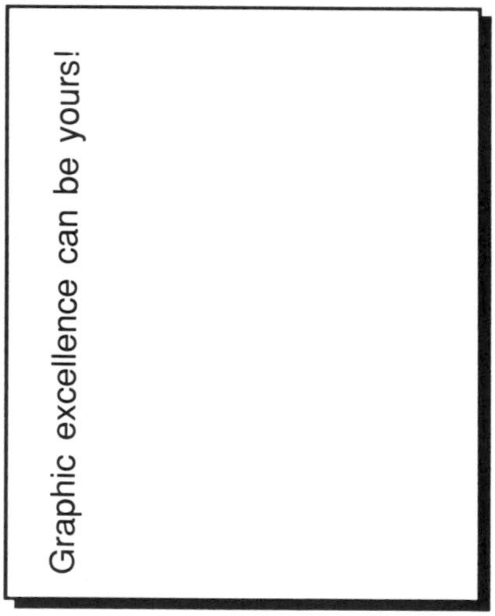
Graphic excellence can be yours!

Creating a Reversed Headline

A new generation of color printers is on the horizon. In anticipation of their appearance, WordPerfect allows you to "mix" ink colors to create the exact shade and intensity you want.

However, until low-cost color printers become available, you can use this feature to create shaded type—or even reversed type (white words against a black background or dark gray background). Reversed type can add drama and impact to your documents by making your headline stand out from others on the same page.

Creating a reversed headline with a PostScript printer involves four steps. (Instructions for each step follow.)

1. Changing the default for USER BOX from a white background to a black background.
2. Creating a USER BOX in the proper position on the page.
3. Centering the headline, selecting the appropriate typeface, type size, type style and entering the text of the headline.
4. Changing the color of the headline text to white, so it will stand out against the black background of the USER BOX.

Remember that a USER BOX won't appear in a compiled list of figures, text or tables.

TIP: You may change the USER BOX option from white to black before you create the box. You may also create the box first, then change the option from white to black. Be sure that in REVEAL CODES your cursor is placed *on or before* your box code and not after it.

WordPerfect's REVEAL CODES command [ALT-F3] can be very useful in helping you locate the precise position for making those changes.

Although some of the following steps are repetitive, you will not only learn how to create a reversed headline, but also will review many important WordPerfect commands used in creating boxes and manipulating type.

Step One: Changing the Default for User Boxes

The first step is to change the background of the *next* USER BOX you create to solid black.

Press: (ALT-F9) (GRAPHICS)

Select: 4 (USER BOX)

Select: 4 (OPTIONS)

Select: 9 (GRAY SHADING (% OF BLACK))

Response: 0%

Type: 100

Press: (ENTER)

Press: (F7) (EXIT)

This creates a totally black box. (Choose 75 percent if you want a dark gray background. As you choose smaller percentages, the background shade becomes lighter.)

Step Two: Placing the Box

Next, place the USER BOX where you want your reversed headline to appear. Let's assume you want the headline to be centered in a black box 3 inches deep that spans the top of your publication. To create the box,

Press: (ALT-F9) (GRAPHICS)

Select: 4 (USER BOX)

Select: 1 (CREATE)

Select: 4 (3 in 5.0) (ANCHOR TYPE)

Select: 2 (PAGE)

Response: Number of pages to skip: 0

Press: (ENTER)

This "locks" the box to a specific point on a specific page, instead of having it "float" with surrounding text.

Select: 6 (5 in 5.0) (HORIZONTAL POSITION)

Select: 1 (MARGINS)

Select: 4 (FULL)

This is WordPerfect's way of creating a box that extends from one margin to the other.

Select: 7 (6 in 5.0) (SIZE)

Response: You're presented with the following alternatives:
1 (SET WIDTH/AUTO HEIGHT)
2 (SET HEIGHT/AUTO WIDTH)
3 (SET BOTH)
4 (AUTO BOTH)

Select: 3 (SET BOTH)

Response: Width = 6.5"

The width of the box is established by the page margins. The use of inches is based on the measuring system you've previously chosen.

Press: (ENTER)

Response: Height = 6.5"

Type: 3

Press: (ENTER)

Press: (F7) (EXIT)

This returns you to your editing screen.

Step Three: Adding Headline Words

Now it's time to place the reversed words within the black box you've created. Position your cursor *on or before* the USER BOX code using the REVEAL CODES command [ALT-F3].

Press: (ALT-F9) (GRAPHICS)

Select: 4 (USER BOX)

Select: 2 (EDIT)

Response: User Box number: 2 (or one number higher than the last USER BOX created so far.)

Type: 1 (or the appropriate number of the reversed USER BOX you've just created.)

Press: (ENTER)

Select: 9 (8 in 5.0) (EDIT)

Any words you now type will be placed in the reversed USER BOX you've just created. Before you enter the words that will be contained in your reversed headline box, enter the font codes that correspond to the appropriate typeface, type size and type style.

Press: (CTRL-F8) (FONT)

Select: 4 (BASE FONT)

Response: You're presented with an alphabetical list of all available resident and downloaded fonts.

Press: Up/down cursor control keys until BOLD HELVETICA is highlighted.

Select: 1 (Select)

Response: Point size: 10 (or the last type size chosen.)

Type: 36

Press: (ENTER)

Press: (CTRL-F8) (FONT)

Select: 5 (PRINT COLOR)

Select: 2 (WHITE)

Press: (F7) (EXIT)

Type: Reversed headlines add impact to your publications!

Before moving on, however, let's break the headline into three lines by pressing [ENTER] immediately after the word headlines and deleting the space before add.

Likewise, press [ENTER] immediately after the word "to" and delete the space before "your."

Return to the beginning of the headline.

Press: (ALT-F4) (BLOCK)

Move the cursor to the end of the headline.

Press: (SHIFT-F6) (CENTER)

Response: (Center) No (Yes)

Type: Y (Yes)

These steps ensure that the headline will be properly centered.

The next step is to center the headline vertically within the reversed box. Since the command CENTER PAGE (TOP TO BOTTOM) doesn't work in graphics boxes, you have two options here. You could simply move the cursor to the top of the headline and press [ENTER] several times to move the headline down. Or you could use the ADVANCE command [SHIFT-F8, 4, 1] to position the headline at a precise location from the top of the box.

The headline now is set up to be both vertically and horizontally centered within the reversed box. The final step is to change the normally black type to white type, so that it will form a dramatic contrast against its black background.

Step Four: Creating White Type

Now we come to the crucial step in creating a reversed headline. With the cursor still on the first letter of the headline,

Press: (CTRL-F8) (FONT)

Select: 5 (PRINT COLOR)

Response: You're presented with WordPerfect's PRINT COLOR menu.

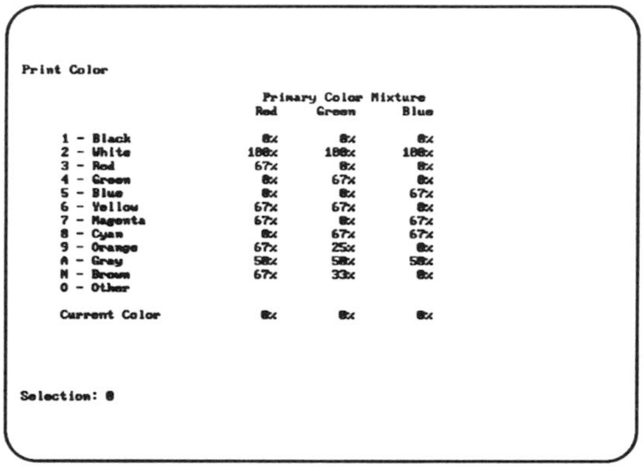

Print Color

	Primary Color Mixture Red	Green	Blue
1 - Black	0%	0%	0%
2 - White	100%	100%	100%
3 - Red	67%	0%	0%
4 - Green	0%	67%	0%
5 - Blue	0%	0%	67%
6 - Yellow	67%	67%	0%
7 - Magenta	67%	0%	67%
8 - Cyan	0%	67%	67%
9 - Orange	67%	25%	0%
A - Grey	50%	50%	50%
N - Brown	67%	33%	0%
O - Other			
Current Color	0%	0%	0%

Selection: 0

Select: 2 (WHITE)

Press: (F7) (EXIT) three times.

This returns you to your editing screen.

Use WordPerfect's VIEW DOCUMENT command [SHIFT-F7, 6]. Depending upon your monitor, you might see only a black box. But if you PRINT the page [SHIFT-F7, 2], you'll find that your words appear in white against a black background! The headline should look like this:

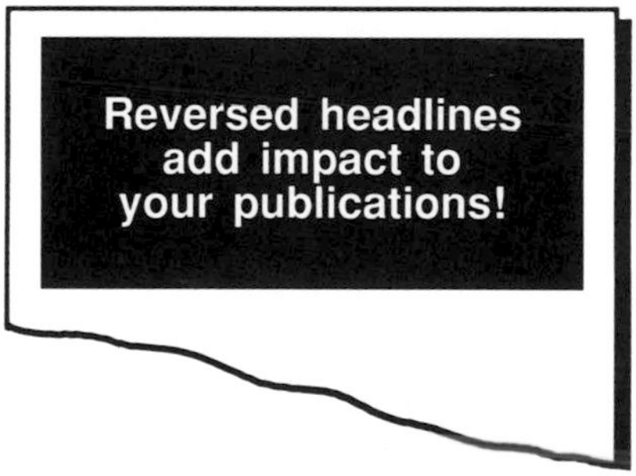
Reversed headlines
add impact to
your publications!

Because you'll be returning to the example later in this chapter, save it. You'll use it again when you experiment with improving the appearance of this headline.

Press: (F10) (SAVE)

Response: Document to be saved:

Type: REVHEAD

Press: (ENTER)

Returning User Boxes to White Background

To return to normal USER BOXes with white backgrounds, repeat the steps used to change the background to black, with the exception of the last step. Specifically,

Press: (ALT-F9) (GRAPHICS)

Select: 4 (USER BOX)

Select: 4 (OPTIONS)

Select: 9 (GRAY SHADING (% OF BLACK))

Response: 100% (selected above)

Type: 0 (zero)

Press: (ENTER)

Response: USER BOXes, once again, will be created with no borders and a white background.

Creating Shaded Type

Shaded type can add two-color impact to your publications at a one-color price. Shaded type is particularly valuable when used to create large, bold, sans-serif headlines, consisting of a few words surrounded by lots of white space.

To create shaded text,

Press: (CTRL-F8) (FONT)

Select: 5 (PRINT COLOR)

Select: O (OTHER)

Response: The cursor jumps to the 0% under Red.

Type: 60

Press: (ENTER)

Response: The cursor jumps to the 0% under Green.

Type: 60

Press: (ENTER)

Response: The cursor jumps to the 0% under Blue.

Type: 60

Press: (ENTER)

Press: (F7) (EXIT)

Press: (CTRL-F8) (FONT)

Select: 4 (BASE FONT)

Response: A list of all available resident and downloadable fonts.

Scroll down until you reach HELVETICA BOLD.

Select: 1 (Select)

Response: Point size: 10 (or last point size chosen.)

Type: 24

Press: (ENTER)

Type: Exciting Headlines

Press: (ENTER)

When printed, your page should be similar to the illustration below:

Exciting Headlines

Shaded type can range from very dark to very light. When printed, type appears darker as the "percentage" approaches 100. Type appears lighter as the "percentage" approaches 0. In most cases, you'll probably vary shadings at 20 percent intervals.

Shaded type can be particularly attractive when used in conjunction with shaded boxes. As the examples below show, interesting effects can be achieved by placing light gray type in a dark gray box, or dark gray type in a light gray box.

ONE DAY SALE

ONE DAY SALE

Moving On

This chapter introduced you to many of the tips and tricks of typography. Great advances are being made in this area. It pays to stay up-to-date as WordPerfect continues to enhance its ability to accurately place and fine-tune text.

Many of the steps described in Chapter 5 and in this chapter involve entering long sequences of keystrokes that might have to be frequently repeated in a long document (e.g., a book containing numerous reversed headlines).

In Chapter 7, you'll see how WordPerfect's powerful STYLE command [ALT-F8] can help you reduce these complicated keyboard sequences. In Chapter 8, you'll learn how WordPerfect's powerful MACRO command [ALT-F10] can expedite page formatting and layout of your document.

CHAPTER 7

USING STYLESHEETS FOR CONSISTENCY AND SPEED

Consistency of style is an important goal when producing print communications. Consistent type treatments, letter and line spacing, and page formatting improve both the appearance and the effectiveness of your projects.

For example, typeface, type size and type style options should be consistent throughout your publication, particularly in the following areas:

- Headlines
- Kickers (short phrases that introduce headlines)
- Bylines (authors' credits)
- Subheads
- Body copy
- Jumplines (e.g., "Continued on page 38" and "Continued from page 29")
- Captions
- Header and footer information (e.g., publication title, section or chapter divisions, author's name, page numbers)
- Footnotes and endnotes

WordPerfect's STYLE command [ALT-F8] makes consistency easy. By using STYLEs you can create stylesheets, containing your choice of type characteristics, as well as alignment and line spacing.

You even can include sophisticated typographic refinements, such as kerning, shading, word and letter spacing, and precise adjustments of margins, tabs and hyphenation zones in the STYLEs you create. These settings can be stored as separate files and accessed as needed. That minimizes the chances of choosing the wrong type characteristics or entering an inconsistent setting.

More important, if you're producing a series of advertisements, books, brochures, newsletters or training materials, WordPerfect's STYLEs can be re-used, making it easy to achieve consistency throughout a series.

It's important to note that WordPerfect's powerful STYLE command can be used any time, even while you're writing or editing your document.

A Shortcut to Achieving Consistent Design

If properly used, WordPerfect's STYLE command can save you a lot of time. Complicated sequences of keystrokes can be reduced to simple files, and accessed quickly and easily. For example, instead of entering a series of FONT and FORMAT commands each time you want to change from body copy to headline type and back again, you can invoke those command sequences by selecting the appropriate macro.

Styles are commonly used to

- Adjust type size and style.
- Change margins.
- Align text.
- Set tabs.
- Insert headers and footers.
- Position text with the ADVANCE command.
- Add graphic elements such as lines and boxes.

Finally, because STYLEs can be edited, you quickly can make major revisions throughout your publication by simply changing the STYLE definition. That's a lot faster than reformatting every headline, subhead and caption.

As you grow accustomed to WordPerfect's STYLE command, you'll wonder how you ever did without it!

Creating a Style

Let's create a STYLE that determines headline treatment for a newsletter.

Press: (ALT-F8) (STYLE)

Response: The STYLE menu is displayed.

Select: 3 (CREATE)

Select: 1 (NAME)

Type: MAINHEAD

Press: (ENTER)

You can include up to 11 letters in a STYLE's name, which should relate logically to its function. As you become comfortable using STYLEs, you'll undoubtedly come up with your own "shorthand" for naming them. The name will appear first in the listing of STYLEs when you execute the STYLE command and the REVEAL CODES command [ALT-F3].

Select: 2 (TYPE)

Response: You're given three options:
1 (PAIRED)
2 (OPEN)
3 (OUTLINE)

You'll probably use 1 (PAIRED) more often than 2 (OPEN). PAIRED STYLEs are used for selected word groups—headlines, subheads, body copy or captions. PAIRED STYLEs are applied to text that you've blocked using [ALT-F4] (BLOCK).

When you select 2 (OPEN), the STYLE remains active throughout the rest of your publication. OPEN STYLEs usually are used to establish formats, such as margins, that will be maintained throughout the publication.

Select: 1 (PAIRED)

Select: 3 (DESCRIPTION)

You can use as many as 59 characters to define the purpose and use of this STYLE. The DESCRIPTION feature is there to remind you of the intended use of the STYLE. It also can be used to remind you of the kind of project a particular STYLE has been assigned (e.g., customer newsletter, employee handbook, etc.).

Type: Defines newsletter headline treatment.

Press: (ENTER)

Select: 4 (CODES)

Now you define the typeface, type size, type style, alignment and line spacing—or any other formatting options—that you want for your newsletter headlines. This section can be as lengthy as necessary to accommodate all your typographic refinements described in the previous chapter. (However, let's make this example relatively short.)

Response: The screen divides in half, with a box containing the words, Place Style On Codes above, and Style Off Codes below.

This screen lets you specify the type characteristics you want applied when you turn the style on and off. The "on" codes go above the Comment box, and the "off" codes go below. Use your right/left cursor control keys to switch between the STYLE ON and STYLE OFF side of the Comment box. To help you visualize this better, notice how the CODES screen is divided in half and the REVEAL CODES command [ALT-F3] is activated automatically.

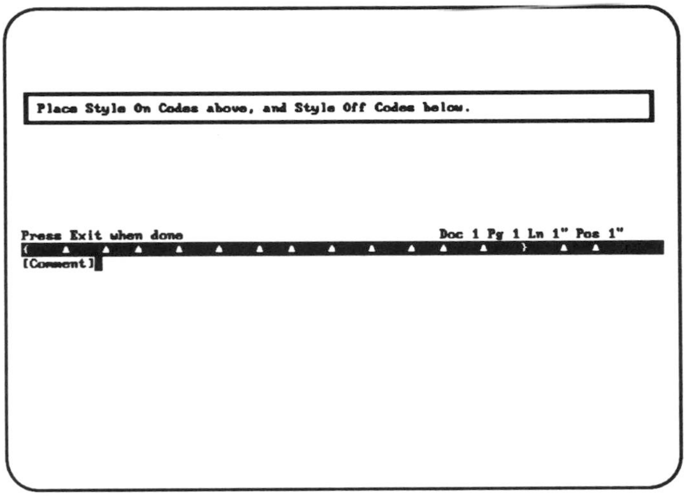

Press: (CTRL-F8) (FONT)

Select: 4 (BASE FONT)

Response: You're presented with a list of all typefaces, type sizes and type styles currently available with the selected printer. Options include resident fonts, downloaded fonts and—if you're using an HP-compatible printer—font cartridges. If you're using a PostScript printer, for example, scroll down the list until you come to HELVETICA.

Select: 1 (Select)

Response: Point Size:

Type: 24

Press: (ENTER)

You also can define the placement and line spacing of the headline at this point. For example, if you want to center the headline,

Press: (SHIFT-F6) (CENTER)

If you want the headline double-spaced,

Press: (SHIFT-F8) (FORMAT)

Select: 1 (LINE)

Response: The screen displays the FORMAT: LINE menu.

Select: 6 (LINE SPACING)

Response: The blinking cursor highlights the currently active default, in this case, 1.

Type: 2

Press: (ENTER)

This replaces the default single-line spacing with double-line spacing.

When you've finished formatting headline type characteristics and line spacing, move the cursor below the Comment box by pressing the right cursor control key. Then enter the formatting choices for text when the STYLE is deactivated.

When you're satisfied with your choices,

Press: (F7) (EXIT)

Response: This returns you to the STYLES: EDIT menu.

The final step in creating a STYLE is to define the purpose of the [ENTER] key when the PAIRED STYLE is turned on.

Select: 5 (ENTER)

Response: 1 (HRT)
2 (OFF)
3 (OFF/ON)

Option 1 (HRT) doesn't affect the function of the [ENTER] key, which operates as a normal hard return. It doesn't affect the way the stylesheet performs.

Option 2 (OFF) lets you use the [ENTER] key to turn off the STYLE definition.

Option 3 (OFF/ON) allows you to use the [ENTER] key as a toggle to turn the STYLE on and off.

Select: 2 (OFF)

To end the style creation process,

Press: (F7) (EXIT) twice

Creating Styles by Example

You also can create a STYLE by using WordPerfect's BLOCK command [ALT-F4]. Start by highlighting a previously formatted group of words including all necessary codes. This can save you time, because you can easily replicate a format that took a lot of trial and error until it appeared just right.

Press: (ALT-F4) (BLOCK)

Use your left/right cursor control keys to choose the formatted words you want saved as a STYLE. Remember that [CTRL]-right and [CTRL]-left cursor control keys advance the cursor one word at a time. When the passage you want saved as a formatted STYLE has been highlighted,

Press: (ALT-F8) (STYLE)

Select: 3 (CREATE)

Select: 1 (NAME)

Type: SUBHEAD

Press: (ENTER)

Select: 3 (DESCRIPTION)

Type: Provides headline/body copy transition

Press: (ENTER)

To return to editing your document,

Press: (F7) (EXIT)

Applying Styles as You Write New Text

STYLEs can be applied while you're writing new text or editing existing text. To apply STYLEs as you write new text,

Press: (ALT-F8) (STYLE)

Response: You're presented with an alphabetical listing of the STYLEs you've previously created.

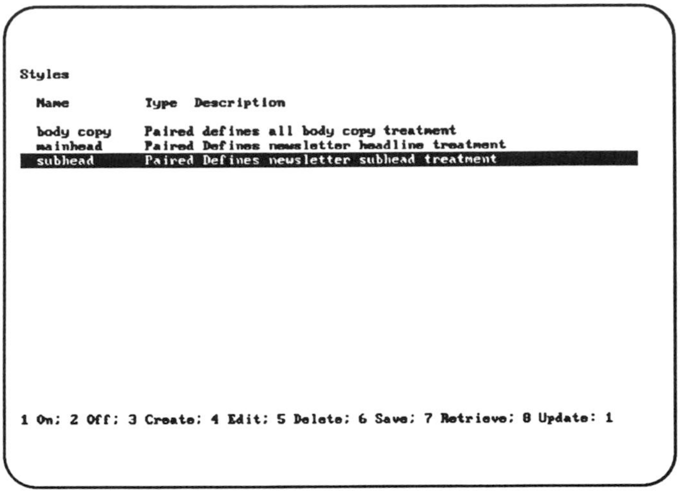
Styles
Name Type Description
body copy Paired defines all body copy treatment
mainhead Paired Defines newsletter headline treatment
subhead Paired Defines newsletter subhead treatment
1 On; 2 Off; 3 Create; 4 Edit; 5 Delete; 6 Save; 7 Retrieve; 8 Update: 1

Press: The up/down cursor control keys until you've highlighted the STYLE you want to use for the next group of words. In this case, MAINHEAD.

Select: 1 (ON)

Type: WordPerfect's Styles Save Time!

Press: (ALT-F8) (STYLE)

Select: 2 (OFF)

To continue the example,

Press: (ALT-F8) (STYLE)

Press: Up/down cursor control keys until SUBHEAD STYLE is highlighted.

Select: 1 (ON)

Type: And they're easy to apply.

Press: (ALT-F8) (STYLE)

Select: 2 (OFF)

Use WordPerfect's VIEW DOCUMENT [SHIFT-F7, 6] or PRINT [SHIFT-F7, 2] commands to see how the STYLEs formatted your words.

Applying Styles to Previously Entered Text

You also can apply previously created STYLEs to existing text. Start by placing the cursor at the beginning of a word group that you want to format.

Press: (ALT-F4) (BLOCK)

Press: The right cursor control key, or [CTRL]-right cursor control key, to select the letters or words you want to format.

Press: (ALT-F8) (STYLE)

Response: You're presented with an alphabetical list of previously created STYLEs.

Press: The down cursor control key to advance to the STYLE you want to apply to the highlighted words.

Select: 1 (ON)

Response: The words are formatted and you return to your editing screen.

Editing a Style

If you want to modify the appearance of your publication by changing previously chosen typeface, type size, type style or alignment alternatives, you easily can edit a STYLE. You also might want to edit a STYLE if you've purchased new downloadable fonts that you want to substitute for previously chosen typefaces.

Editing lets you quickly change typeface, type size, type style or alignment formats throughout the document. By editing the STYLE, you automatically can modify the appearance of every word, or group of words, to which the STYLE relates. With a few simple keystrokes, you can make major changes in the appearance of your document.

To edit a STYLE,

Press: (ALT-F8) (STYLE)

Response: You're presented with an alphabetical list of previously defined STYLEs.

Press: The down cursor control key to highlight the STYLE you want to edit.

Select: 4 (EDIT)

Response: You're presented with the name, description, codes and [ENTER] key options for the STYLE you've chosen. Although you can edit the name or description, in most cases you'll probably want to edit the codes.

Select: 4 (CODES)

Response: Notice how WordPerfect's REVEAL CODES command [ALT-F3] automatically is activated to help you.

Type: Your changes. Remember, the "on" codes go above the Comment box, and the "off" codes go below. When you're finished,

Press: (F7) (EXIT) three times.

That returns you to your editing screen and changes the formatting of all word groups to which the STYLE relates.

Deleting a Style

You can delete a STYLE. You might want to do so because a format doesn't look good when printed or relates to a downloadable font you no longer want to use.

You also may want to delete a STYLE that's unique to a single document and doesn't belong in a STYLE library you're creating for several different publications (see below).

To delete a previously defined STYLE,

Press: (ALT-F8) (STYLE)

Response: You're presented with an alphabetical list of previously defined STYLEs.

Press: The down cursor control key to highlight the STYLE you want to delete.

Select: 5 (DELETE)

Response: Delete Styles: 1 Leaving Codes
2 Including Codes
3 Definition Only

In Version 5.0, your choices are Yes and No.

Select: 2 (INCLUDING CODES) (or type Y in Version 5.0)

Response: The deleted STYLE no longer appears in the listing of available STYLEs. This act is irrevocable. You can't retrieve a deleted STYLE.

Creating a Style Library

STYLEs normally are saved with the document for which they've been designed. It's possible, however, to create STYLE libraries, which let STYLEs created for one publication be used again for other publications.

To create a STYLE library,

Press: (ALT-F8) (STYLE)

Response: You're presented with an alphabetical list of previously defined STYLEs.

Select: 6 (SAVE)

Response: You're prompted to enter a file name. Let's assume you want to re-use the STYLEs in future newsletters.

Type: NEWSTYLS

Press: (ENTER)

To avoid confusion, choose a "shorthand" file name that explains the contents of the file in just eight letters.

To return to text entry and editing,

Press: (F7) (EXIT)

Retrieving a Style Library

Later, when you're working on a different document and want to use a previously defined STYLE library,

Press: (ALT-F8) (STYLE)

Response: The STYLEs menu appears without any defined STYLEs.

Select: 7 (RETRIEVE)

Response: Filename:

Type: The name of your previously stored STYLE library (in this case, NEWSTYLS).

Press: (ENTER)

Response: The STYLE menu now displays an alphabetical list of STYLEs created for your original document that now are available with your current document.

TIP: You might want to create a STYLE library in a separate subdirectory. When retrieving a previously stored STYLE library, you have to enter its full pathname (e.g., \STYLIB\NEWSTYLS).

Creating Open Styles

In addition to using STYLEs to establish typographic formats, you can also use them to create page layouts. Let's create an OPEN style, which features a page layout for a three-column newsletter.

Press: (ALT-F8) (STYLE)

Select: 3 (CREATE)

Select: 1 (NAME)

Type: 3COLGRID

Press: (ENTER)

Select: 2 (TYPE)

Response: 1 (PAIRED)
2 (OPEN)
3 (OUTLINE)

Select: 2 (OPEN)

Select: 3 (DESCRIPTION)

Type: Creates three-column newsletter grid

Press: (ENTER)

Select: 4 (CODES)

Response: You'll see the STYLE codes screen.

Press: (ALT-F7) (COLUMNS/TABLES)

Select: 1 (COLUMNS) (not used in Version 5.0)

Select: 3 (4 in 5.0) (DEFINE)

Response: You're presented with the TEXT COLUMN definition menu.

Accept the NEWSPAPER format, as described in Chapter 3.

Select: 2 (NUMBER OF COLUMNS)

Response: The cursor under 2 will blink.

Type: 3

Press: (ENTER)

This replaces the default two-column format with a three-column format.

Response: Notice how the column widths are computed automatically.

Press: (ENTER)

Finally, to activate the three-column format, turn columns on:

Select: 1 (ON) (or 3 (COLUMN ON/OFF) in Version 5.0.)

Press: (F7) (EXIT) three times

The three-column format now is saved, and the style 3COLGRID is added to the list of styles. In a similar way, you can create STYLEs that define margins, create headers and footers, assign page number locations, center title pages and customize page layouts in many other ways.

Moving On

In Chapter 8, you'll look more closely at the way macros and stylesheets can work together with WordPerfect's desktop publishing tools to help you create good-looking publications. You'll also examine how desktop publishing features work with other hardware and software options, such as the WordPerfect Library and expanded memory boards.

CHAPTER 8

ADVANCED TECHNIQUES

By now you're familiar with WordPerfect's basic desktop publishing tools and how they interact.

To review, desktop publishing with WordPerfect is based on a combination of six major features introduced in Version 5.0:

1) The ability to create and accurately locate boxes for placing text and graphics files created with other programs.

2) The ability to control the placement of text on a page, including mixing multiple typefaces, sizes and styles.

3) The use of macros and STYLEs to expedite page layout and select and change type characteristics.

4) Organizational capabilities, such as generating automatic references, endnotes, footnotes, index entries and tables of contents, as well as detailed lists of graphs, drawings, tables and illustrations.

5) A page preview feature that lets you view your work on your computer screen at varying degrees of magnification.

6) An enhanced REVEAL CODES feature that allows on-screen editing and formatting.

To move beyond basic desktop publishing, let's look at advanced macros, which let you assemble those features into quick routines that establish page layouts, add graphic accents and choose type attributes.

Using Nested Macros

WordPerfect lets you nest macros within macros. Thus, you can combine your existing macros in various ways to simplify page layouts and text formatting. This technique works only with [ALT]-key macros.

In earlier chapters, you learned how to use macros to create a border, a multicolumn page layout and boxes of various sizes. In Chapter 7, you examined STYLEs and their use in selecting a given typeface, type size and type style.

A macro can consist of other nested macros and STYLEs that operate in sequence automatically. Thus, by executing one macro, you simultaneously can

- Add page borders.
- Add white space.
- Establish multicolumn layouts.
- Choose a particular typeface, type size and type style.

You can even use repeating macros to lay out a multipage newsletter automatically, complete with page numbers alternating on the left- and right-hand pages. Let's go through a sample exercise to see how macros can be nested within "master" macros.

Assume you want to create a macro that will lay out the first page of a newsletter and that you've already created several individual macros that perform the functions described. Let's assume you've created these macros:

- [ALT-M] imports a newsletter masthead or nameplate.
- [ALT-B] places a .25-inch line across the bottom of the page.
- [ALT-C] creates a three-column page and turns on the column-formatting feature.
- [ALT-V] places vertical lines between the columns.

In the exercise below, these four macros will be nested within a new macro called [ALT-N].

Start by opening a practice document that includes several prepared macros and STYLEs.

Press: (CTRL-F10) (MACRO DEFINE)

Response: You're prompted to name the macro.

Press: (ALT-N)

Response: You're prompted to describe the macro.

Type: Creates front page of 3-col newsletter

Press: (ENTER)

Response: The MACRO DEF prompt indicates that the following keystrokes will be recorded.

Press: (ALT-F10) (MACRO)

Response: Macro:

You're prompted to name a previously prepared macro you want to include in the [ALT-N] macro.

Press: (ALT-M)

Press: (ALT-F10) (MACRO)

Response: Macro:

Again, you're asked to enter the name of a previously created macro.

Press: (ALT-B)

Press: (ALT-F10) (MACRO)

Response: Again, you're prompted to enter the name of a previously created macro.

Press: (ALT-C)

Press: (ALT-F10) (MACRO)

Response: Again, you're prompted to enter the name of a previously created macro.

Press: (ALT-V)

At this point, you've completed laying out the front page. To end the macro,

Press: (CTRL-F10) (MACRO DEFINE)

This concludes the macro creation process. You're returned to your editing screen.

In a similar way, you can create macros for each page in your newsletter. You might create separate macros for left- and right-hand pages in order to alternate header and footer information. These macros could be called [ALT-R] and [ALT-L].

Using a Nested Macro

To quickly lay out the front page of your newsletter with the chained macro,

Press: (ALT-F10) (MACRO)

Response: Macro:

Press: (ALT-N)

Press: (ENTER)

Response: All the nested macros included in the macro [ALT-N] will be applied in the order they were entered. The result will be a formatted page ready for your words.

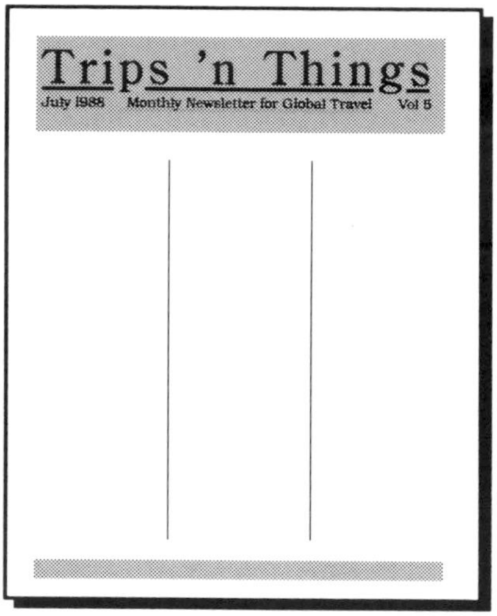

Editing a Macro

There may be occasions when you'll want to change your macro definition. You might find that the vertical lines extend into the masthead box or that a different column layout is needed. WordPerfect makes it easy to edit previously created macros.

Press: (CTRL-F10) (MACRO DEFINE)

Response: Define macro:

This prompts you to enter the macro name. For purposes of illustration, let's enter the name of one of the macros used in the previous exercise.

Press: (ALT-V)

Response: ALTV.WPM Already Exists: 1 Replace; 2 Edit; 3 Description: 0

Select: 2 (EDIT)

Response: You're presented with the MACRO: ACTION screen, which lists the file name and the description. The cursor moves automatically to the box containing the codes (in Version 5.0, you'll have to select 2 (ACTION) to position the cursor in the box).

Notice how this MACRO: EDIT box is similar to WordPerfect's REVEAL CODES [ALT-F3] screen.

Press: (CTRL-F10) (MACRO DEFINE)

Any key you press now will be added to the macro. When you need to move the cursor, or when you're finished editing the macro,

Press: (CTRL-F10) (MACRO DEFINE)

Press: (F7) (EXIT)

You now are returned to the editing screen. The macro you've edited has been revised and saved.

Repeating a Macro

WordPerfect's MACRO feature makes it easy to create multiple page layouts. Macros can be set up to repeat as many times as you want. The ESCAPE key (ESC) is used to repeat macros automatically.

Using the above example, let's say that within a macro you want to repeat a nested macro two times. Before you press [ALT-F10] to enter the macro name, press the [ESCAPE] key.

Press: (CTRL-F10) (MACRO DEFINE)

Press: (ESCAPE)

Response: Repeat Value = 8

Type: 2 (do not press [ENTER])

Press: (ALT-F10) (MACRO)

Press: The [ALT]-key name of the macro you want repeated.

Press: (CTRL-F10) (MACRO DEFINE)

This ends the macro creation process. When the macro is invoked, the chained macro inside is repeated as many times as you've indicated.

Sharing Macros with Other Documents

Unlike STYLEs, macros are stored in separate files, independent of the document in which they were created. Thus, macros can be shared with more than one document without having to go through the saving and retrieving process required when STYLEs are shared.

WordPerfect macros are easily identified by their .WPM suffix. You can use WordPerfect's SETUP command [SHIFT-F1, 6, 2] (or [SHIFT-F1, 7, 3] in Version 5.0) to identify a previously created subdirectory where all macros are stored.

Creating Compound Documents

As you begin to create detailed publications with WordPerfect, you'll find yourself placing a previously written file inside your current document. WordPerfect's RETRIEVE TEXT command [SHIFT-F10] lets you do this without destroying your original file. Thus, when you edit the retrieved file within your current document, the original file remains intact. (Of course, any changes you make won't appear in the original file.)

To retrieve a previously prepared file, place your cursor at the position in your document where you want to insert the file.

Press: (SHIFT-F10) (RETRIEVE TEXT)

Response: Document to be retrieved:

If you know the file name you want to place in your current document, enter it. If you're not sure of the file name or are unsure of which subdirectory the file is located in,

Press: (F5) (LIST FILES)

Response: You're shown the currently active subdirectory.

If it's the correct subdirectory, press [ENTER]. If the file you want to retrieve is in a different subdirectory, type in the name of the correct subdirectory and press [ENTER].

In either case, scroll through the files using your up/down/left/right cursor control keys. When you locate the file,

Select: 1 (RETRIEVE)

Response: Retrieve into current document? No (Yes)

Type: Y (Yes)

Response: The text of the file you saved will flow into your current document. If you've selected a multicolumn newsletter format with newspaper-type columns, for example, the text will be reformatted as you defined.

TIP: Remember that the text will be imported using the typeface, type size, type style and alignment it was saved in, *not* the type characteristics currently active in your file.

Reformatting a Retrieved File

You may want to reformat the retrieved file to correspond to the type characteristics of your current document. To do this, position your cursor at the point in the document where the file was retrieved.

Press: (ALT-F3) (REVEAL CODES)

Response: The screen is divided. You'll see that the contents of the retrieved file follow a description of the formatting (page layout and type specifications) of the imported file.

To reformat the retrieved file to make it conform with your current file,

Press: The backspace or [DELETE] keys to erase the formatting commands of the retrieved file.

Response: Instantly, the file is reformatted to reflect the typeface, type size and alignment of your currently active document.

Expanded Memory and the WordPerfect Library

Although WordPerfect has powerful built-in desktop publishing features, it also can be used in conjunction with other software programs. Examples of this might include

a) Creating sophisticated newsletter nameplates or business logos with separate "draw" or "paint" programs to place in various kinds of boxes. Typical programs include Windows Draw, GEM Draw and PC Paintbrush.

b) Creating graphs and charts with spreadsheet programs, such as WordPerfect's PlanPerfect, Lotus 1-2-3 or SuperCalc 4.

c) Importing scanned photographs created with such programs as Aldus Snapshot.

The WordPerfect Corporation publishes a supplementary software program, the WordPerfect Library, which makes it easy to locate and place files created with other software programs. It's an excellent supplement to WordPerfect for several reasons.

On the most elementary level, the WordPerfect Library is valuable because it lets you access WordPerfect, or any other software program, by pressing a single letter that corresponds to the program you want to load. Instead of facing a blank screen with a naked C:\> prompt, for example, you're shown a list of up to 20 programs available on your hard disk.

When you press the letter corresponding to the program you want to use, the WordPerfect Library automatically selects the proper subdirectory in which the program has been saved and loads the program.

The WordPerfect Library is further enhanced when used with expanded memory boards, such as the Intel AboveBoard. By using them together, you temporarily can leave the WordPerfect document you're working on, load and operate another software program and, when you're finished, immediately return to the exact cursor position where you left your original WordPerfect document.

The WordPerfect Library, in other words, lets you "swap" programs between your computer's working memory and a special memory storage area. An optional memory board will let you work around the normal memory limitations of the DOS operating system.

Returning to DOS

If you have the WordPerfect Library, you'll appreciate the ability to leave the WordPerfect document you're working on—without closing the file—and exit to DOS. Then you can format a new diskette or create a subdirectory for a new project.

To use this feature,

Press: (CTRL-F1) (SHELL)

Response: 1 Go to DOS; 2 DOS Command: 0

Select: 1 (Go to DOS)

You'll now be able to execute any DOS command. When you're finished and want to return to your place in the WordPerfect document,

Type: EXIT (Note that you must spell it out. The EXIT command [F7] doesn't work.)

Press: (ENTER)

You'll be returned to the exact cursor position in the WordPerfect document you were editing when you executed SHELL [CTRL-F1].

Using WordPerfect with Other Library Programs

To temporarily leave WordPerfect and enter another program in the library,

Press: (ALT-SHIFT) and the letter that corresponds to the new software program you want to enter.

Response: WordPerfect and the document you've been working on are placed in expanded memory, and the new program is loaded.

When you've finished working with the program, exit it in the normal way. You'll then be returned to the Library Shell program.

Type: A (the letter normally assigned to WordPerfect in the WordPerfect Library.)

Response: The WordPerfect program and the document(s) you've been working on will be returned to active status.

TIP: If the second program is a WordPerfect program, such as the PlanPerfect spreadsheet or DataPerfect database management system, you can go directly from the program back to WordPerfect.

Press: (ALT-SHIFT) and A (assuming A is the letter referring to WordPerfect.)

This technique bypasses the Shell and directly returns you to your WordPerfect document.

Other Library Features

In addition to letting you swap WordPerfect with other programs, the WordPerfect Library contains a powerful calculator and a versatile calendar that you easily can enter and leave.

The latest version of the WordPerfect Library, Version 2.0, also has a time management module that lets you keep track of time spent working with various software programs or on specific projects. Consultants and writers will appreciate these enhancements at billing time! Version 2.0 of the WordPerfect Library also includes a telephone dialing utility, handy for modem users.

Working with the Clipboard

The latest version of the WordPerfect Library, Version 2.0, has a Clipboard feature that lets you easily exchange text from one software program to another without storing and retrieving complete files.

For example, let's say you're working on a WordPerfect document and want to insert drop caps for the first letter of the first word of each major section of your document.

Press: (SHIFT-ALT-H)

H is based on the assumption that your favorite draw or paint program is accessed through this letter of the WordPerfect Library Shell.

Using the drawing program, create an alphabet of special characters to be used as drop caps.

Highlight, or outline, the letter you've created, and copy it to the Library's Clipboard.

Exit the drawing program and re-enter WordPerfect.

Position the cursor in the CHARACTER BOX you've created at the beginning of the first paragraph in the new section of your document.

Press: (CTRL-F1) (SHELL)

Select: 2 (CLIPBOARD)

Select: 4 (RETRIEVE A GRAPHICS FILE)

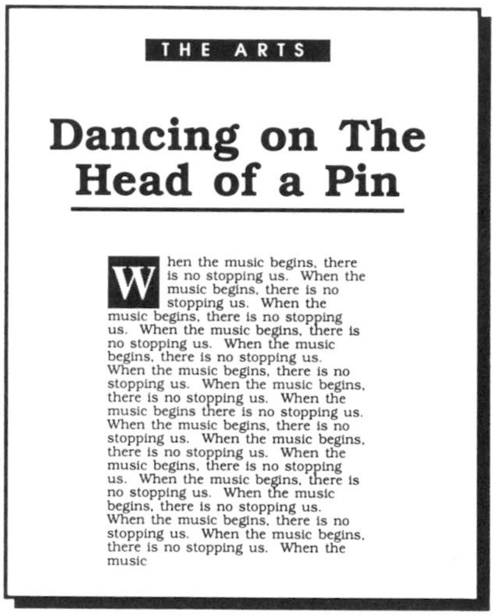

THE ARTS

Dancing on The Head of a Pin

When the music begins, there is no stopping us. When the music begins, there is no stopping us. When the music begins, there is no stopping us. When the music begins, there is no stopping us. When the music begins, there is no stopping us. When the music begins, there is no stopping us. When the music begins, there is no stopping us. When the music begins there is no stopping us. When the music begins, there is no stopping us. When the music begins, there is no stopping us. When the music begins, there is no stopping us. When the music begins, there is no stopping us. When the music begins, there is no stopping us. When the music begins, there is no stopping us. When the music begins, there is no stopping us. When the music

In a similar way, you can add graphs and charts created with PlanPerfect to proposals and reports you're creating with WordPerfect. The Clipboard feature also allows you to import segments of a PlanPerfect spreadsheet into a formal proposal or presentation.

More WordPerfect Library Uses

If you created a graphics file but forgot its file name, the WordPerfect Library makes it easy to enter the draw or paint-type file quickly to use the program's particular "open file" command to see which files have been created.

Or you can leave WordPerfect temporarily and enter DOS, select the subdirectory in which you may have stored the file, and use the DOS DIR command to scan the subdirectory.

You'll quickly grow to appreciate the flexibility the library adds to WordPerfect's basic word processing and desktop publishing capabilities. By using the library, you can consolidate several programs into good-looking, effective print communications.

Moving On

You now know how to use WordPerfect macros and styles to simplify the layout and formatting of your documents. In the next chapter, you'll look at how WordPerfect's organizing tools help readers quickly locate information such as graphs, illustrations or tables of data.

As you'll see, WordPerfect offers document organizing power that rivals that available in many conventional desktop publishing programs.

CHAPTER 9

DOCUMENT ORGANIZATION

If you can't judge a book by its cover, you probably can judge it by its organizational features. A thorough table of contents and index help readers find information quickly and efficiently. Yet, developing such tools can be an arduous task.

WordPerfect, however, has strong document organizational capabilities. As you write, edit or format your document, you can insert commands that automatically compile

- Table of contents.
- Lists of subjects.
- Lists of tables, charts and graphs.
- Lists of illustrations and photographs.
- Word index.

Regardless of the size of the book or training manual, readers can use these tools to quickly locate the words or graphic information they need.

Creating a Table of Contents

WordPerfect's document organization features make it easy to create a table of contents—perhaps positioned strategically on the front cover of your catalog, newsletter or formal report—to entice readers and help them locate information. But creating a table of contents involves more than just listing chapter headings and subheads. You also must design and generate it.

WordPerfect lets you include as many as five levels of detail, which organize information into a hierarchy—ranging from "very important" to the "supporting detail" level. Readers in academic or technical fields, in particular, appreciate this format, which allows them to skim the table of contents to locate information quickly.

To create a table of contents, highlight the chapter titles and subheadings you want to include. Move the cursor to the first word in your first chapter title.

Press: (ALT-F4) (BLOCK)

Select: Using the left and right cursor control keys by themselves or in conjunction with [CTRL] (which advances the cursor one word at a time), highlight the first title you want included in your table of contents.

Press: (ALT-F5) (MARK TEXT)

Select: 1 (ToC)

Response: ToC Level:

Type: 1, 2, 3, 4 or 5 (depending on the priority of the highlighted information; 1 is the highest level, 5 is the lowest).

Press: (ENTER)

TIP: Assign chapter headings to Level 1, subheadings to Level 2 and secondary subheadings to Level 3.

Go through your entire document and mark all the words and phrases to be included in your table of contents.

Next, define the table's appearance. Let's assume you want to create a table with three levels of detail. Place the cursor at the end of the page before the table of contents begins.

Press: (CTRL-ENTER) (HARD PAGE)

Type: The title of your table of contents.

Move: The cursor to the position where you want the table of contents to begin.

Press: (ALT-F5) (MARK TEXT)

Select: 5 (DEFINE)

Select: 1 (DEFINE TABLE OF CONTENTS)

Response: The TABLE OF CONTENTS definition screen appears.

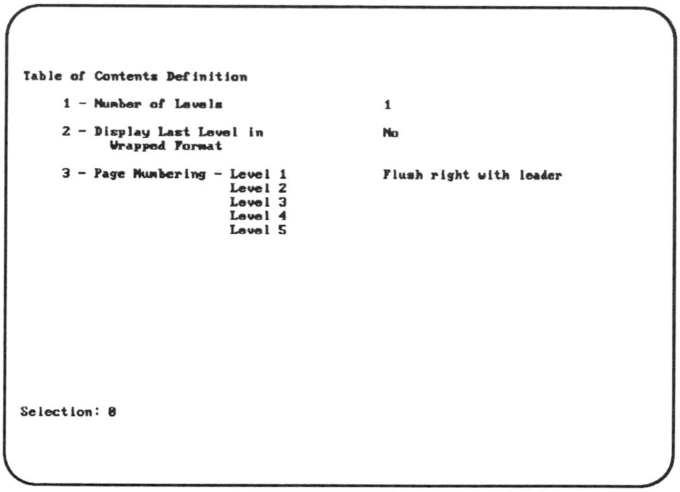

Select: 1 (NUMBER OF LEVELS)

Type: 3

Select: 2 (DISPLAY LAST LEVEL IN WRAPPED FORMAT) if you're using the lowest level of detail and want long phrases continued from the right-hand end of one line to wrap around—or to be indented properly at the beginning of the next line. Otherwise, accept the No default.

If you want to accept the default page-number option Flush Right with Leader dots for your table of contents,

Press: (F7) (EXIT)

But if you want to use a different page-numbering option,

Select: 3 (PAGE NUMBERING)

Response: You're offered several options for each of the table of contents levels you selected in 1 (NUMBER OF LEVELS):

1 (NONE)
2 (PAGE # FOLLOWS) without parentheses around the page number.
3 ((PAGE #) FOLLOWS) with the page number in parentheses.
4 (FLUSH RT) without a row of dots connecting the entry and the page number.
5 (FLUSH RT WITH LEADER) with a row of dots, which helps the reader relate entries to page numbers.

Make your choice for each level and then press [F7] (EXIT) twice.

To generate your table of contents,

Press: (ALT-F5) (MARK TEXT)

Select: 6 (GENERATE)

Select: 5 (GENERATE TABLES, INDEXES, CROSS REFERENCES, ETC.)

Response: Existing tables, lists, and indexes will be replaced.
Continue? Yes (No)

Type: Y (Yes)

The table of contents appears:

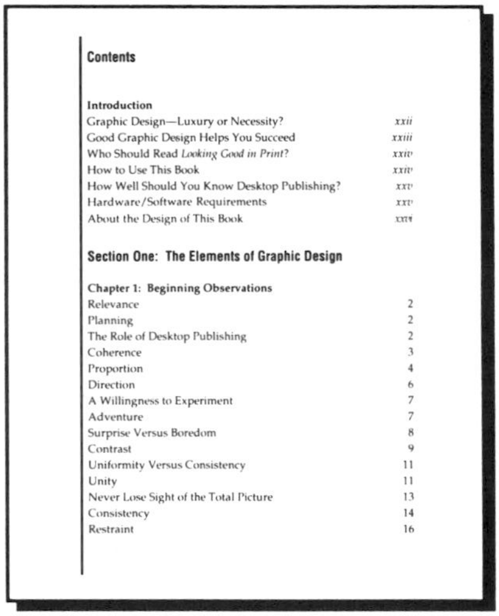

Contents

Keeping Track of Drawings and Illustrations

As described in Chapter 2, illustrations and scanned photographs are added to WordPerfect documents by being placed in previously created FIGURE, TABLE, TEXT or USER graphics boxes. These boxes are numbered automatically as you create them and renumbered if you add or delete other boxes.

When creating these graphics boxes, WordPerfect prompts you to write a caption for each chart, graph, table, illustration or scanned image. These captions are the basis of compiled lists of illustrations and photographs, which form separate files that can be placed anywhere in your document. For example, a list of illustrations might appear at the front or back of your book or training manual.

TIP: Remember that WordPerfect compiles a list starting at the beginning of your document and working toward the end, where the list will appear. If you want a list to appear at the beginning of the document, follow the procedure outlined below to generate the list. Then use WordPerfect's BLOCK [ALT-F4] and MOVE [CTRL-F4, 2] commands to move the list from the end of your document to the beginning. To place your list on the page on which you want it, move the cursor to the desired position, use the MOVE command [CTRL-F4, 1] to retrieve the list. Then press [ENTER].

To generate a list of illustrations, place the cursor at the end of your document. At this point, use the [ENTER] key to add as much space as you want between the top of the page and the heading for your list.

Type: The heading you assign your list (e.g., ILLUSTRATIONS).

To center your heading, use WordPerfect's CENTER command [SHIFT-F6].

TIP: When entering headings, you can choose any available typeface, type size or type style by using WordPerfect's FONT command [CTRL-F8], described in Chapter 5.

Next, select the type of list you want to generate.

Press: (ALT-F5) (MARK TEXT)

Select: 5 (DEFINE)

Select: 2 (DEFINE LIST)

Response: List Number (1 - 10):

Options 1 through 5 let you create lists based on any category of information. However, if you want your list based on captions created for FIGURE, TABLE, TEXT, USER or EQUATION BOXes, choose from Options 6 through 10, respectively.

Select: 6 (FIGURE CAPTIONS)

Press: (ENTER)

Select: Choose from the following alternatives:

1 (NO PAGE NUMBERS)
2 (PAGE NUMBERS FOLLOW ENTRIES)
3 (PAGE NUMBERS) FOLLOW ENTRIES
4 (FLUSH RIGHT PAGE NUMBERS)
5 (FLUSH RIGHT PAGE NUMBERS WITH LEADERS)

Finally, generate the list.

Press: (ALT-F5) (MARK TEXT)

Select: 6 (GENERATE)

Select: 5 (GENERATE TABLES, INDEXES, CROSS-REFERENCES, ETC.)

Response: Existing tables, lists, and indexes will be replaced.
Continue? Yes (No)

Type: Y (Yes)

The following is a typical FIGURE LIST that can be placed at the front of a book or training manual.

ILLUSTRATIONS

Figure 1. Map of Poland - 1945

Figure 2. Map of Russia - 1980

Figure 3. Diagram of Battle Fields

Figure 4. Map of Separation

Figure 5. Map of Italy - 1966

Figure 6. Diagram of Truck Routes

Figure 7. Map of Italy - 1940

Figure 8. Map of Europe - 1980

Keeping Track of Tables, Charts and Graphs

Regardless of whether you're producing a book, financial proposal or formal report, lists of tables, charts and graphs add further credibility to your document and help readers quickly inventory and locate information. Many readers like to turn first to pages containing tables, charts and graphs, since they provide concise, visual displays of important numbers.

To create these lists, you use a procedure similar to the one used to compile lists of illustrations. Follow the same process of defining the location and appearance of a file that is assembled automatically, based on the captions you added when creating the box.

When making your choice, remember the following:

- 6 creates a list of FIGURE BOXes.
- 7 creates a list of TABLE BOXes.
- 8 creates a list of TEXT BOXes.
- 9 creates a list of USER BOXes.
- 10 creates a list of EQUATION BOXes.

Keeping Track of Sidebars and Articles

If your publication includes numerous short articles or features, WordPerfect's ability to keep track of TEXT BOXes can be of value. For example, you might use TEXT BOXes for sidebars—short articles that elaborate upon information contained in the body copy of a book or newsletter.

You also can use WordPerfect's ability to create an index of TEXT BOXes to identify departments within a newsletter (e.g., a calendar of events, or a list of recent promotions, awards and outstanding accomplishments).

You even can create a list based on WordPerfect's USER BOXes, which give you greater flexibility by letting you create lists of more than one type of TEXT BOX.

TIP: If you create a box and don't give it a caption, it won't be included in a compiled list. The FIGURE, TABLE, TEXT, USER or EQUATION BOX number will be omitted from the list.

Creating an Index

You can create a subject index by *marking* words and phrases as index entries. You then can generate the index by using WordPerfect's LIST GENERATE command [ALT-F5, 6, 5].

While writing or editing your document, locate each word or phrase you want included in the index. If you want to include a multiple word entry in your index, use WordPerfect's BLOCK command [ALT-F4] and the cursor control keys to highlight the words you want to include. But if an entry consists of a single word, there's no need to block the word—just position the cursor anywhere in the word.

Then, to identify the chosen word or phrase as an index entry,

Press: (ALT-F5) (MARK TEXT)

Select: 3 (INDEX)

Response: Index heading: and the word or words you've highlighted.

If you want to accept the word or phrase as it stands, press [ENTER]. However, if you want to use a different word or phrase summarizing the highlighted word or phrase,

Type: Words summarizing the word or phrase you want added to your index.

When you've finished,

Press: (ENTER)

Response: Subheading:

If you don't want to include a subheading in your index,

Press: (ENTER)

If you want a subheading, type in the words that describe the original highlighted word or phrase. Then press [ENTER].

When you've marked all the words and phrases you want to include, you can generate the index. First you must define the appearance of the index. Move the cursor to the end of your document, and start a new page.

Press: (CTRL-ENTER) (HARD PAGE)

Type: A title for the index. (Add any extra line spaces you might want between the title and the references.)

Press: (ALT-F5) (MARK TEXT)

Select: 5 (DEFINE)

Select: 3 (DEFINE INDEX)

Response: Concordance Filename (Enter=none):

Press: (ENTER)

Next, select a numbering style for your index.

Select: One of the following five alternatives:

1 (NO PAGE NUMBERS)
2 (PAGE NUMBERS FOLLOW ENTRIES)
3 (PAGE NUMBERS) FOLLOW ENTRIES
4 (FLUSH RIGHT PAGE NUMBERS)
5 (FLUSH RIGHT PAGE NUMBERS WITH LEADERS)

Now, generate the index.

Press: (ALT-F5) (MARK TEXT)

Select: 6 (GENERATE)

Select: 5 (GENERATE TABLES, INDEXES, CROSS REFERENCES, ETC.)

Response: Existing tables, lists, and indexes will be replaced.
Continue? Yes (No)

Type: Y (Yes)

Working with a Concordance File

A concordance file simplifies and expedites the process of creating an index. It's used when a word or phrase appears frequently in your document. After a word is added to a concordance file, WordPerfect automatically searches and adds other occurrences of that word to your index, saving you a lot of time.

To create a concordance file, you must let WordPerfect know which words or phrases you want it to find automatically. For convenience, you can switch to Doc 2, the second editing screen, to type the words and phrases.

Press: (SHIFT-F3) (SWITCH)

Type: The words and phrases you want WordPerfect to search. Press [ENTER] after each.

Press: (F7) (EXIT)

Response: Save document? Yes (No)

Type: Y (Yes) or press (ENTER)

Response: Document to be saved:

Type: CONCORDA or any other easily remembered name for the concordance file.

Press: (ENTER)

Be sure to erase this file after you've used it to compile the index for a particular project. Alternately, if you're working on more than one project at a time, you could name your concordance files 1CONCORD, 2CONCORD, 3CONCORD, etc.

After you've saved your concordance file, you're prompted to return to your main document.

Response: Exit doc 2? No (Yes)

Type: Y (Yes)

Alternately, you can return to your main document by using WordPerfect's SWITCH command [SHIFT-F3].

Creating an Index with a Concordance File

To create an index that includes a concordance file, enter the name of the concordance file when you define the index.

Press: (ALT-F5) (MARK TEXT)

Select: 5 (DEFINE)

Select: 3 (DEFINE INDEX)

Response: Concordance Filename (Enter=none):

Type: CONCORDA (or the file name you've chosen.)

Press: (ENTER)

Select: The page number definition you want, as described above.

To generate the list,

Press: (ALT-F5) (MARK TEXT)

Select: 6 (GENERATE)

Select: 5 (GENERATE TABLES, INDEXES, CROSS REFERENCES, ETC.)

Response: Existing tables, lists, and indexes will be replaced.
Continue? Yes (No)

When the file is completed, every word in it is listed automatically in the index, with references to page numbers.

TIP: While writing and editing, try to be as consistent as possible in using singular and plural versions of the same word. If both are included in your manuscript, remember to include them in your concordance file. Unassisted, WordPerfect doesn't know that "books" is the plural of "book," for example.

Footnotes and Endnotes

WordPerfect's document-organizing features also make it easy to provide readers with ancillary information in footnotes and endnotes to further strengthen your message.

To create a FOOTNOTE or ENDNOTE, place the cursor where you want the note number inserted. When your cursor is located next to the word or phrase you want amplified,

Press: (CTRL-F7) (FOOTNOTE)

Response: You'll see the following options:

1 (FOOTNOTE) if you want the supporting material to be included on the same page as the reference.
2 (ENDNOTE) if you want the supporting material to be gathered together at the end of your document.
3 (ENDNOTE PLACEMENT) if you want to place an [Endnote Placement] code at the cursor's position.

Select: 1 (FOOTNOTE)

Select: 1 (CREATE)

Type: The words you want included in the footnote.

Press: (F7) (EXIT) when you've finished entering the text.

TIP: Use WordPerfect's FONT command [CTRL-F8] if you want footnotes or endnotes to appear with a different typeface, type size, type style or line spacing from the body copy of your document. Remember that FONT choices must be entered before the footnote number.

Editing Footnotes and Endnotes

You can edit footnotes and endnotes at any point.

Press: (CTRL-F7) (FOOTNOTE)

Select: 1 (FOOTNOTE)

Select: 2 (EDIT)

Response: Footnote number? 2 (The number that appears is one higher than the number of the last footnote created.)

Type: The number of the footnote you want to edit.

Press: (ENTER)

Now edit the note and press [F7] (EXIT).

Renumbering Footnotes and Endnotes

You can renumber footnotes and endnotes at any point (for example, when you start a new chapter or section of a book or training manual). Using the above example, press [CTRL-F7] and then select Option 1 or 2.

Then choose NEW NUMBER (Option 3). WordPerfect responds with "Footnote number?" It assigns the number you enter to the next footnote or endnote you create.

Cross-References

Often when creating books and training materials, you'll want to refer the reader to topics covered at an earlier or later point. Or, you might want to refer the reader to illustrations, graphs or numeric tables in other chapters. WordPerfect's CROSS REFERENCE feature lets you reference other text—even if you don't know the final page location of the reference, or *target*, text. WordPerfect keeps track of the correct page. Each time you regenerate the cross-references (using [ALT-F5, 6, 5]), it automatically updates and renumbers the page reference if words, paragraphs or pages are added or deleted.

Likewise, it updates the box number if you reference a specific FIGURE or TABLE BOX as intervening boxes are added or deleted (for example, "See Figure 31, Population Changes 1900-1950").

WordPerfect can even create multiple references that list both box numbers and page numbers: "See Figure 31, Population Changes, 1900-1950, Page 149."

Generating Cross-References

By automatically creating references, WordPerfect can save you a lot of time. If a reader is impatient to learn more about a subject, or how you arrived at a conclusion, a cross-reference identifies the page containing the information.

To create a cross-reference,

Type: An introductory phrase, such as "See Population Growth, page," and add a space.

Press: (ALT-F5) (MARK TEXT)

Select: 1 (CROSS REF)

Select: 3 (MARK BOTH REFERENCE AND TARGET) if you know the location of your target text.

Select: From the following types of references:

1 (PAGE NUMBER)
2 (PARAGRAPH/OUTLINE NUMBER)
3 (FOOTNOTE NUMBER)

4 (ENDNOTE NUMBER)
5 (GRAPHICS BOX NUMBER)

Move: The cursor to the word or graphics box on the page to which you want to refer (the target).

Press: (ENTER)

Response: Target Name:

Type: A word that identifies the reference, or highlight the word by using WordPerfect's BLOCK command [ALT-F4] and the cursor control keys.

Press: (ENTER)

TIP: Incomplete references are indicated by a question mark on your screen. This serves as a reminder that you haven't defined a target location. Use WordPerfect's SEARCH command [F2] to locate incomplete references quickly.

Updating References

You should update your CROSS REFERENCEs frequently, particularly before printing. Otherwise, the page numbers may not be correct.

To update a CROSS REFERENCE list,

Press: (ALT-F5) (MARK TEXT)

Select: 6 (GENERATE)

Select: 5 (GENERATE TABLES, INDEXES, CROSS REFERENCES, ETC.)

Response: Existing tables, lists, and indexes will be replaced.
Continue? Yes (No)

Type: Y (Yes)

Creating Master Documents

As you begin to create more ambitious desktop publishing projects, such as books or training manuals, your working files will become larger and larger. That can slow down document editing because numerous pages must be repaginated every time you enter or delete a word or paragraph. In addition, FIGURE, TEXT and other boxes, as well as footnotes and endnotes, have to be renumbered when you add or delete boxes or notes.

Large files also slow down the spell-checking process, since you're forced to recheck pages (unless you confine spell-checking to just one page at a time).

However, WordPerfect's MASTER DOCUMENT feature ensures that editing and spell-checking will clip along at a fast pace. With it, you can create a relatively small master document that includes numerous subdocuments—such as individual chapters in a book.

To create a master document that will organize a series of individual files, open a new file. Then,

Press: (ALT-F5) (MARK TEXT)

Select: 2 (SUBDOC)

Type: The name of the first subdocument file and press [ENTER]. Then enter the names of other subdocuments you want to include. When you're finished,

Press: (F10) (SAVE)

Type: The name you want to give the master document.

TIP: Be sure to give your master document an easily identifiable file name, so you won't have trouble locating it at a later date. The name should differ dramatically from subdocument file names (for example, WPBOOK instead of CHAP1 or CHAP2, etc.).

Generating a Master Document

A master document has to be expanded before you can edit or print it. To expand it,

Press: (ALT-F5) (MARK TEXT)

Select: 6 (GENERATE)

Select: 3 (EXPAND MASTER DOCUMENT)

Because a single large file is created out of several individual files, expanding a master document can take several minutes. As this is occurring, pages are being renumbered, as are footnotes, endnotes and lists of FIGURE, TEXT, TABLE and USER BOXes.

TIP: Remember that tables of contents, footnotes, endnotes, indexes and lists of boxes are recompiled and renumbered when master documents are created.

Condensing a Master Document

To return to a smaller, more manageable master file,

Press: (ALT-F5) (MARK TEXT)

Select: 6 (GENERATE)

Select: 4 (CONDENSE MASTER DOCUMENT)

Response: Save Subdocs? Yes (No)

Press: (ENTER) to accept the default.

Response: Replace (name of Subdoc 1)?
1 Yes; 2 No; 3 Replace All Remaining: 0

Select: 3 (REPLACE ALL REMAINING)

Response: Replace All Remaining.

With Option 3, all subdocuments will be saved with any editing changes you've made. Option 1 lets you save subdocuments one by one. Option 2 doesn't save editing changes.

Moving On

This concludes Section One of *Desktop Publishing with WordPerfect*. You now have learned what WordPerfect can do. However, knowing the basic commands and functions is just part of the overall picture.

Section Two completes the picture by focusing on the design considerations involved in creating newsletters, brochures, advertisements and other documents.

You'll realize the importance of planning your documents—making accurate, actual-size layouts you can use to set up margins and column widths. You also can plan the size and placement of the various types of boxes used in your desktop publishing activities.

SECTION TWO

DESIGN TIPS AND TRICKS

CHAPTER 10

PLANNING AND PRODUCING DOCUMENTS

Desktop publishing with WordPerfect differs from desktop publishing with dedicated page layout programs in several important ways. To use WordPerfect successfully, a thorough understanding of these differences is crucial. Although you can create publications that are virtually indistinguishable from those created with page layout programs, you have to be comfortable working in a different way.

Because it doesn't have an on-screen grid, WordPerfect demands more planning than do dedicated page layout programs. A grid is a background of horizontal and vertical lines that helps define the location of the various elements (borders, headlines and columns, etc.). Most grids have a "magnetic attraction," which helps align text and graphic elements precisely.

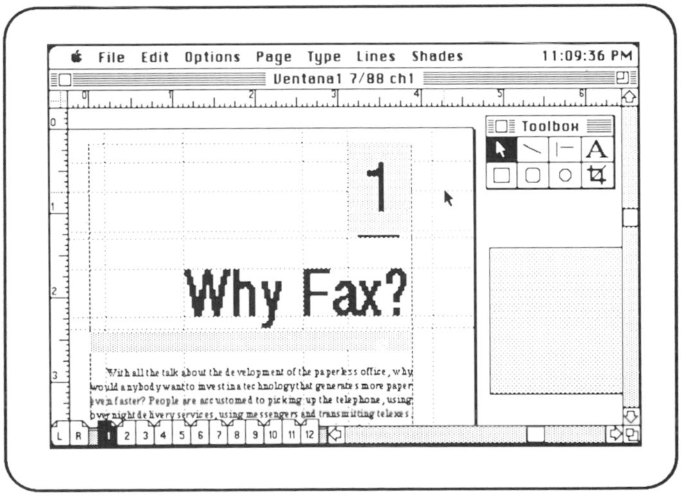

In addition, the WordPerfect screen doesn't include the horizontal and vertical rulers found on page layout programs. You can compensate for the lack of a background grid and on-screen rulers in two ways:

- Your initial layouts should be planned more precisely. Place headlines, columns of text and graphics boxes mathematically instead of empirically "grabbing" and placing them.
- Train yourself to pay attention to the location of the cursor, as indicated in the lower right-hand corner of the screen. It's important to know the "longitude" and "latitude" of the cursor because, in many cases, you're not able to see all the elements on a page until you use VIEW DOCUMENT [SHIFT-F7, 6] or PRINT [SHIFT-F7, 2].

All this can work to your advantage, as increased planning often results in a more cohesive design than the "free-form" designs sometimes generated from dedicated page layout programs.

You also must learn to handle text differently. Unless you've chosen a big-screen monitor or the Hercules RamFont graphics card (described in Appendix B), you won't see accurate on-screen representations of different typefaces, type sizes or type styles as you work (for example, 36-point Helvetica bold headlines appear to be the same size as 11-point Times Roman body copy on the screen).

Again, you can use WordPerfect's STYLE command [ALT-F8] to turn this into an advantage. Often, documents produced with page layout programs include too many typefaces, sizes and styles. By carefully limiting your type choices and storing them as STYLEs, you can increase consistency within your documents and improve the appearance of your publications.

As a result of training yourself to plan and measure, you'll produce attractive, easy-to-read publications that will reflect well upon you and your company. In addition, you'll be able to readily use such features as WordPerfect's extensive document-organizing tools and spelling checker that will give your projects thoroughness and professionalism.

Planning Your Project

Planning a desktop publishing project can be divided into four distinct stages. The first two require conventional graphic design materials: tissue paper, soft pencils and plenty of erasers. The last two stages are executed on your computer using WordPerfect.

The first stage involves creating "thumbnail sketches" (reduced-size rough layouts) that convey the overall effect you want to achieve.

Translating those rough layouts into accurate, actual-size drawings is the second stage.

The third stage involves translating the dimensions and type specifications of your sketched layouts into electronic page layouts. In many cases, you'll use WordPerfect's extensive macro and stylesheet capabilities to do that.

The fourth and final step is to produce your document and add the refinements that make the document's design quality leap from "adequate" to "outstanding." Changes undoubtedly will suggest themselves as your project evolves. Some changes will become obvious as you preview your project, using WordPerfect's VIEW DOCUMENT command [SHIFT-F7, 6]. Other changes only will become obvious when you PRINT either individual pages [SHIFT-F7, 2] or your entire project [SHIFT-F7, 1]. In either case, WordPerfect's REVEAL CODES command [ALT-F3] makes it easy to incorporate last-minute design changes.

As you refine your design, you'll probably find that being able to edit previously created macros and STYLEs greatly simplifies the process of making formatting changes.

Let's review these stages in greater detail.

Developing Thumbnail Sketches

This step could be called "The Cocktail Napkin School of Design." Its purpose is to establish a rough idea of how you want your finished project to look.

Because this layout is for your eyes only, you can work as quickly and roughly as you want. Use heavy curly lines to indicate headlines, thin parallel lines to show captions and body copy, and boxes to indicate where you'll insert charts, graphs, drawings or photographs.

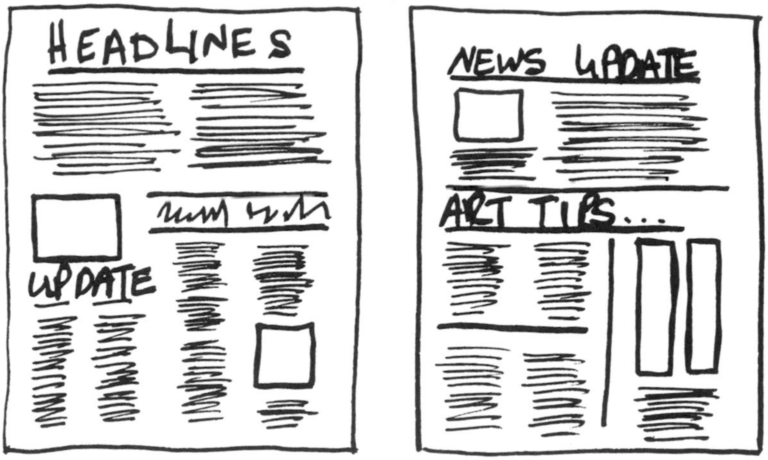

At this stage of the game, previously published ads, brochures or newsletters can offer a wealth of ideas and solutions to design problems. To get your creative juices flowing, you might consider skimming through such publications as *Communications Arts*, *Print* or your daily newspaper. During this "inspiration" phase, you might want to pay special attention to your industry's trade journals and magazines. Or you might leaf through books, such as the annual *The One Show* (which highlights the nation's best advertising and brochures).

TIP: Many graphic artists maintain "swipe files," more politely termed "idea files." Devote a drawer in your file cabinet to examples of "good" and "bad" design. Add to it every time you find a document containing elements you like or dislike.

Use hanging file folders to divide the drawer into ads, brochures and newsletters. Use Post-it notes attached to each project to jot down the reasons you chose each piece (for example, "good border treatment," "masthead overwhelms page and fights with headline," etc.). By referring to your file whenever you start a new project, you'll find your ideas begin to flow more quickly.

The reason for maintaining an idea file isn't to copy the work of others, but to learn from and be inspired by it. It's important to note that as you plan and produce a document, it inevitably will change, taking on a life of its own. By the time you've finished, your project probably will bear little resemblance to its original "inspiration."

Generating Accurate Layouts

After you've created a satisfying reduced-size thumbnail sketch of your project, translate it to full-size sample pages. Work as precisely as possible, using a ruler and triangle to create vertical lines. Be particularly careful to establish accurate

- Top, bottom and side margins.
- Border size and placement.
- Number and location of columns.
- Placement of headers and footers.
- Occurrences of white space, such as "sinks" (extra white space at the top of each page or some pages).

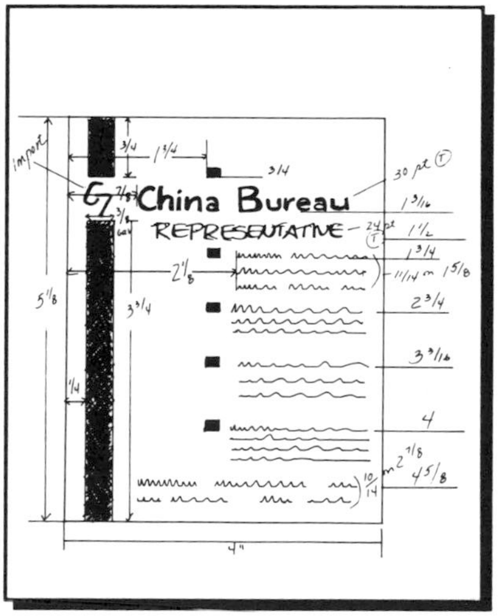

Chances are, you'll create more than one page setup for each project. For example, if you're working on a newsletter, you'll probably create separate page layouts for

- Front page (with your nameplate and firm's logo).
- Inside pages.
- Back page.

If you're producing a book, you'll probably establish separate page layouts for

- Table of contents page.
- Lists of figures, graphs and drawings.

- Introduction.
- The first page of each chapter.
- Typical chapter left- and right-hand pages.
- Bibliography and index.

Save those drawings for future reference.

Creating Electronic Page Layouts

The third step is to translate the dimensions of your final layouts into macros and STYLEs for each project. For example, you might want to create your layout in the following sequence:

- Accurately measure the top, bottom and side margins of your layout, open a new document and create a macro that establishes the appropriate page layout.
- Measure the column widths you established on your page layout, as well as the placement of each column and the distance between them. Create a macro that establishes these column specifications.
- Measure the size and placement of page borders, and create a macro that places these borders on each page.
- Likewise, if necessary, create macros for placing vertical lines between columns on each page.
- Select the typefaces, sizes and styles to be used in your document. Create a macro that quickly chooses the BASE FONT for your project. Then, create STYLEs for each time you change type characteristics. For example, STYLEs can be used for headlines or chapter headings, primary subheads, secondary subheads, body copy, captions and footnotes.
- Develop macros for creating and placing any necessary FIGURE, TABLE, TEXT or USER BOXes. For example, if you're going to include a USER BOX for placing your logo on each page, create a macro that quickly adds the box to each page.

TIP: At this point, you might want to review the information in Chapter 7 showing how STYLEs created for one document can be shared by other documents.

After you've created macros to define basic page layout specifications for the various aspects of each page, create nested macros—macros that contain other macros—that quickly set up more than one specification simultaneously.

For example, if you're producing a monthly newsletter, create an [ALT-N] macro that sets up the front page of your newsletter, complete with a USER nameplate box. Then create [ALT-L] and [ALT-R] macros for setting up the inside pages. Finally, create an [ALT-B] macro for the back page of your newsletter, complete with address panel. Each of these macros may contain individual nested macros for establishing margins, borders, columns and vertical rules.

Producing and Refining Your Document

Creating separate macros, and nesting them as described above, simplifies the process of making changes as your work proceeds. By using separate macros for margins, columns, boxes and type selection, you easily can change one or all of those elements as you work.

It's important to understand that you'll rarely achieve perfection on your first attempt. Excellence can be achieved only to the extent that you frequently use WordPerfect's VIEW DOCUMENT [SHIFT-F7, 6] and PRINT [SHIFT-F7, 2] commands and revise your work as you move along. You'll undoubtedly find yourself changing the location and size of such design elements as borders, headlines and text columns.

As you become more comfortable with electronic publishing, you'll become more sensitive to the major impact that slight changes in line placement or line thickness can have.

Templates and Libraries

Templates are formatted, blank documents that contain macros and STYLEs for creating all the necessary page layout elements—headers, footers, column layouts, boxes and type specifications. Created by saving files composed of "empty" page layouts, templates don't contain words or graphics, just the formatted framework in which text and graphics are placed.

Templates also can be developed from previously created documents. For example, you can assemble the February issue of your newsletter using the basic elements of the January issue. You simply change the specific text and illustrations of the earlier issue and save the new version using a different file name, which should be done immediately after opening your template file.

Press: (F10) (SAVE)

Response: File name of original template (for example, NEWSTEMP)

Type: New file name (for example, FEBNEWS)

Press: (ENTER)

TIP: To avoid destroying your original files accidentally, you can store all of your project templates in a separate subdirectory. For further data integrity, you can back up templates on floppy diskettes, stored in a separate location.

Six Steps to Success

It's impossible to cover the subject of graphic design in a single chapter. Nevertheless, a six-step sequence can help you design and produce better-looking, easier-to-read documents.[1]

The following steps can provide a perspective on the sequence of events and some design decisions involved in transforming your pencil-and-paper layouts into more elaborate electronic page layouts.

TIP: As the following sequence shows, when designing your projects, you'll usually find it helpful to start from the page borders and work toward the inside.

Step One: Setting Margins

Start by establishing the page margins. To establish left and right margins,

Press: (SHIFT-F8) (FORMAT)

Select: 1 (LINE)

Select: 7 (MARGINS—LEFT, RIGHT)

Response: The cursor advances to the one-inch, left-hand default, which you can change to the dimension you want.

---

1 For a fuller description of the principles of graphic design, see *Looking Good in Print*, listed in Appendix B.

Press: (ENTER) (if you wish to accept the default; or type in a new number, followed by [ENTER]).

Response: This advances you to the right-hand default.

Press: (ENTER) (if you wish to accept the default; or type in a new number, followed by [ENTER]).

Then press (F7) (EXIT).

To establish top and bottom margins,

Press: (SHIFT-F8) (FORMAT)

Select: 2 (PAGE)

Select: 5 (MARGINS—TOP, BOTTOM)

Response: The cursor appears, blinking under the one-inch default measure for the top margin.

Press: (ENTER) (to accept the default, or type in a new number, followed by [ENTER]).

Response: The cursor is advanced to the bottom margin default.

Press: (ENTER) (to accept the default, or type in a new number, followed by [ENTER]).

Then press (F7) to exit.

TIP: The location of these margins usually will be determined by the borders you create. Remember that the more white space surrounding your publication, the more "open" and readable it will appear. Margins that are too close to the edge of a page "darken" the page. Borders and white space surrounding a document frame and isolate it from its surroundings.

Compare this. . .

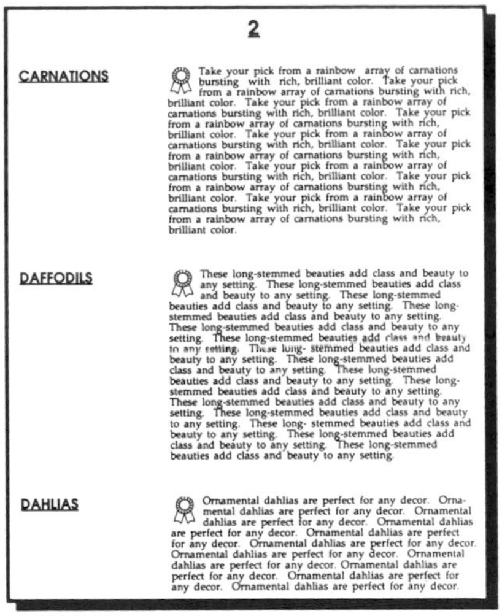

with this. . .

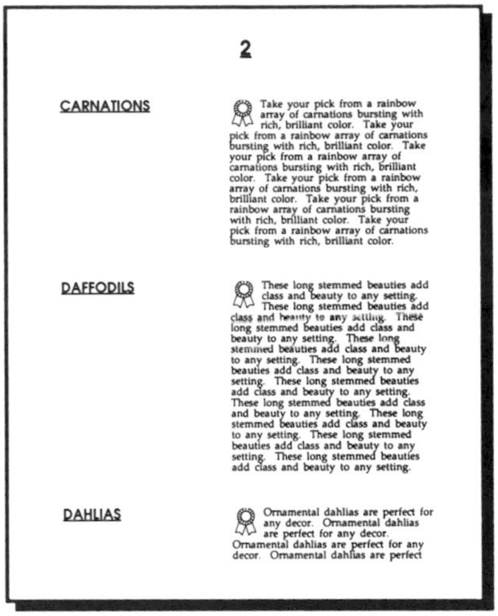

Step Two: Creating Borders

Next, using WordPerfect's GRAPHICS command [ALT-F9], create rules and boxes that will frame your project and draw the reader's eyes into the publication. (Refer to Chapter 2, if necessary, to review the steps involved in creating rules and boxes.)

TIP: If you're going to include headers and footers on each page, be sure to compensate for them by adjusting the vertical placement of the rules and boxes defining your page margins. For example, if you want your headers to appear above the top border of each page, lower the rule or box used to create the top border. If you want footers to appear below the bottom border, raise the rule or box.

Compare this. . .

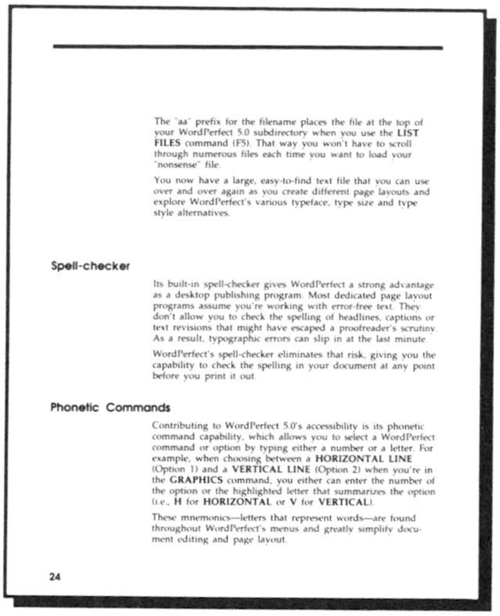

The "aa" prefix for the filename places the file at the top of your WordPerfect 5.0 subdirectory when you use the **LIST FILES** command (F5). That way you won't have to scroll through numerous files each time you want to load your "nonsense" file.

You now have a large, easy-to-find text file that you can use over and over again as you create different page layouts and explore WordPerfect's various typeface, type size and type style alternatives.

Spell-checker

Its built-in spell-checker gives WordPerfect a strong advantage as a desktop publishing program. Most dedicated page layout programs assume you're working with error-free text. They don't allow you to check the spelling of headlines, captions or text revisions that might have escaped a proofreader's scrutiny. As a result, typographic errors can slip in at the last minute.

WordPerfect's spell-checker eliminates that risk, giving you the capability to check the spelling in your document at any point before you print it out.

Phonetic Commands

Contributing to WordPerfect 5.0's accessibility is its phonetic command capability, which allows you to select a WordPerfect command or option by typing either a number or a letter. For example, when choosing between a **HORIZONTAL LINE** (Option 1) and a **VERTICAL LINE** (Option 2) when you're in the **GRAPHICS** command, you either can enter the number of the option or the highlighted letter that summarizes the option (i.e., **H** for **HORIZONTAL** or **V** for **VERTICAL**).

These mnemonics—letters that represent words—are found throughout WordPerfect's menus and greatly simplify document editing and page layout.

24

with this. . .

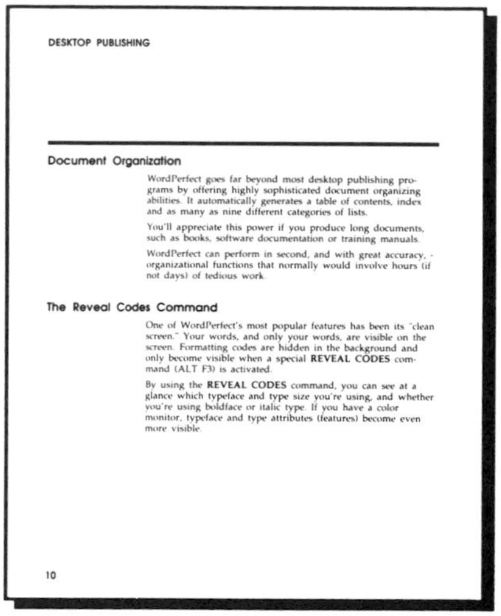

DESKTOP PUBLISHING

Document Organization

WordPerfect goes far beyond most desktop publishing programs by offering highly sophisticated document organizing abilities. It automatically generates a table of contents, index and as many as nine different categories of lists.

You'll appreciate this power if you produce long documents, such as books, software documentation or training manuals.

WordPerfect can perform in second, and with great accuracy, - organizational functions that normally would involve hours (if not days) of tedious work.

The Reveal Codes Command

One of WordPerfect's most popular features has been its "clean screen." Your words, and only your words, are visible on the screen. Formatting codes are hidden in the background and only become visible when a special **REVEAL CODES** command (ALT F3) is activated.

By using the **REVEAL CODES** command, you can see at a glance which typeface and type size you're using, and whether you're using boldface or italic type. If you have a color monitor, typeface and type attributes (features) become even more visible.

10

Then establish the placement of text on each page. Use WordPerfect's COLUMNS/TABLES command [ALT-F7, 1, 3] (or [ALT-F7, 4] in WordPerfect 5.0) to establish column position, column width and the distance between columns. (Review Chapter 3 for more details.)

TIP: Remember to indent your left- and right-hand column margins so that type doesn't overlap or appear too close to your page borders. Pay particular attention to the spacing between columns.

Compare this. . . with this. . .

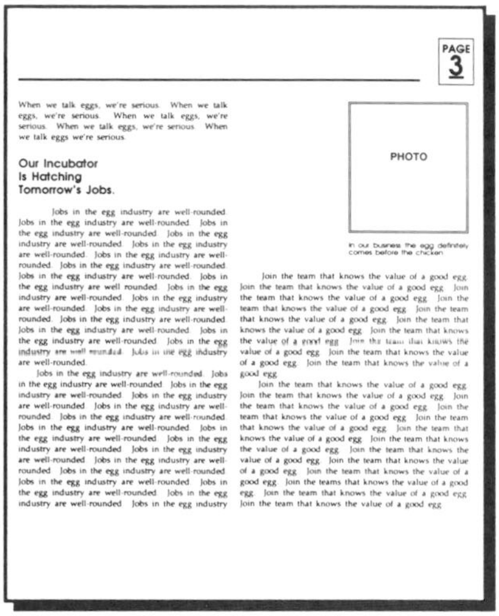

You can use the ADVANCE command to "force" white space at the top of a page, between top and bottom page borders, and at the beginning of a column of type.

Compare this. . . with this. . .

If you're formatting a book, you can use extra white space to emphasize the first page of each chapter.

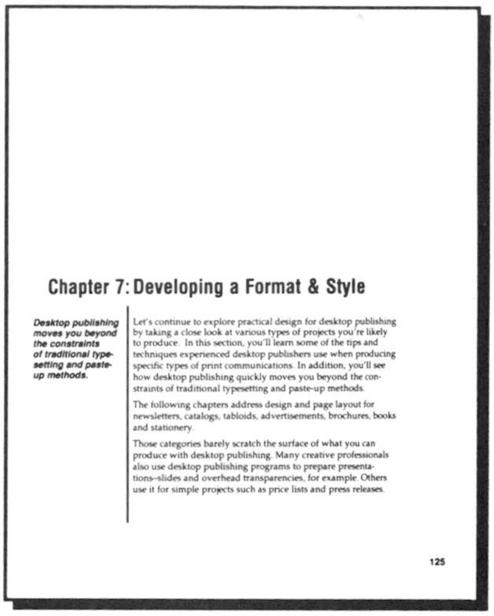
Chapter 7: Developing a Format & Style

Desktop publishing moves you beyond the constraints of traditional typesetting and paste-up methods.

Let's continue to explore practical design for desktop publishing by taking a close look at various types of projects you're likely to produce. In this section, you'll learn some of the tips and techniques experienced desktop publishers use when producing specific types of print communications. In addition, you'll see how desktop publishing quickly moves you beyond the constraints of traditional typesetting and paste-up methods.

The following chapters address design and page layout for newsletters, catalogs, tabloids, advertisements, brochures, books and stationery.

Those categories barely scratch the surface of what you can produce with desktop publishing. Many creative professionals also use desktop publishing programs to prepare presentations–slides and overhead transparencies, for example. Others use it for simple projects such as price lists and press releases.

125

Step Three: Typography

Use WordPerfect's FONT [CTRL-F8] and STYLE [ALT-F8] commands to choose the typefaces, type sizes and type styles for your document. Also, use the FORMAT command [SHIFT-F8] to adjust line spacing and tab settings, and to choose between flush-left/ragged-right and justified type. You might want to refer to Chapter 5 to review the basic commands used in setting type with WordPerfect.

As described in Chapter 7, WordPerfect's STYLEs help you save time and achieve consistency as you change type attributes for headlines, subheads, body copy and captions.

When establishing STYLEs, decide how you want type placed in columns. Justified type, in which the right- and left-hand edges of each column are aligned, is often chosen for "formal" documents. It increases word density—the number of words that fit in a given space.

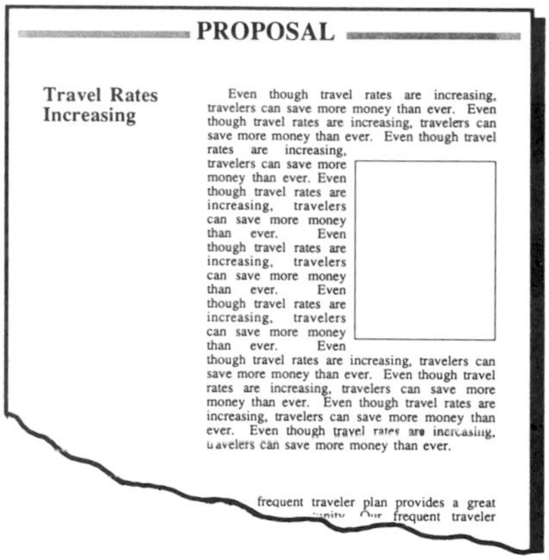
PROPOSAL

Travel Rates Increasing

Even though travel rates are increasing, travelers can save more money than ever. Even though travel rates are increasing, travelers can save more money than ever. Even though travel rates are increasing, travelers can save more money than ever. Even though travel rates are increasing, travelers can save more money than ever. Even though travel rates are increasing, travelers can save more money than ever. Even though travel rates are increasing, travelers can save more money than ever. Even though travel rates are increasing, travelers can save more money than ever. Even though travel rates are increasing, travelers can save more money than ever. Even though travel rates are increasing, travelers can save more money than ever. Even though travel rates are increasing, travelers can save more money than ever.

frequent traveler plan provides a great

Our frequent traveler

For a more informal, "contemporary" document, flush-left/ragged-right type gives an "open" feeling, because of the irregular amounts of white space that appear at the end of each line.

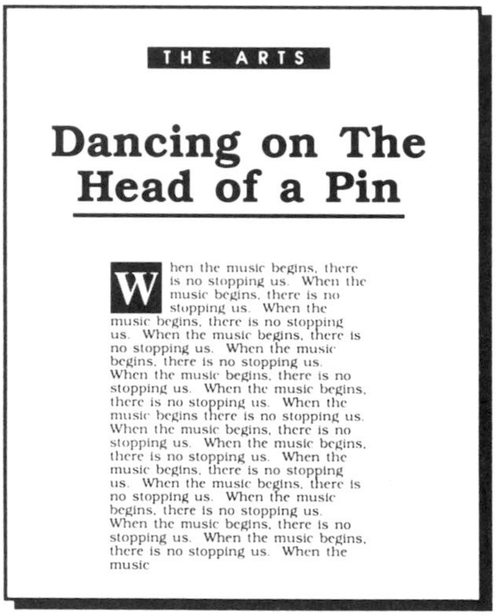
THE ARTS

Dancing on The Head of a Pin

When the music begins, there is no stopping us. When the music begins, there is no stopping us. When the music begins, there is no stopping us. When the music begins, there is no stopping us. When the music begins, there is no stopping us. When the music begins, there is no stopping us. When the music begins, there is no stopping us. When the music begins there is no stopping us. When the music begins, there is no stopping us. When the music begins, there is no stopping us. When the music begins, there is no stopping us. When the music begins, there is no stopping us. When the music begins, there is no stopping us. When the music begins, there is no stopping us. When the music begins, there is no stopping us. When the music

In deciding whether to use WordPerfect's HYPHENATION feature, remember that even flush-left/ragged-right columns can benefit from hyphenation. It can help prevent unnaturally large gaps of white space at the end of lines.

We observed the brownish fox
jumping happily around the
sleeping puppy. We observed the
brownish fox jumping happily
around the sleeping puppy. We
observed the brownish fox
jumping happily around the
sleeping puppy. We observed the
brownish fox jumping happily
around the sleeping puppy. We
observed the brownish fox

Hyphenated justified type increases word density and cuts down on the amount of white space between words. However, hyphenation used in narrow columns with large type often results in too many hyphenated words, making columns difficult to read. As a rule of thumb, avoid having more than three consecutive hyphenated lines.

Remember to always
be courteous, attentive,
responsive and knowl-
edgeable about your prod-
uct. Remember to al-
ways be courteous, atten-
tive, responsive, and

As a final typographic refinement, use WordPerfect's TAB SET command [SHIFT-F8, 1, 8] to adjust the depth of indention. Remember that the standard half-inch tab setting that looks good on a typed manuscript often looks exaggerated when text is typeset in a multicolumn format. This is particularly true as type size decreases.

2
Satisfied Customers Keep Coming Back

An interesting correlation exists between column width and type size. Large type in narrow columns often is difficult to read.

16-point text placed on a 12-pica column is also very difficult to read.

Similarly, small type in wide columns can be difficult to read. The reader's eyes have to make too many "jumps" and can become "lost" when moving from the right-hand end of one line to the beginning of the next line.

> **7-point text placed on a 24-pica column is very difficult to read. 7-point text placed on a 24-pica column is very difficult to read. 7-point text placed on a 24-pica column is very difficult to read. 7-point text placed on a 24-pica column is very difficult to read. 7-point text placed on a 24-pica column is very difficult to read. 7-point text placed on a 24-pica column is very difficult to read. 7-point text placed on a 24-pica column is very difficult to read. 7-point text placed on a 24-pica column is very difficult to read. 7-point text placed on a 24-pica column is very difficult to read. 7-point text placed on a**

Line spacing, or leading, also should enter the equation. Narrow columns with small type often work best with WordPerfect's automatic line spacing. But, as line lengths become longer, extra space should be added between the lines of type.

Compare this. . .

> Typography is a craft that requires careful attention to detail. Typography is a craft that requires careful attention to detail. Typography is a craft that requires careful attention to detail.

with this. . .

> Typography is a craft that requires careful attention to detail. Typography is a craft that requires careful attention to detail. Typography is a craft that requires careful attention to detail. Typography is a craft that requires careful attention to detail. Typography is a

As a rule of thumb, small type works best in narrow columns with normal or tight line spacing. As columns become wider, larger type and extra leading look best.

This relationship depends upon the particular typeface you choose, because each typeface has its own horizontal length and colors the page in a different way. In the example below, note how different typefaces set in the same size have vastly different word density levels.

The quick brown fox
jumped over the lazy dog.

The quick brown fox
jumped over the lazy dog.

The quick brown fox
jumped over the lazy dog.

The quick brown fox
jumped over the lazy dog.

Spacing Between Columns

Space between columns should be correctly proportioned to column width. Large type set in wide columns requires more space between columns than small type set in narrow columns.

Compare this. . . with this. . .

Step Four: Graphic Accents

The next step is to create macros for the various sizes of rules and boxes you're likely to need throughout your document. For example, if you're working on a multicolumn newsletter and are using horizontal bars to separate adjacent articles, create a macro that quickly creates the bar each time you need it. (See Chapter 3 for a review.)

Remember to use WordPerfect's GRAPHICS command [ALT-F9] to create the type of TEXT, TABLE, FIGURE or USER BOX you want in your documents. You might want to review the techniques described in Chapter 4 regarding the modification of border style, caption placement and positioning, background shading, as well as the spacing of text inside and around the boxes.

Step Five: Document Organization

Next, add organizing elements, such as page numbers, headers and footers. These commands are grouped under WordPerfect's FORMAT command [SHIFT-F8]. Remember that header and footer information, including page numbers, usually differs on left- and right-hand pages.

Step Six: Final Touches

If you're preparing a long document, such as a book or training manual, review the sections of Chapter 9 that describe how WordPerfect automatically generates an index, table of contents, automatic references, lists of figures, tables, drawings and photographs, as well as endnotes and footnotes. You can save a lot of last-minute writing and editing by including the proper commands in your document as you write it.

TIP: As you go through the six-step process outlined above, use WordPerfect's MACRO and STYLE features to store your project specifications. As described in earlier chapters, you easily can modify them as you go along.

Moving On

The following chapters provide detailed descriptions and illustrations of some types of desktop publishing projects you're likely to design and produce with WordPerfect. The chapters are organized by projects of increasing complexity.

CHAPTER 11

WORDPERFECT IN ACTION

When you've learned to use WordPerfect's graphics features, you'll find that the appearance of nearly any document can be enhanced. In this chapter, you'll examine a potpourri of documents that can be created with WordPerfect, and you'll learn valuable design techniques and shortcuts as well.

These documents shouldn't be interpreted as rigid prototypes of appropriate design; rather use them to glean ideas on making your project more effective.

Remember that experimentation and "creative dissatisfaction" are stepping stones that lead to good design. An element from an advertisement might work well in your newsletter, just as a stylesheet for a training manual might suit your in-house tabloid.

Let's briefly examine some of the ways you're likely to use WordPerfect's graphics features. The following examples contain design tips and suggestions. However, you'll undoubtedly add your own expertise to refine the design of these documents.

Business Correspondence

All types of business correspondence—letterheads, proposals, invoices, forms, memos and reports—can be made more readable, persuasive and enjoyable by using simple desktop publishing techniques.

You can produce attractive stationery and envelopes with WordPerfect, particularly if you import images using other graphics software. Remember that your company identity is all-important. If necessary, use the services of a graphic artist to design lasting professional images.

You also can create forms, reports and other documents that require constant updating. Strive to attain an overall company image by incorporating similar visual features in all your documents, particularly those that will be seen outside the company.

Advertisements

If you regularly run sales-oriented advertising in daily or weekly publications, you'll find that desktop publishing offers you a way to quickly update specifics and still retain the overall format of the ad. This can save many hundreds of dollars in traditional typesetting and paste-up costs. And it's easier to meet deadlines on last-minute sales and other time-sensitive advertising.

Remember that desktop publishing can't do everything yet. If your ads include photographs or illustrations, don't try to scan them in or import them. Instead, create a bordered box that indicates the size of your graphic. Then give your sales representative instructions on how to drop it into your ad. (Most magazines and newspapers will strip in artwork for a small fee.) Your all-important graphic images will be sharper and look more appealing.

Newsletters

The timeliness and relative simplicity of newsletters make them a natural for WordPerfect's new desktop publishing features. Stylesheets and macros can speed your work, particularly for longer newsletters with high page-to-page consistency.

If your nameplate is more complicated than WordPerfect can handle, have it produced by other means, and your printer can drop it into your camera-ready art. You can create a blank USER BOX to indicate position.

Consider having a graphic artist help you with the nameplate and overall design of your newsletter—it's a worthwhile, one-time cost.

Always save old newsletters—the copy, as well as the macros and stylesheets. You'll be surprised how many times you'll use repeating elements, such as lists of sales offices, revised products or annual events.

Catalogs

Because catalogs require constant revisions and often are formatted rigidly, you'll find WordPerfect to be a prolific production tool.

First, decide which pages you want to produce with WordPerfect and which are better suited for production by other methods. For example, catalog covers are often multicolored, with elaborate graphics and unusual type treatments—inappropriate for WordPerfect at this time.

If your catalog is to be produced on glossy ("slick") paper, consider outputting your work on a Linotronic or a similar machine that produces typeset-quality material.

Training Manuals, Books and Longer Documents

Although long, unwieldy documents, such as user manuals, pamphlets and books, can be created successfully, your work will be speeded greatly if you use WordPerfect macros and stylesheets for repetitive, complex page layouts.

For large projects, you may want to contract a designer to plan the overall appearance, then use WordPerfect to produce the final product. A designer is a one-time expense that will more than return your investment, particularly if you're planning large print runs or multiple printings.

Moving On

As you'll see in the following pages, WordPerfect can create or duplicate hundreds of different kinds of documents—resumés, warranty cards, menus, invoices, purchase orders, spec sheets, announcements, invitations and more. The following examples show only a few of the many effects that can be achieved.

The importance of developing accurate sketches before executing your design can't be overemphasized. Future versions of WordPerfect probably will allow you to edit graphics features directly on your screen. Until then, avoid bouncing back and forth between text and VIEW DOCUMENT. The more thoroughly you develop your design beforehand, the more successful you'll be in creating your documents.

As with any new technology, you must balance the time spent obtaining a result with the time saved having it done the "old way." The solution often lies somewhere in the middle, and you'll probably find yourself using a combination of desktop publishing and traditional cut-and-paste techniques to get the job done quickly and inexpensively.

Keep experimenting, and always be on the lookout for new graphics ideas. Your design skills will grow as WordPerfect desktop publishing features become more versatile and powerful with each new version.

Advertisements

Display Classified Advertising

Newspapers often allow you to furnish camera-ready artwork, which puts you in control of copy and design. You can create eye-catching borders, headlines and typefaces for smaller classifieds that will make them stand out among competing advertisements.

The screens were created using two separate figure boxes.

When boxes touch each other, be sure to specify any matching border styles you might want. In this example, the top screen had 0 border for the bottom, right and left, but Single for the top. Otherwise, a borderless screen would have hurt continuity.

Bullets were dropped in using WordPerfect's character sets. Check your printer to see which sets it recognizes.

REPRESENTATIVE
for our China Bureau
Exciting career opportunity for talented, outgoing individual. Must be experienced travel representative.
Position includes 20% travel to various cities in China. Must have flexible schedule.
Generous benefit program including paid vacations, sick leave, insurance plan, and other benefits.
Applications being accepted immediately. Apply in person at the Global Travel office at 100 Side Street, Los Angeles, CA 00010.
Global Travel is an equal opportunity employer and does not discriminate on the basis of race, religion, sex, handicap, or non-specific jet lag afflictions.

Display Classified Advertising

Remember that graphics boxes must be created and positioned separately. You can't create a box within a box or manipulate graphics within a box. Additional boxes must be layered over the master figure box and "jockeyed" into position, often using trial-and-error methods.

If you develop a sketch before producing the ad, you'll have a better idea of how many boxes you need, as well as your required measurements.

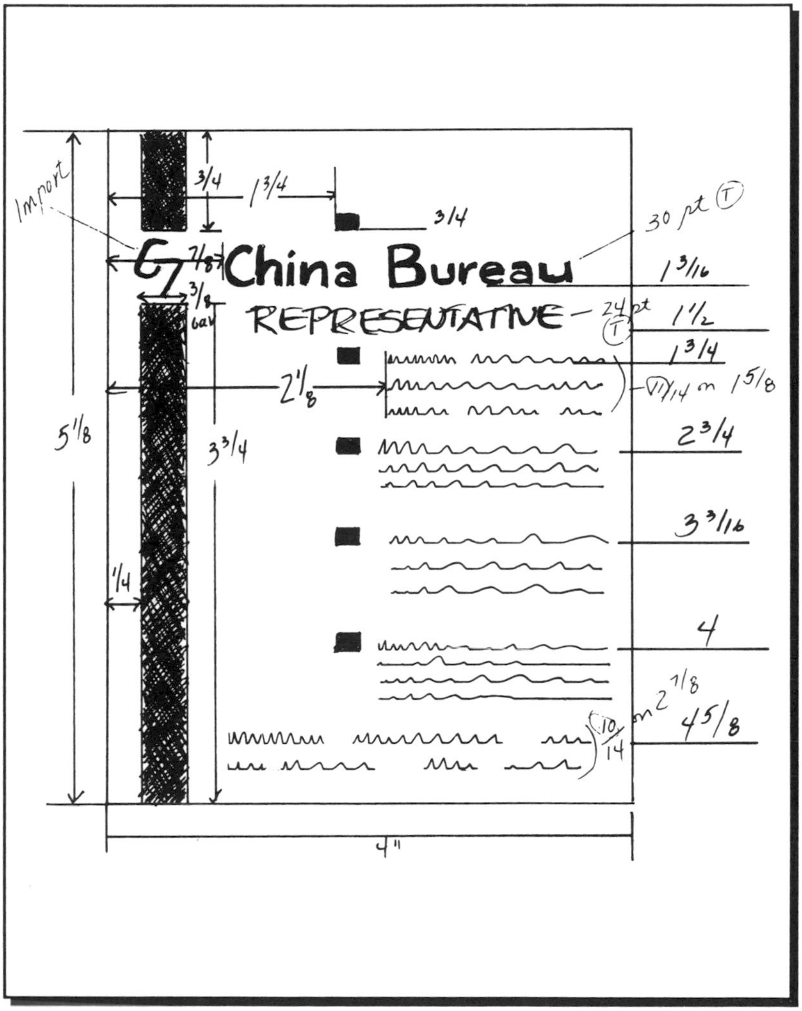

Flyers

This example shows how the simple juxtaposition of boxes and thick rules can create sophisticated effects.

First, create three boxes. Then position lines around them, either by using a ruler or by noting horizontal positions of the boxes.

Four separate vertical lines were created, uniformly spaced from borders of boxes.

Often it's easier to print out unfinished work, then measure the remaining elements, rather than to try to position graphics on-screen.

Flyers

Don't be discouraged if you initially fail to produce the effect you want with more complex visuals. Remember, all graphic design is a series of trial-and-error steps. Often you must rely on a combination of intuition and well-established rules.

Note how different type sizes and weights call attention to *SummerFair* and the date.

The S and F are different-sized fonts (rather than an uppercase and lowercase font) creating a more uniform, stylized headline.

Remember to maintain uniform distances between rules and boxes, and always check with a ruler to make certain they're aligned on the final printout.

Note that boxes are transparent and don't cover up overlapping lines or screens when placed over other boxes.

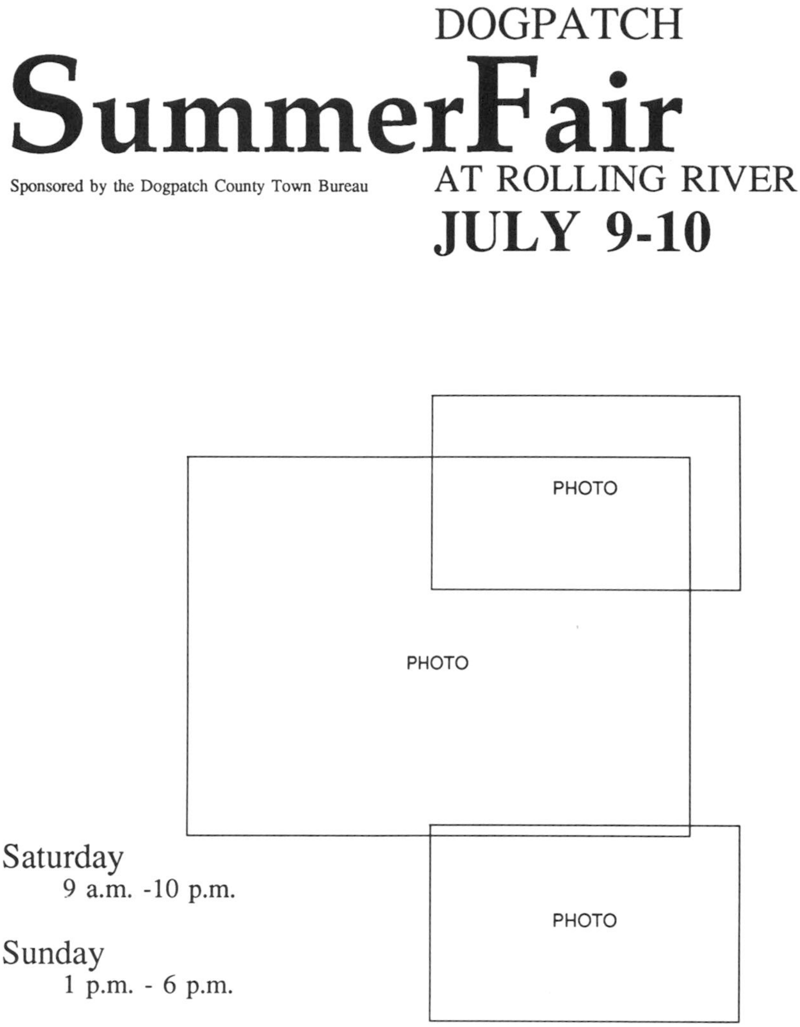
DOGPATCH
SummerFair
Sponsored by the Dogpatch County Town Bureau
AT ROLLING RIVER
JULY 9-10
PHOTO
PHOTO
Saturday
9 a.m. -10 p.m.
Sunday
1 p.m. - 6 p.m.
PHOTO

Business Correspondence

Letterheads

Keep stationery design simple and uncluttered, with a clearly defined writing area. Envelopes should reflect the same elements and style as your letterhead.

Clip art was imported from WordPerfect's graphics files.

You can use the ADVANCE command to specify a position when creating white space.

The Seafood Barn

1001 Main Street SE, Miami, Ohio 48900 (919) 922-2222

Business Cards

If you have a number of employees, you can group business cards on the same page and change names and addresses when appropriate. This can save time and cuts preparation and printing costs.

You'll save time if you know your vertical and horizontal positions before importing graphics.

Either all or none of the image area can be screened. Because the graphic was imported with a FIGURE BOX, attempting to screen only the logo would create undesirable results.

The logo was imported from a WordPerfect graphics file using a FIGURE BOX with the None border option.

You may need to play around with size and position until you get the desired result.

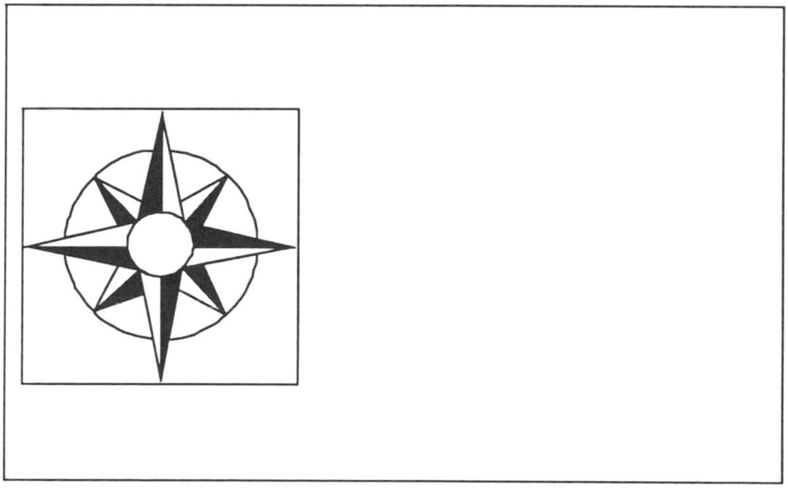

Reports and Proposals

Typewritten reports and proposals are dull, although they often need to be persuasive and quickly read.

PROPOSAL

INVESTMENT OPPORTUNITIES
FOR THE FREQUENT TRAVELER

To:

Board of Directors

Stock Holders

New Investors

Loan Sharks

September 19, 1988

Reports and Proposals

One of the most attractive aspects of using WordPerfect for desktop publishing is that simple graphic elements can be added while the document is being produced with little or no extra time and effort expended.

Use thick horizontal lines, screened at 20 percent, to create interesting borders, headers and footers.

Experiment with letter spacing to provide breathing room for short headlines with big type.

Work with horizontal lines creatively to provide "quick and dirty" graphic design.

PROPOSAL

Investment Opportunities
for the Frequent Traveler

To:

Board of Directors

Stock Holders

New Investors

Loan Sharks

September 19, 1988

Reports and Proposals

These examples show two ways you can make documents more readable by manipulating graphic elements.

A photo or illustration placed within the text area helps break up monotonous type.

Headlines placed in margins allow readers to obtain critical information at a glance.

PROPOSAL

Travel Rates Increasing

Even though travel rates are increasing, travelers can save more money than ever. Even though travel rates are increasing, travelers can save more money than ever. Even though travel rates are increasing, travelers can save more money than ever. Even though travel rates are increasing, travelers can save more money than ever. Even though travel rates are increasing, travelers can save more money than ever. Even though travel rates are increasing, travelers can save more money than ever. Even though travel rates are increasing, travelers can save more money than ever. Even though travel rates are increasing, travelers can save more money than ever. Even though travel rates are increasing, travelers can save more money than ever.

Better Buys

Our frequent traveler plan provides a great investment opportunity. Our frequent traveler plan provides a great investment opportunity. Our frequent traveler plan provides a great investment opportunity. Our frequent traveler plan provides a great investment opportunity. Our frequent traveler plan provides a great investment opportunity. Our frequent traveler

Reports and Proposals

Although these two examples differ considerably, there's no "right" or "wrong" solution. Either is acceptable, depending on your particular document.

WordPerfect lets you specify the exact vertical position of horizontal lines to the nearest hundredth of an inch.

Pull-quotes create visual appeal and promote readership.

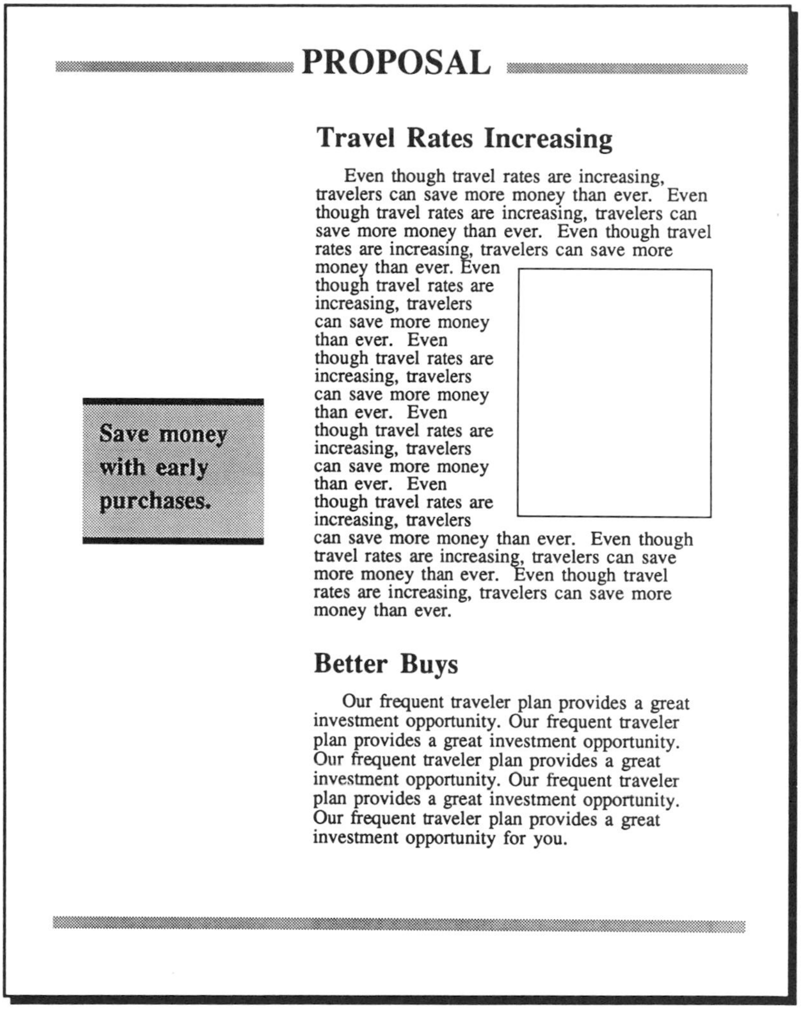

PROPOSAL

Travel Rates Increasing

Even though travel rates are increasing, travelers can save more money than ever. Even though travel rates are increasing, travelers can save more money than ever. Even though travel rates are increasing, travelers can save more money than ever. Even though travel rates are increasing, travelers can save more money than ever. Even though travel rates are increasing, travelers can save more money than ever. Even though travel rates are increasing, travelers can save more money than ever. Even though travel rates are increasing, travelers can save more money than ever. Even though travel rates are increasing, travelers can save more money than ever. Even though travel rates are increasing, travelers can save more money than ever.

Save money with early purchases.

Better Buys

Our frequent traveler plan provides a great investment opportunity. Our frequent traveler plan provides a great investment opportunity. Our frequent traveler plan provides a great investment opportunity. Our frequent traveler plan provides a great investment opportunity. Our frequent traveler plan provides a great investment opportunity for you.

Newsletters

WordPerfect is capable of producing any number of nameplates and formats, depending upon your tastes. Experiment with column widths and the number of columns, and the position of the contents box, headlines and subheads.

Note that the nameplate screen is borderless. Outside rules would have fought with internal horizontal lines. Yet the contents are framed in a box to clearly set them off from the text.

If you want headlines to extend more than one column, create a box with wraparound text. That will help you align columns more easily when placing text.

The top rule above the headline was created by making a box and specifying a thick border at the top, with no border on the remaining sides.

Trips 'n Things

July 1988 Monthly Newsletter for Global Travel Vol 5

JetAir Offers Weekend Getaways to Lebano

You can now fly direct from Raleigh You can now fly direct from Raleigh You can now fly direct from Raleigh You can now fly direct from Raleigh You can now fly direct from Raleigh You can now fly direct from Raleigh You can now fly direct from Raleigh You can now fly direct from Raleigh You can now fly direct from Raleigh You can now fly direct from Raleigh You can now fly direct from Raleigh You can now fly direct from Raleigh You can now fly direct from Raleigh You can now fly direct from Raleigh You can now fly direct from Raleigh You can now fly direct from Raleigh You can now fly direct from Raleigh

You can now fly direct from Raleigh You can now fly direct from direct from Raleigh You can now fly direct from Raleigh You can now fly direct from Raleigh You can now fly direct from Raleigh You can now fly direct from Raleigh You can now fly direct from Raleigh You can now fly direct from Raleigh You can now fly direct from Raleigh

Get Away

Get away from it all Get away from it all Get away from it all Get away from it all Get away from it all Get away from it all Get away from it all Get away from it all Get away from it all Get away from it all Get away from it all Get away from it all Get away from it all Get away from it all Get away from it all Get away from it all Get away from it all Get

continued on page 4

What's Inside

Newsletters

Your newsletter nameplate is the single most important visual element. Take a look at other newsletters—perhaps those of your competitors—for ideas on developing or improving your own nameplate.

In this example, it's much easier to underline *Trips 'n Things* three times than to create horizontal lines.

Experimentation with letter spacing was required to make *Monthly Newsletter for Global Travel* fit snugly between the p and the g.

Trips 'n Things

July 1988 Monthly Newsletter for Global Travel Vol 5

JetAir Offers Weekend Getaways to Lebano

You can now fly direct from Raleigh You can now fly direct from Raleigh You can now fly direct from Raleigh fly direct from

Raleigh You can now fly direct from Raleigh You can now fly direct from Raleigh You can now fly direct from Raleigh You can now fly direct from Raleigh You can now fly direct from Raleigh You can now fly direct from Raleigh You can now fly direct from Raleigh You can from Raleigh direct from

Raleigh You can now fly direct from Raleigh You can now fly direct from Raleigh You can now fly direct from Raleigh You can now fly direct from Raleigh You can now fly direct from Raleigh You can now fly direct from Raleigh You can now fly direct from Raleigh

Get Away

Get away from it all Get away from it all Get away from it all Get away from it all Get away from it all Get away from it all Get away from it all Get away from it all Get away

Newsletters

As with any graphics project, the final result may be a hybrid of several first-draft sketches. Have a good idea of how your document will look before trying to produce it using WordPerfect.

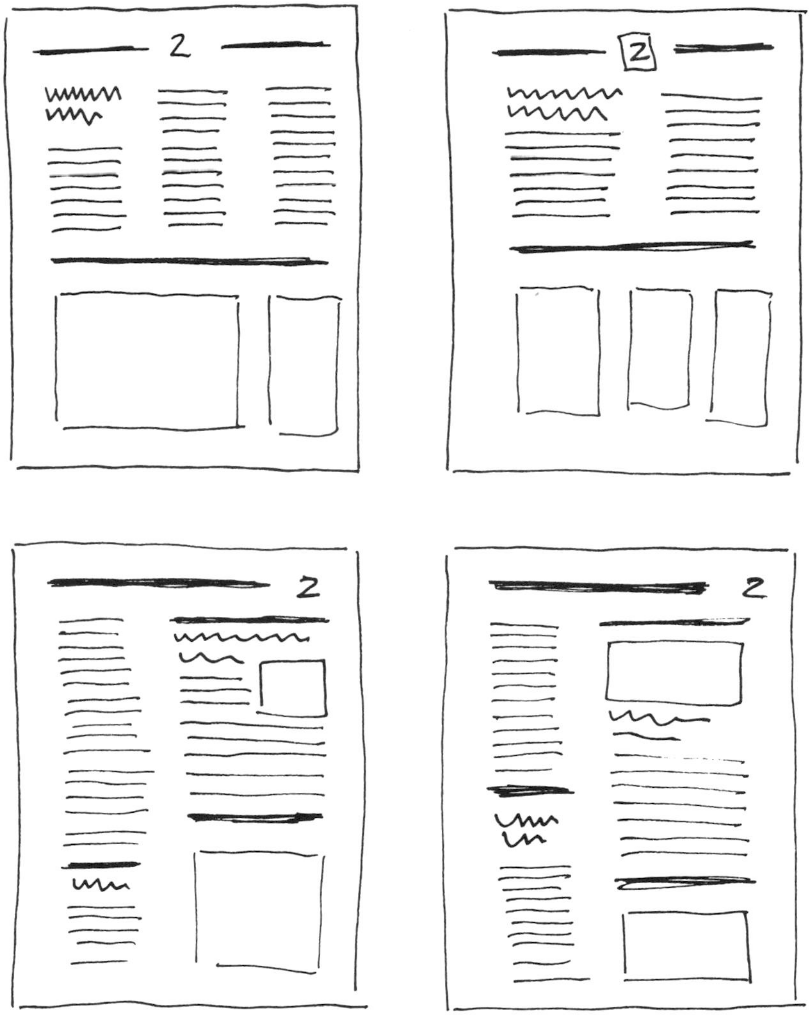

Newsletters

Graphic elements from the original cover page should carry over to inside newsletter pages. Note how the thickness and width of horizontal lines remain the same, as do screen values, type sizes and rules around boxes.

Avoid justified type in narrow columns. It can create excessive hyphenation and uneven word spacing.

Because you can't put horizontal lines in a USER BOX, the UNDERLINE command was used to create rules.

Screens call attention to important material and provide contrast on all-type pages.

Hard returns often produce either too little or too much space between headlines and copy. Experiment with line spacing and the ADVANCE command to align type with other visual elements.

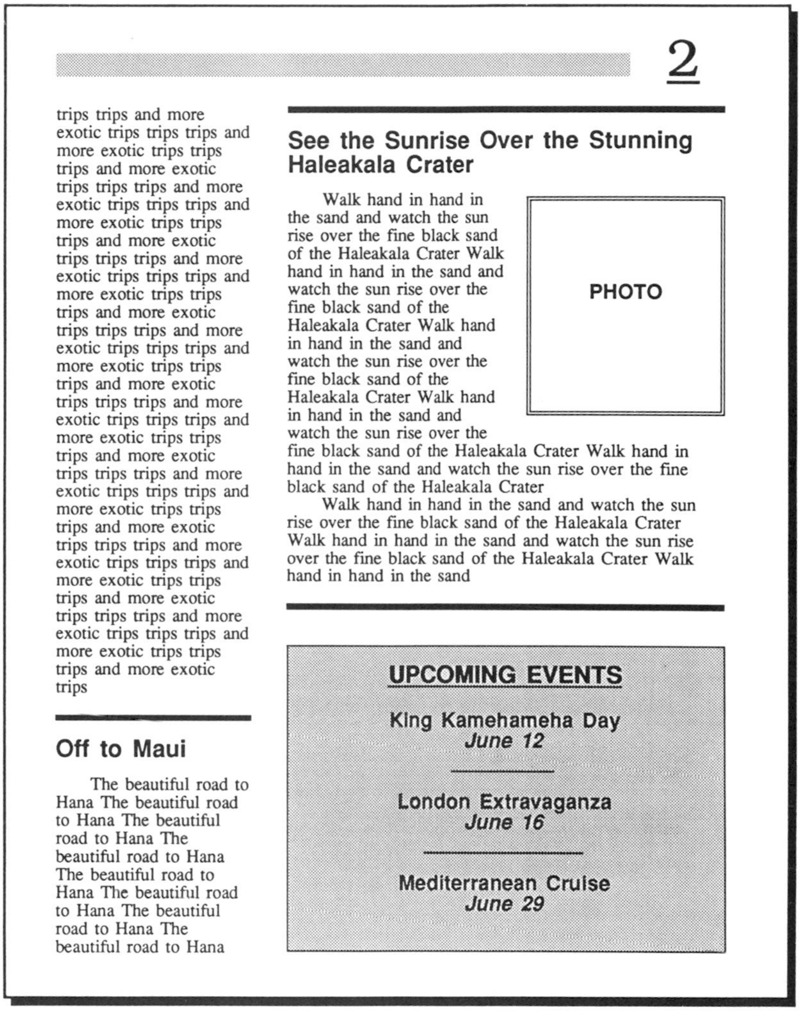

2

trips trips and more exotic trips trips trips and more exotic trips trips trips and more exotic trips trips trips and more exotic trips trips trips and more exotic trips trips trips and more exotic trips trips trips and more exotic trips trips trips and more exotic trips trips trips and more exotic trips trips trips and more exotic trips trips trips and more exotic trips trips trips and more exotic trips trips trips and more exotic trips trips trips and more exotic trips trips trips and more exotic trips trips trips and more exotic trips trips trips and more exotic trips trips trips and more exotic trips trips trips and more exotic trips trips trips and more exotic trips

Off to Maui

The beautiful road to Hana The beautiful road to Hana The beautiful road to Hana The beautiful road to Hana The beautiful road to Hana The beautiful road to Hana The beautiful road to Hana The beautiful road to Hana

See the Sunrise Over the Stunning Haleakala Crater

PHOTO

Walk hand in hand in the sand and watch the sun rise over the fine black sand of the Haleakala Crater Walk hand in hand in the sand and watch the sun rise over the fine black sand of the Haleakala Crater Walk hand in hand in the sand and watch the sun rise over the fine black sand of the Haleakala Crater Walk hand in hand in the sand and watch the sun rise over the fine black sand of the Haleakala Crater Walk hand in hand in the sand and watch the sun rise over the fine black sand of the Haleakala Crater

Walk hand in hand in the sand and watch the sun rise over the fine black sand of the Haleakala Crater Walk hand in hand in the sand and watch the sun rise over the fine black sand of the Haleakala Crater Walk hand in hand in the sand

UPCOMING EVENTS

King Kamehameha Day
June 12

London Extravaganza
June 16

Mediterranean Cruise
June 29

Catalogs

Always create accurate sketches, including measurements, *before* creating your image on-screen. Until WordPerfect is fully WYSIWYG ("What You See Is What You Get"), rough sketches prepared beforehand are preferable to playing peek-a-boo with VIEW DOCUMENT.

Catalogs

Creative use of type and white space often can result in simple yet elegant catalog cover designs.

Use repeating lines of slightly different widths to produce subtly pleasing visual effects.

The CS logos were imported from a graphics package.

The lower "multiple line" image can be repeated by blocking and moving the appropriate codes from the image above.

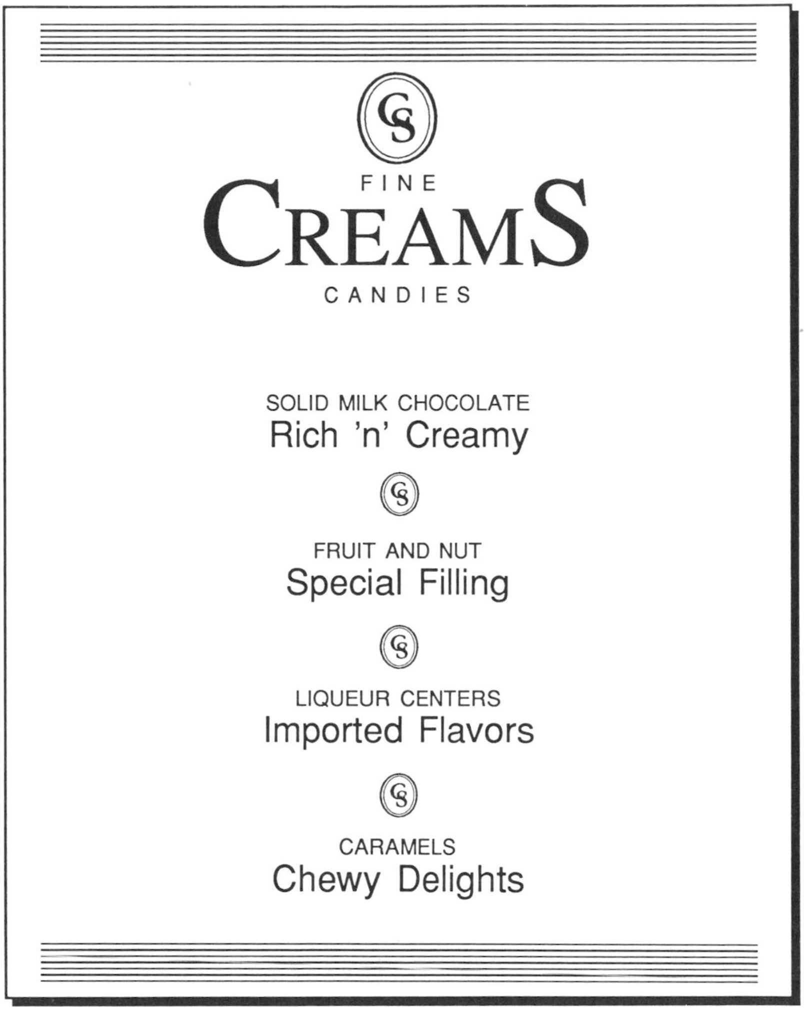

Catalogs

Trial-and-error experimentation with kerning, leading and font sizes will achieve a pleasing, unified image. The REVEAL CODES example below shows the many steps required to produce a seemingly simple all-type image.

By reducing line height for the word CREAMS, you're able to drop the word FINE below the ascenders C and S.

F I N E

CREAMS

C A N D I E S

Rather than using uppercase and lowercase type, specify a larger point size of the same font to create more interesting all-type effects.

[HRt]
[Center][Font:Helvetica 12 pt]F I N E[Ln Height:0.01"][HRt]
[Center][Font:Times Roman 66 pt]C[Font:Times Roman 44 pt]REAM
[Font:Times Roman 66 pt]S[Ln Height:0.9"][HRt]
[Font:Helvetica 12 pt][Center]C A N D I E S[Ln Height:Auto]
[HRt]
[HRt]

Catalogs

In these examples, type was positioned on inside pages, then boxes were used to indicate position of photos or illustrations.

To create the top header, first type FRUITS, then create separate horizontal lines to the left and right.

One box was created, then blocked and copied five more times. The handy CAPTION feature allows you to create text that automatically attaches to specific boxes.

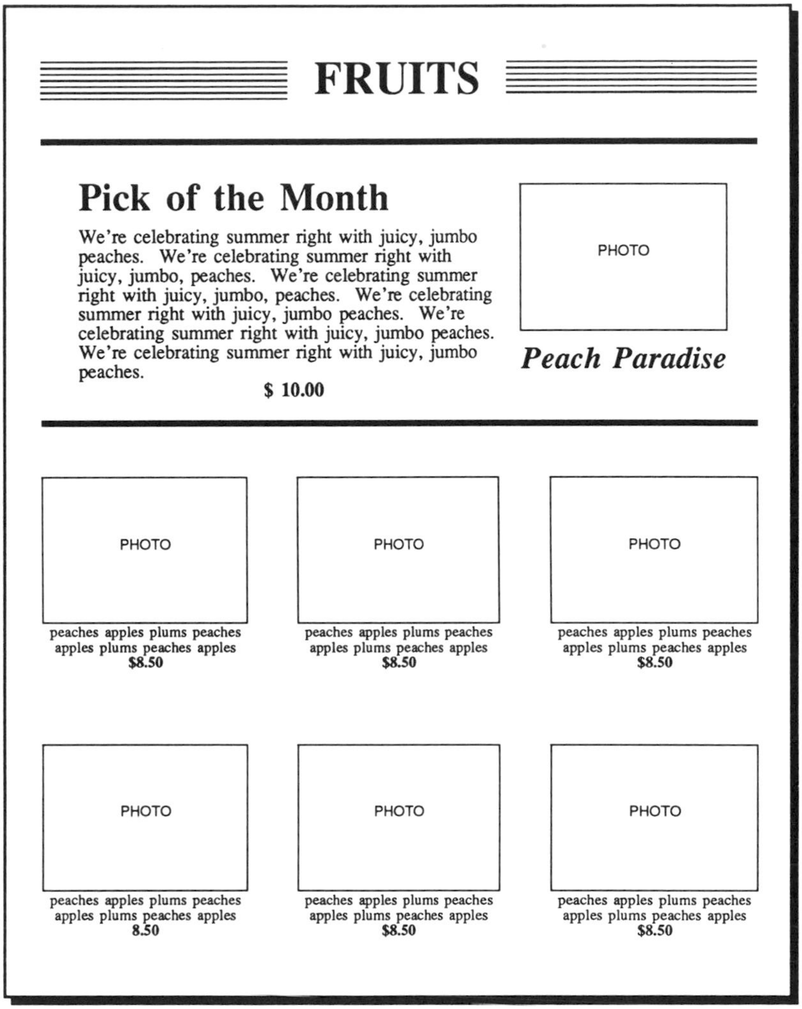

FRUITS

Pick of the Month

We're celebrating summer right with juicy, jumbo peaches. We're celebrating summer right with juicy, jumbo, peaches. We're celebrating summer right with juicy, jumbo, peaches. We're celebrating summer right with juicy, jumbo peaches. We're celebrating summer right with juicy, jumbo peaches. We're celebrating summer right with juicy, jumbo peaches.

$ 10.00

PHOTO

Peach Paradise

PHOTO

peaches apples plums peaches apples plums peaches apples
$8.50

PHOTO

peaches apples plums peaches apples plums peaches apples
$8.50

PHOTO

peaches apples plums peaches apples plums peaches apples
$8.50

PHOTO

peaches apples plums peaches apples plums peaches apples
8.50

PHOTO

peaches apples plums peaches apples plums peaches apples
$8.50

PHOTO

peaches apples plums peaches apples plums peaches apples
$8.50

Long Documents

Covers for training manuals often appear in straight typewritten format. With a little extra effort, your message can be enhanced by the creative use of fonts, screens and rules.

A borderless screen was created. Then the text was underlined to create offsetting rules.

Horizontal lines cannot be created within a box, so use the UNDERLINE command to create rules.

You can center text automatically left and right within a box. To center it top to bottom, use inside border space or the ADVANCE command.

Experiment with letter and word spacing to align type vertically.

KEEPING
THE
CUSTOMER
SATISFIED

Employee Training Manual

CLOTHES OUT WORLD, INC.
190 Sun Drive, Denver, Colorado 96200

Long Documents

Simple use of horizontal lines and screens can greatly enhance any cover sheet.

First, create the screened box and note horizontal positions of the box, left and right.

Also note vertical positions of each text line.

Then go outside the box, space down to that position and create lines to the left and right of the box, using page borders and box borders as margins.

Boxes are transparent when laid over other boxes, so horizontal lines were created separately to the left and right of the screened area.

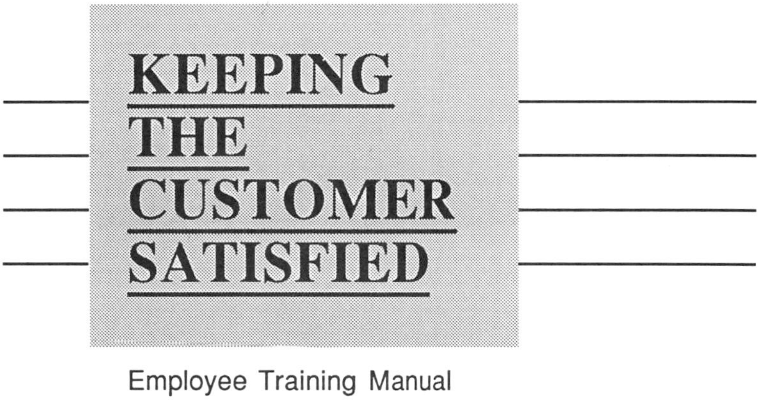

Long Documents

Note how the simple placement of six horizontal rules and two vertical rules makes this document more lively and readable.

To reverse type, create a 100 percent black box, choose color White, then type text.

To avoid uneven column wrapping, place the COLUMN ON code at the point where you actually want text to begin.

2

The Satisfied Customer

The satisfied customer is one who is greeted with a smile, treated like a v.i.p., and leaves with exactly what he or she was looking for. The satisfied customer is one who is greeted with a smile, treated like a v.i.p., and leaves with exactly what he or she was looking for.

The satisfied customer is one who is greeted with a smile, treated like a v.i.p., and leaves with exactly what he or she was looking for. The satisfied customer is one who is greeted with a smile, treated like a v.i.p., and leaves with exactly what he or she was looking for. The satisfied customer is one who is greeted with a smile, treated like a v.i.p., and leaves with exactly what he or she was looking for. The satisfied customer is one who is greeted with a smile, treated like a v.i.p., and leaves with exactly what he or she was looking for. The satisfied customer is one who is greeted with a smile, treated like a v.i.p.,

Satisfied Customers Keep Coming Back

and leaves with exactly what he or she was looking for. The satisfied customer is one who is greeted with a smile, treated like a v.i.p., and leaves with exactly what he or she was looking for. The satisfied customer is one who is greeted with a smile, treated like a v.i.p., and leaves with exactly what he or she was looking for.

The satisfied customer is one who is greeted with a smile, treated like a v.i.p., and leaves with exactly what he or she was looking for. The satisfied customer is one who is greeted with a smile, treated like a v.i.p., and leaves with exactly what he or she was looking for. The satisfied customer is one who is greeted with a smile, treated like a v.i.p., and leaves with exactly what he or she was looking for.

The satisfied customer is one who is greeted with a smile, treated like a v.i.p., and leaves with exactly what he or she was looking for. The satisfied customer is one who is greeted with a smile, treated like a v.i.p., and leaves with exactly what he or she was looking for. The satisfied customer is one who is greeted with a smile, treated like a v.i.p., and leaves with exactly what he or she was looking for. The satisfied customer is one who is greeted with

Long Documents

Pull-quotes are an effective way to break up long runs of text and "pull" the reader's attention into the document.

Use outside border space, instead of hard returns, to create white space above and below pull-quotes.

To force the text to wrap correctly, set up pull-quotes as boxes with borders at the top and bottom.

Then anchor them to a paragraph, not to a page.

for. The satisfied customer is one who is greeted with a smile, treated like a v.i.p., and leaves with exactly what he or she was looking for. The satisfied customer is one who is greeted with a smile, treated like a v.i.p.,
Satisfied Customers Keep Coming Back
and leaves with exactly what he or she was looking for. The satisfied customer is one who is greeted with a smile, treated like a v.i.p., and leaves with exactly what he or she was looking for. The satisfied customer is one who is greeted with a smile, treated like a v.i.p., and leaves with exactly what he or she was looking

Long Documents

Watch out for "visual overkill"—too many visual elements placed on one page. Note how the reverses and screens in the body copy are repeated appropriately above with the horizontal rules and page numbers.

Note how even and odd page numbers are positioned opposite each other at the outside of the page. Stylesheets and macros can make short work of repetitive headers and footers.

Use line spacing, not hard returns, to adjust white space around the headlines.

Vertical rules between columns help frame type and visual elements within the text.

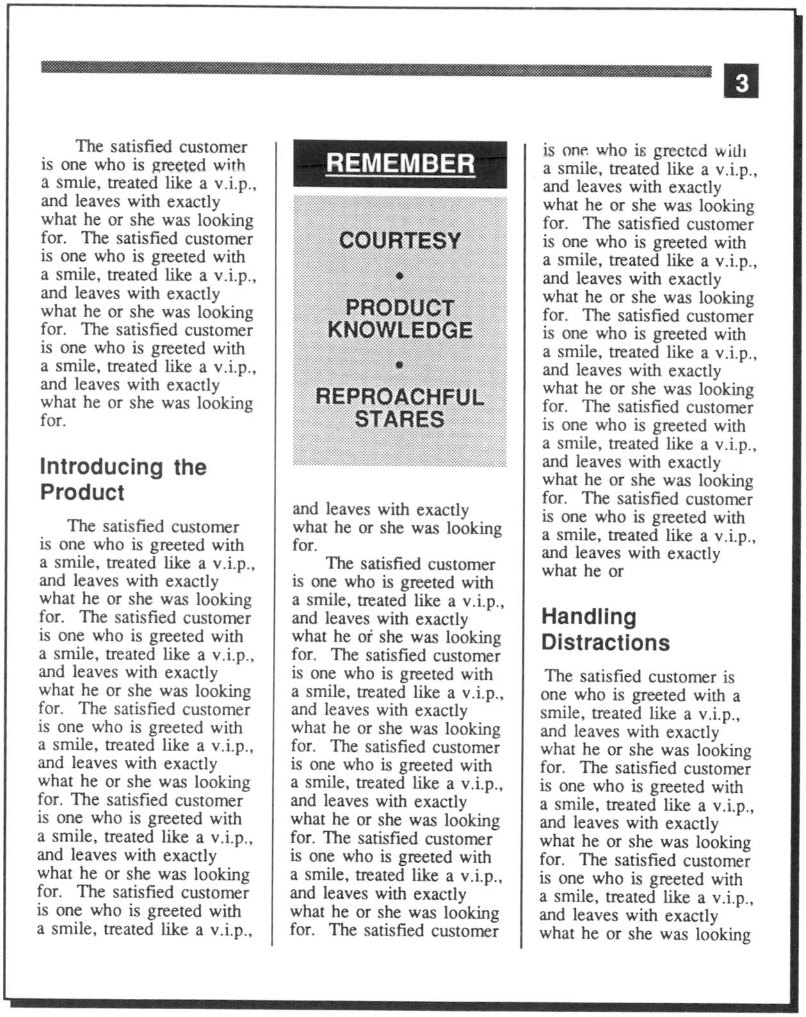

3

The satisfied customer is one who is greeted with a smile, treated like a v.i.p., and leaves with exactly what he or she was looking for. The satisfied customer is one who is greeted with a smile, treated like a v.i.p., and leaves with exactly what he or she was looking for. The satisfied customer is one who is greeted with a smile, treated like a v.i.p., and leaves with exactly what he or she was looking for.

Introducing the Product

The satisfied customer is one who is greeted with a smile, treated like a v.i.p., and leaves with exactly what he or she was looking for. The satisfied customer is one who is greeted with a smile, treated like a v.i.p., and leaves with exactly what he or she was looking for. The satisfied customer is one who is greeted with a smile, treated like a v.i.p., and leaves with exactly what he or she was looking for. The satisfied customer is one who is greeted with a smile, treated like a v.i.p., and leaves with exactly what he or she was looking for. The satisfied customer is one who is greeted with a smile, treated like a v.i.p.,

REMEMBER

COURTESY
•
PRODUCT KNOWLEDGE
•
REPROACHFUL STARES

and leaves with exactly what he or she was looking for.

The satisfied customer is one who is greeted with a smile, treated like a v.i.p., and leaves with exactly what he or she was looking for. The satisfied customer is one who is greeted with a smile, treated like a v.i.p., and leaves with exactly what he or she was looking for. The satisfied customer is one who is greeted with a smile, treated like a v.i.p., and leaves with exactly what he or she was looking for. The satisfied customer is one who is greeted with a smile, treated like a v.i.p., and leaves with exactly what he or she was looking for. The satisfied customer is one who is greeted with a smile, treated like a v.i.p., and leaves with exactly what he or she was looking for. The satisfied customer is one who is greeted with a smile, treated like a v.i.p., and leaves with exactly what he or she was looking for. The satisfied customer is one who is greeted with a smile, treated like a v.i.p., and leaves with exactly what he or she was looking for. The satisfied customer is one who is greeted with a smile, treated like a v.i.p., and leaves with exactly what he or

Handling Distractions

The satisfied customer is one who is greeted with a smile, treated like a v.i.p., and leaves with exactly what he or she was looking for. The satisfied customer is one who is greeted with a smile, treated like a v.i.p., and leaves with exactly what he or she was looking for. The satisfied customer is one who is greeted with a smile, treated like a v.i.p., and leaves with exactly what he or she was looking

Long Documents

Multiple graphics boxes can create a nearly endless variety of contrasting yet appealing graphic images.

Always create separate boxes when using different graphics options. Here, two boxes were produced, one to create reversed type and one for a screen.

It's easier to use outside border space to create the white space between boxes than to specify that space mathematically.

REMEMBER

COURTESY

•

PRODUCT
KNOWLEDGE

•

REPROACHFUL
STARES

REMEMBER

COURTESY

•

PRODUCT
KNOWLEDGE

•

REPROACHFUL
STARES

Other Graphics

Menus

WordPerfect allows you to import illustrations from graphics libraries and other software programs. You may want to invest in libraries of clip art and other visual enhancements.

Creative use of vertical rules creates a "barn" effect.

Use Border Options to enhance interest with borders of varying widths.

Use justified margins and dot leaders to align type with dots automatically.

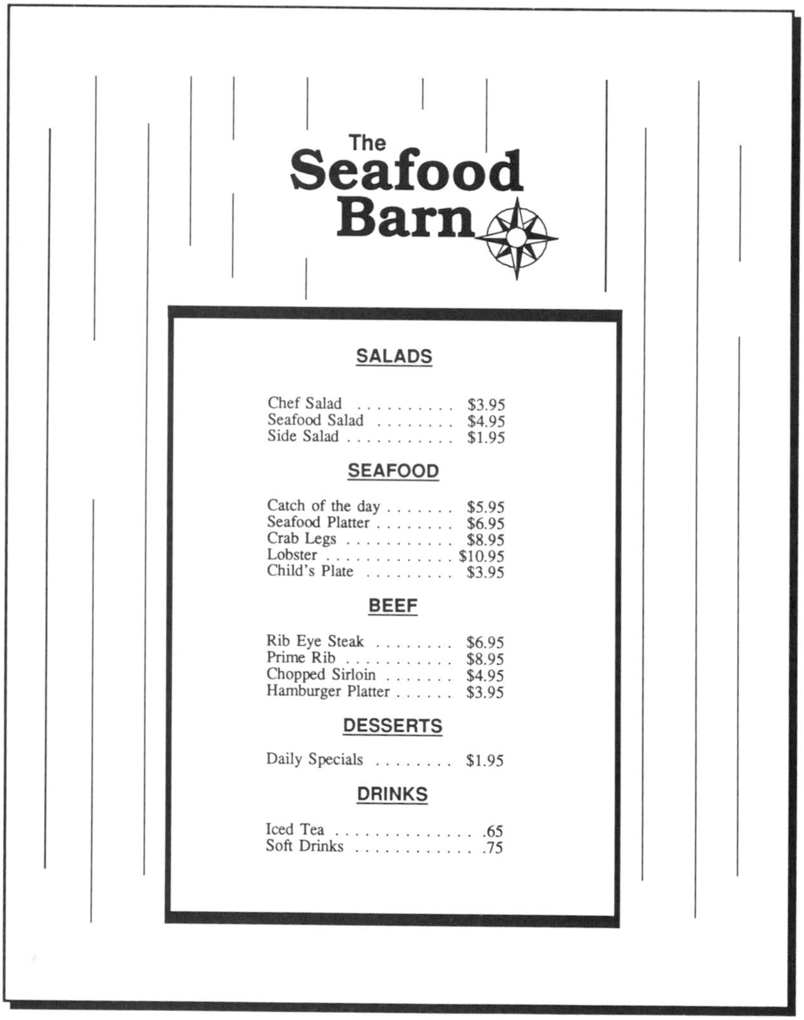

The
Seafood Barn

SALADS

Chef Salad $3.95
Seafood Salad $4.95
Side Salad $1.95

SEAFOOD

Catch of the day $5.95
Seafood Platter $6.95
Crab Legs $8.95
Lobster $10.95
Child's Plate $3.95

BEEF

Rib Eye Steak $6.95
Prime Rib $8.95
Chopped Sirloin $4.95
Hamburger Platter $3.95

DESSERTS

Daily Specials $1.95

DRINKS

Iced Tea 65
Soft Drinks 75

Menus

Logos can be tedious to produce, and you may need design expertise to achieve satisfactory results. As this example shows, WordPerfect is capable of producing excellent logos and icons.

Type *Seafood* first to anchor your position on the page. Then position other words above and below.

Line spacing between *Seafood* and *Barn* was changed to 0.8".

Line spacing was reduced to 0.6" from 1.0" to allow *The* to go below ascenders S and f.

The

Seafood

Barn

Invoices and Purchase Orders

Although the working section in the illustration below looks like a box, it was actually created from a series of horizontal and vertical lines, since WordPerfect won't let you use the LINE DRAW command within a GRAPHICS box.

Two separate boxes were used, one with a reversed screen and one with black type placed within.

If you have trouble making corners meet, just print the document and use good old white-out!

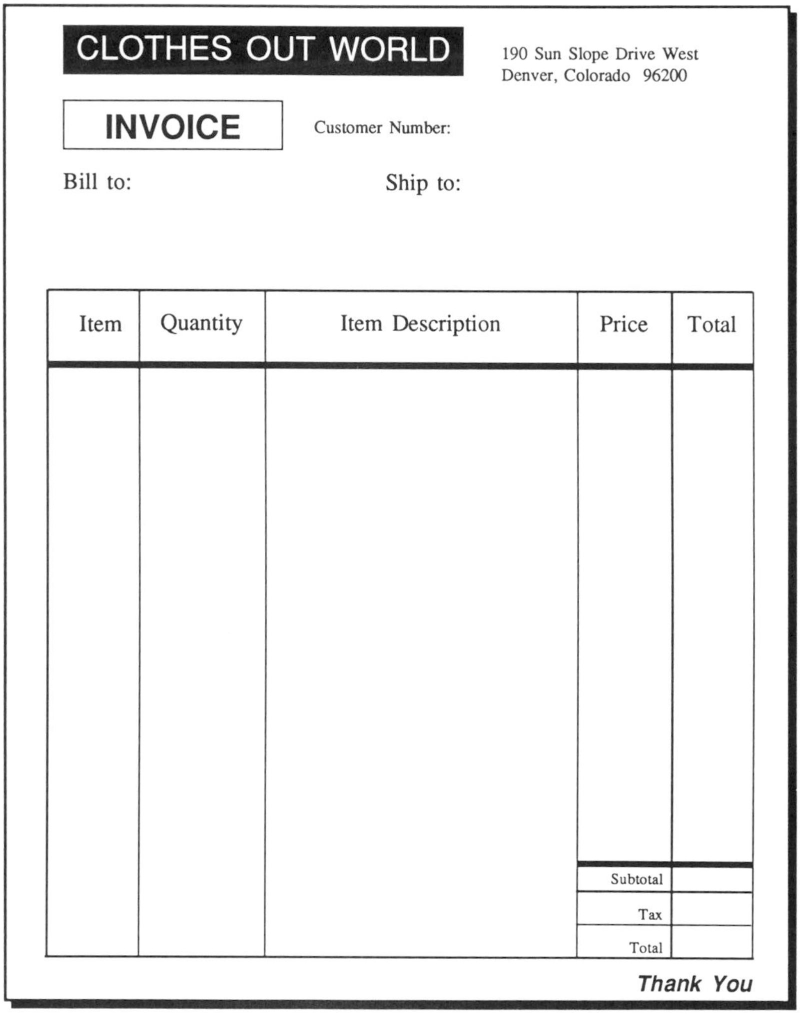
CLOTHES OUT WORLD

190 Sun Slope Drive West
Denver, Colorado 96200

INVOICE

Customer Number:

Bill to:

Ship to:

Item	Quantity	Item Description	Price	Total
			Subtotal	
			Tax	
			Total	

Thank You

Price Lists, Order Forms, Spec Sheets

Timely information can be updated almost daily, making sure sales and customer service personnel have access to the most current information.

Horizontal rules are used to break up type and provide easy reading.

Additional white space between rules also makes documents easier to read.

10

ITEM	PRICE	DESCRIPTION
Lawn Darts	$11.99 each set	Safety-tipped rubber lawn darts designed for easy aim and safe play. In bright colors that are easy to see. Made for beginning players yet enjoyable for all ages. Precise balanced design allows great control and accuracy in throwing for professional-style dart action.
Rubber Duckies	$4.95 each	Jumbo-sized duckies that fit the pool rather than the bathtub. Bright yellow classic design, water resistant to float, make noises when squeezed.
Beach Towels	$11.95 each	Thick, plush towels in extra-large sizes and an assortment of colorful designs such as favorite cartoon characters and movie stars.
Flip-Flops	$1.95 a pair	Assorted sizes and colors of durable, comfortable flip-flops.
T-Shirts	$5.99 each	100% cotton t-shirts in an assortment of designs and sizes.

CHAPTER 12

PRESENT AND FUTURE PERFECT

As you've seen in the preceding chapters, WordPerfect offers a wealth of powerful and easily accessible graphic, text and layout features.

WordPerfect lets you design and produce attractive multicolumn documents, enhanced with a wide variety of graphic accents, such as borders, rules and bars. It lets you control white space and easily integrate your words with imported graphic images, such as charts, graphs, illustrations and scanned photographs. Once placed in a WordPerfect document, these images can be easily resized, moved or distorted until the effect is "just right."

WordPerfect's graphics handling ability is matched by its strong document organizing features and its control over typography. You can easily compile a table of contents, an index, and lists of imported graphics and text files. You can edit a text file with the knowledge that imported graphics files (and their captions) will remain adjacent to the text to which they relate. You can include numerous typefaces on a page. You can adjust line and letter spacing to tolerances close enough to please the most exacting art director or typesetter.

Once created, WordPerfect PostScript files can be set in type on such high-resolution output devices as the Linotronic 100 or 300. Phototypesetting at 1270 or 2540 dots per inch, instead of the 300 dots per inch offered by most laser printing, allows documents such as this book to rival the quality of yesterday's best composition methods.

This isn't to say that WordPerfect should be the only software program you'll ever use. Design-intensive projects (e.g., logos, posters or single-page image advertisements) may require the use of outside drawing programs, such as Arts & Letters, Micrografix Designer and PC Paintbrush—all of which are excellent partners for WordPerfect.

WordPerfect Versus Dedicated Page Layout Programs

At what point should you consider moving beyond WordPerfect and investigate a dedicated page layout program? The answer depends upon both the design sophistication of your project and the point at which the added productivity of a dedicated page layout program makes the purchase of the program economically feasible.

The type of work you do should be a major deciding factor. If you're a designer who spends a lot of time creating one-of-a-kind projects like logos, posters or single-page advertisements, you may find that the continuous WYSIWYG (What-You-See-Is-What-You-Get) screen display of a dedicated page layout program is worth the added expense.

If you're like most people, however, your work probably involves a combination of writing, formatting and text organization. During the course of a week, you probably work on many types of multi-page documents, including brochures, newsletters, proposals, price lists and other projects. For you, WordPerfect probably offers all the desktop publishing power you need. It lets you format your words and enhance them with imported graphics, without having to leave WordPerfect and load another program.

The Dangerous Job of Attempting to Predict the Future

It's also important to recognize that WordPerfect will be continually enhanced to increase the desktop publishing power of its basic word processing "engine." The differences between WordPerfect and dedicated page layout programs will become fewer and fewer with each new WordPerfect release.

Possible enhancements may include improved on-screen display, on-screen rulers and a more interactive VIEW DOCUMENT mode, which would allow you to edit while viewing all, or magnified portions, of a single page or two-page spread.

Future versions probably will allow you to create oversized documents and will expand WordPerfect's color-handling capabilities. As a new generation of color laser printers begins to appear, WordPerfect undoubtedly will keep pace by allowing you to "mix" colors on-screen and prepare spot-color overlays or even four-color separations.

As image-scanners grow in popularity, WordPerfect perhaps will add a capability that lets you modify the contrast range of scanned photographs so they'll reproduce best on the type of paper you use to print your project.

All of the above should be classified as conjecture rather than as authorized predictions. They're included here to emphasize that as your desktop publishing needs become more sophisticated, WordPerfect will grow right along with you. The above enhancements, in short, are simply based on common sense and WordPerfect's proven tradition of "listening to the market."

So, jump on the WordPerfect desktop publishing bandwagon. Today's WordPerfect and its future versions promise to have a profound impact on the appearance of printed documents of all types. Desktop publishing has never been easier or more affordable. By becoming familiar with WordPerfect's desktop publishing capabilities now, you can easily keep up with the program as its powers become stronger and stronger.

APPENDIX A

Using a Mouse with WordPerfect

Mouse support is one of the key new features of WordPerfect 5.1. With a mouse, routine tasks such as blocking text and selecting commands are simplified. Pointing and clicking the mouse can often save you a number of keystrokes.

Pull-down menus make the mouse especially useful. Unlike the regular WordPerfect menus, these menus pop open in response to a click of the mouse, and then close after you've selected a command. Using pull-down menus does not prevent you from using the regular menus.

Although pull-down menus are most appropriate for mouse users, they're available to everyone using Version 5.1. If you don't have a mouse, press [ALT] and [=] together to display the main pull-down menu. Then use the arrow keys to move the pointer to the desired command, and press [ENTER] to select the command.

Mouse Setup

The first step is to set up the mouse for your system and your personal preferences. To set up the mouse,

Select: (SHIFT-F1) (SETUP)
1 (Mouse)

Response: You'll see the mouse setup menu:

1 (Type) lets you specify the type of mouse you are using.
2 (Port) lets you specify the port to which a *serial* mouse is connected (for example, Com 1).

3 (Double Click Interval) lets you specify the time interval that distinguishes a "click" from a "drag" (see "Basic Skills" below for an explanation of these terms).
4 (Sub-Menu Display Time) determines the delay between your selection of a menu option and the display of the next submenu.
5 (Acceleration Factor) determines how closely the movement of the mouse pointer on-screen matches the physical movement of the mouse. A larger number here makes the mouse pointer more responsive to the movement of the mouse.
6 (Left-Handed Mouse) reverses the functions of the left and right mouse buttons.

The most important option is 1 (Type), which lets you identify the type of mouse you're using. If the default settings for the other options are acceptable, you won't have to select them.

Basic Skills

Using a mouse involves two activities: clicking and dragging.

A *click* is a quick press and release of one of the mouse buttons. Clicks are used to open menus, select options from menus, and reposition the cursor.

A *drag* involves pressing a mouse button (without releasing it) and moving the mouse. Drags are used to block text and to move the cursor dynamically through the text.

The table below explains how to accomplish routine tasks in WordPerfect 5.1. With a little practice, you'll be mousing like a pro.

Button	Location	Action	Response
Left	In text	Click	Repositions the editing cursor at the mouse pointer's position.
		Drag	Blocks text.
	In a menu	Click	Selects the command to which the mouse pointer is pointing.
Right	In text	Click	Opens the main pull-down menu.

Button	Location	Action	Response
		Drag	Moves the editing cursor dynamically through the text.
	In a menu	Click	Exits all menus and returns to the editing screen.
Left + Right			Cancels the current operation.

Note: If your mouse has three buttons, the center button accomplishes the same effect as pressing the left and right buttons together.

APPENDIX B

The following is a list of just a few hardware and software enhancements that can help you get the most out of desktop publishing with WordPerfect 5.0 and 5.1.

Adobe Systems, Inc., P.O. Box 7900, Mountain View, CA 94039-7900. 415-961-4400.

Adobe publishes one of the largest collections of downloadable fonts for PostScript printers, such as the Apple LaserWriter IINT, as well as for Linotronic 100 and 300 phototypesetters. Most Adobe fonts are licensed by the International Typographic Corporation (ITC), which ensures quality and compatibility with typefaces available from conventional phototypesetters.

Adobe publishes *Font & Function*, a free quarterly newsletter that contains illustrations of character sets for all of its typefaces, as well as samples of typical applications for each particular typeface.

Adobe's Publisher's Packages should be of interest to those who are taking their first steps beyond resident fonts. These specially priced packages consist of two or more typeface families that work well together and are appropriate for particular categories of projects.

For example, Adobe's "Package Number One: Newsletters" consists of three typefaces—two serif and one sans-serif—that can add a distinct appearance to your newsletter.

Bitstream, Inc., Athenaeum House, 215 First Street, Cambridge, MA 02142. 617-497-6222.

Bitstream produces digital type of ITC quality for users of both PostScript and HP-compatible printers. Bitstream also has designed several typefaces, created to work particularly well in a variety of sizes with laser-output devices. More than 100 typefaces are available, with more being added each month.

Because Bitstream outline fonts can be used with either family of laser printers, your investment is preserved if you change from a printer that is HP-compatible to a PostScript printer.

Bitstream publishes a free catalog showing sample alphabet sets from its wide selection of typefaces.

Computer Support Corporation, 15926 Midway Road, Dallas, TX 75244. 214-661-8960.

This company's Arts & Letters software is a combination of a Microsoft Windows-based drawing program and a clip art library consisting of 1,100 sample symbols and drawings. These can be combined in various ways and stored in a variety of formats, including an encapsulated PostScript file, and placed in a WordPerfect document.

Data Products, 6404 Nancy Ridge Drive, San Diego, CA 92121. 619-552-0880.

This company makes plug-in PostScript boards for Hewlett-Packard LaserJet printers. They feature a variety of type sizes, including large headline type.

Goldsmith Communications Company, 3759 Pioneer Place, San Diego, CA 92103. 619-294-7570.

Designed for general word processing applications, Goldsmith Communication's Perfect Keys software also lets you use WordPerfect as a desktop publishing tool. Single keystrokes let you move the cursor from sentence to sentence, paragraph to paragraph or page to page; delete or block text; select among 13 fonts and many font sizes; retrieve any of 10 style libraries and apply any of 14 styles from a library; and much more.

Hercules Computer Technology, Inc., 921 Parker Street, Berkeley, CA 94710. 415-540-6000.

Hercules manufactures several graphics cards, including a black and white version, a network version and the In-Color RamFont Card. These cards and accompanying software expedite page layout and formatting by giving you an on-screen representation of increased or decreased type size, as well as such attributes as boldface, italics, underlining and boldface italicized type.

The Hercules RamFont cards should be of special interest to those preparing long documents that are designed to use a few type sizes and type styles consistently.

Hewlett-Packard Company, 16399 W. Bernardo Drive, San Diego, CA 92127-1899. 619-592-8010.

Hewlett-Packard, a manufacturer of measurement and computation products and systems, makes PC-compatible printers and products for desktop publishing.

The LaserJet IIP printer produces four pages per minute and provides 300-dot-per-inch resolution. It fits on the corner of a desk and weighs about 25 pounds (it also costs less than other HP printers). Compatible with the LaserJet Series II and IID printers, the IIP's features include 512K of memory, two slots for boards that can expand memory to 4.5 megabytes, 14 internal fonts and an input tray that adjusts for different paper sizes. Optional cartridges let the IIP emulate your old dot-matrix printer or give you access to Adobe PostScript fonts.

The LaserJet III printer costs less than the LaserJet II series and was designed to replace it. Compatible with all LaserJet printers, the LaserJet III uses the HP PCL 5 printer language and features improved resolution, due to a change in dot size and placement. Other new features include more built-in, scalable fonts in more sizes; increased page layout flexibility; and faster graphics printing. The printer's standard one-megabyte memory is upgradable to four megabytes with additional boards.

HP DeskJet PLUS printers are alternatives to 24-wire dot-matrix printers. The DeskJet PLUS produces a page of text up to twice as fast and a page of graphics up to five times as fast as the original DeskJet printer did in 1988. The printer comes with 10 fonts; fonts up to 30 points are available in cartridge and soft-font formats. The DeskJet PLUS works with a variety of HP, IBM and IBM-compatible computers and is supported by (in addition to WordPerfect) Microsoft Word and Windows; Lotus 1-2-3 and Freelance; Wordstar Professional; Harvard Graphics; and Multimate software packages.

Type Director typeface scaling and font management software can be used with all HP disk-based, scalable-typeface products to create bit-mapped fonts for printers.

Type Director Version 2.0 works with Microsoft Word 4.0 and 5.0; WordPerfect 5.0 and 5.1; Xerox Ventura Publisher; and all Microsoft Windows applications.

Version 2.0 also supports a wider range of printers than the first version; these include DeskJet and DeskJet PLUS, PaintJet XL text and color graphics printers, and Epson and IBM 9- and 24-wire dot matrix printers. Features that support the LaserJet III let users install cartridge and disk-based scalable typefaces into applications and download disk-based scalable typefaces for on-the-fly scaling.

LaserMaster Corporation, 7156 Shady Oak Road, Eden Prairie, MN 55344. 612-944-9330.

LaserMaster print controllers allow the use of Adobe PostScript fonts in documents produced on HP LaserJet printers. These control cards can increase print resolution up to 1,000 dots per inch, and permit on-the-fly font scaling. LaserMaster also makes a large-screen monitor whose level of clarity matches that of the Adobe Typeface Manager in the Macintosh environment.

Micrografx, 1820 N. Greenville Avenue, Richardson, TX 75801. 214-234-1769.

Micrografx Designer is a sophisticated, Windows-based drawing program that can be used to create logos and drawings for placement in WordPerfect documents.

Okidata, 532 Fellowship Road, Mount Laurel, NJ 08054. 609-235-2600.

Okidata is a supplier of PC peripherals: impact and nonimpact printers, high-speed and PC modems and facsimile equipment.

The company's laser printers include the OkiLaser 800, 820 and 840. The OkiLaser 800 prints at eight pages per minute and includes 26 resident fonts in four typefaces (with two font card slots for expansion). The printer has 512K of memory, expandable up to 4.5 megabytes of RAM. It can be upgraded to a font-scaling or full Adobe PostScript configuration.

The OkiLaser 820 printer features on-the-fly font scaling, using 13 Bitstream scalable-outline fonts and 26 resident bit-map fonts for HP compatibility. The OkiLaser 840 includes a PostScript interpreter and provides Hewlett-Packard Series II and Diablo emulations as standard. The 840 has 35 scalable typefaces and 26 HP-compatible bit-map fonts in four typefaces, and features 2 megabytes of memory, expandable to 4 megabytes.

Pacific Data Products, 6404 Nancy Ridge Drive, San Diego, CA 92121. 619-552-0880.

Pacific Data Products produces software, cartridges and memory expansion boards for Hewlett-Packard LaserJet and compatible printers including IBM, Canon and Olivetti.

25 Cartridges in One! is a cartridge containing 172 fonts and symbol sets combined from all Hewlett-Packard font cartridges. Headlines in a Cartridge provides 18 proportionally spaced display fonts, 14 to 18 points in size, in both Times Roman and Helvetica bold and italics.

PacificPage cartridges provide complete PostScript language emulation for LaserJet printers, offering 35 scalable fonts and graphics capabilities. Plotter in a Cartridge emulates Hewlett-Packard graphics plotters, letting laser printers output high-resolution graphics faster than pen plotters can.

Upgradable memory boards include the 1-2-4 Plus for LaserJet II and IID printers; the 2 Plus 2, which allows the addition of 1 to 4 megabytes of memory to Laserjet IIP printers; and the sqmsLP memory board for IBM printers, available in 1-, 2- or 3.5-megabyte configurations.

QMS, One Magnus Pass, Mobile, AL 36618. 205-633-4300.

QMS JetScript is a hardware/software upgrade that lets Hewlett-Packard LaserJet Series II owners add PostScript capability to their printer. JetScript consists of printed circuit boards to be added to your printer and to your computer, plus appropriate software.

The primary advantage of JetScript is that it lets LaserJet Series II owners make laser proofs of documents that will later be phototypeset on a Linotronic 100 or 300. Installation doesn't void Hewlett-Packard's warranty and, once installed, the LaserJet can be used as either an HP PCL printer or a PostScript printer.

Softcraft, Inc., 16 North Carroll Street, Suite 500, Madison, WI 53703. 608-257-3300.

Softcraft publishes several programs which, when used in conjunction with Bitstream's bit-mapped fonts, make many PostScript features accessible to users of HP-compatible printers.

Softcraft's Font Effects program, for example, lets you add special effects such as shadows, outlines, striped interiors and shaded backgrounds. You also can slant, enlarge, reduce, embolden or lighten a font—creative powers that were previously unavailable on HP-compatible printers.

The Softcraft Font Editor lets you create your own typefaces for special purposes such as logos or headline effects.

Symsoft, Inc., 444 First Street, Suite K, Los Altos, CA 94022. 415-941-1552.

Symsoft's HotShot Plus and HotShot Graphics are two utility programs that will be of special interest to anyone using WordPerfect to create computer or software documentation.

HotShot Plus is a memory-resident screen capture program that can save any text or graphics appearing on the screen of your computer to a file that can be placed in a WordPerfect document. HotShot Graphics is an editing program that lets you modify screen capture images and organize them into easily accessed "picture databases."

T/Maker Company, 1973 Landings Drive, Mountain View, CA 94043. 415-962-0195.

T/Maker publishes several packages of ClickArt pre-drawn illustrations that can be easily imported to newsletters or other projects. One of its most useful packages is Business Images, which includes more than 1,000 industrial and business symbols and borders, including drawings of office equipment and supplies.

T/Maker's newest addition is a series of high-quality EPS illustrations in the form of encapsulated PostScript file images. You can increase or decrease them in size without loss of quality. Included are country/state maps, as well as frequently used symbols such as credit cards, male/female symbols and drawings with seasonal themes. An illustrated index helps you quickly locate any desired image.

Zsoft Corporation, 450 Franklin Road, Suite 100, Marietta, GA 30067. 404-428-0008.

Zsoft's PC Paintbrush is one of the most powerful drawing programs available for MS-DOS computers. It gives virtually unlimited flexibility to manipulating text and graphics, including the creation of color images from black and white scanned images. Its zoom-out editing feature helps you keep track of the "big picture" as you create detailed drawings.

If you're working in the Microsoft Windows environment, Zsoft's Publisher's Type Foundry lets you create your own typeface, starting with a typeface on paper or soft fonts.

BIBLIOGRAPHY

BOOKS

Adobe Systems, Inc. *PostScript Language Tutorial and Cookbook*. Reading, MA: Addison-Wesley, 1986.

Desktop publishing is based on the PostScript programming language. This book and the one that follows are essential to any desktop publisher seeking an advanced understanding of PostScript and the hardware and software that use it.

Adobe Systems, Inc. *PostScript Language Reference Manual*. Reading, MA: Addison-Wesley, 1986.

A companion volume, organized for easy access.

Adobe Systems, Inc. *The Adobe Type Catalog*. Palo Alto, CA: Adobe Systems, 1987.

When you want to move beyond the typefaces built into your laser printer, this book shows which typefaces are available as downloadable fonts. Each typeface is illustrated, along with suggested applications.

Bly, Robert W. *Create the Perfect Sales Piece: A Do-It-Yourself Guide to Producing Brochures, Catalogs, Flyers and Pamphlets*. New York: John Wiley & Sons, 1987.

This book guides entrepreneurs and executives with new responsibilities through the process of planning, copywriting and designing an effective print communication. Places a great deal of emphasis on advance planning and scheduling.

Burke, Clifford. *Type from the Desktop: Designing with Type and Your Computer.* Chapel Hill, NC: Ventana Press, 1990.

A thought-provoking exploration into the world of typography and design. Filled with type examples, this book explores the history, functions and aesthetics of type.

Gedney, Karen, and Fultz, Patrick. *The Complete Guide to Creating Successful Brochures.* Westbury, NY: Asher-Gallant, 1988.

Combines a marketing approach with good advice on design. Topics include post-production, printing and scheduling issues.

Hurlburt, Allen. *Publication Design: A Guide to Page Layout, Typography, Format and Style.* New York: Van Nostrand Reinhold, 1971.

Written for graphics professionals, this book discusses the underlying issues behind the design of major magazines.

Hurlburt, Allen. *The Grid.* New York: Van Nostrand Reinhold, 1978.

Illustrates how grids can be used in developing page layouts for newspapers, magazines and books.

Makuta, Daniel J., and Lawrence, William F. *The Complete Desktop Publisher.* Greensboro, NC: Compute Publications, 1986.

An informed overview of the field, this book emphasizes function rather than specific hardware or software.

Middleton, Tony. *A Desktop Publisher's Guide to Pasteup: A Do-It-Yourself Guide to Preparing Camera-ready Pasteups and Mechanicals.* Colorado Springs, CO: Plusware, 1987.

Provides a practical answer to the question, "What do you do with the pages that come out of your laser printer?" Describes the tools needed to prepare paste-ups and how to use them. Also explains how to choose the right commercial printers for your job and how to work with them.

Mitchell, Joan P. *The New Writer: Techniques for Writing Well with a Computer.* Redmond, WA: Microsoft Press, 1987.

Shows you how to prepare better publications by making the most of the computer's ability to help you quickly organize, edit and rewrite.

Nace, Ted, and Gardner, Michael. *LaserJet Unlimited: Edition II*. Berkeley, CA: Peachpit Press, 1988.

A comprehensive guide to using Hewlett-Packard LaserJet printers. Compares the performance of the various LaserJet models; suggests ways to maximize performance of both popular and hard-to-find software programs with the LaserJet; describes how to upgrade your LaserJet; and surveys available LaserJet font resources.

Nelson, Roy Paul. *The Design of Advertising*. Fifth edition. Dubuque, IA: William C. Brown Company, 1985.

A classic college text, this book succeeds because of its numerous examples and "hands-on" conversational style. Fourteen of its 16 chapters are devoted to print advertising.

Nelson, Roy Paul. *Publication Design*. Dubuque, IA: William C. Brown Company, 1984.

This companion volume concentrates on magazine, newspaper and newsletter design, although Chapter 11, "Miscellaneous Publications," also describes brochures and direct mail.

New York Art Directors Club. *The One Show*. New York: Watson-Guptill Publications, 1989.

A one-stop source for viewing the nation's finest advertising. Each year, the nation's leading art directors submit their best work to a jury of their peers; this book includes the entries in each category and showcases the winners. Because of its inspirational value, this book is an important addition to your collection.

Parker, Roger C. *The Makeover Book: 101 Design Solutions for Desktop Publishing*. Chapel Hill, NC: Ventana Press, 1989.

Contains "before" and "after" examples of how you can put basic design tools to work to make your documents more attractive and persuasive. Each example is accompanied by invaluable tips and techniques for creating better-looking newsletters, ads, brochures, flyers, letterhead, charts and graphs.

Seybold, John, and Dressler, Fritz. *Publishing from the Desktop*. New York: Bantam Books, 1987.

A technical overview of the various aspects of typography and typesetting, with an emphasis on how the various imaging systems differ. Separate chapters cover image scanners and modifying line art and halftones.

Sitarz, Daniel. *The Desktop Publisher's Legal Handbook: A Comprehensive Guide to Computer Publishing Law*. Carbondale, IL: Nova Publishing, 1989.

Explores legal issues involved in establishing a desktop publishing service business, to help you avoid libel and defamation problems. Contains sample client contracts and copyright registration forms.

Strunk, William, Jr., and White, E.B. *The Elements of Style*. Third edition. New York: Macmillan, 1979.

Short, entertaining and extremely focused, this classic deserves its reputation, earned over almost three-quarters of a century, as an indispensable writer's reference.

Swann, Alan. *How To Understand and Use Design and Layout*. Cincinnati, OH: North Light Publishers, 1987.

This handsomely illustrated volume does an excellent job of balancing theory and practical example. Numerous rough layouts illustrate various formats and ways of placing type on a page. Four-color photographs of printed publications show these concepts translated into reality.

University of Chicago. *A Manual of Style* Thirteenth edition. Chicago, IL: The University of Chicago Press, 1982.

Keep this book next to your computer. Its tightly packed, 700-plus pages provide the answers to questions asked by the most conscientious editor, publisher or copywriter. It describes the proper way to handle punctuation, illustrations, quotations and abbreviations as well as design and typography.

White, Jan V. *Editing by Design: A Guide to Effective Word-and-Picture Communication for Editors and Designers*. Second edition. New York: R.R. Bowker, 1982.

Still one of the most valuable resources available to desktop publishers on using graphic design as a tool of communication rather than adornment or decoration. Highly readable; full of interesting examples.

White, Jan V. *Mastering Graphics: Design and Production Made Easy*. New York: R.R. Bowker, 1983.

Elaborates on the ideas first expressed in *Editing by Design*. Although written in pre-desktop-publishing days, it includes numerous do-it-yourself applications examples. It's hard not to be excited or motivated by the way the illustrations relate theory to reality.

Zinsser, William. *On Writing Well*. New York: Harper & Row, 1987.

An excellent contemporary guide to effective writing. Will help newsletter editors develop their inherent abilities and learn to write as clearly and concisely as possible.

Zinsser, William. *Writing with a Word Processor*. New York: Harper & Row, 1983.

Required reading for any typewriter-oriented person who needs help making the transition to preparing copy with a word processor. Warm, friendly and useful.

PUBLICATIONS

Before & After: How To Design Cool Stuff on Your Computer, PageLab, 331 J St., Ste. 150, Sacramento, CA 95814. *Monthly*.

A testament to the vision and talents of John McWade, one of the country's first—and, still, most influential—desktop designers. The emphasis is on design excellence, with an informative, how-you-can-achieve-these-results, tutorial approach.

Communication Arts, Coyne & Blanchard, 410 Sherman Ave., Palo Alto, CA 94303. *Eight issues/year.*

This magazine is best known for its special focus issues, which showcase the year's best design entries in various categories, including advertising, illustration, design and photography.

Font & Function: The Adobe Type Catalog, Adobe Systems, P.O. Box 7900, Mountain View, CA 94039-7900. *Thrice yearly.*

A quarterly publication describing the latest Adobe fonts and reviewing old favorites; also presents interviews with typeface users and designers. If you use a PostScript laser printer, you owe it to yourself to request a free subscription to *Font & Function*.

In-House Graphics, United Communications, 4550 Montgomery Ave., Ste. 700N, Bethesda, MD 20814. *Monthly.*

An advertising-free publication containing a healthy and pragmatic mix of newsletter design and content articles that extend beyond the desktop to the commercial printing environment.

ITC Desktop, International Typeface Corp., 2 Hammarskjold Plaza, New York, NY 10017. *Bimonthly.*

Approaches desktop publishing from a design more than a hardware/ software applications standpoint.

Newsletter Design, The Newsletter Clearinghouse, 44 West Market St., P.O. Box 311, Rhinebeck, NY 12572. *Bimonthly.*

A great source of design inspiration; shows sample pages of all types of newsletters with commentary on what makes them succeed, along with suggestions for improvement.

PC Computing, Ziff-Davis, 4 Cambridge Ctr., 9th Flr., Cambridge, MA 02142. *Monthly.*

Balances coverage of the latest hardware and software with articles of general interest to any reader, regardless of which hardware or software they use. Frequently discusses desktop publishing issues.

PC Publishing, Hunter Publishing Co., 950 Lee St., Des Plaines, IL 60016. *Monthly.*

Produced entirely using desktop publishing techniques, this publication features news about the latest hardware and software advances, as well as tips and tricks for the novice.

Personal Publishing, Hitchcock Publishing Co., 25W550 Geneva Rd., Wheaton, IL 60188. *Monthly.*

Balanced treatment of both Macintosh and MS-DOS desktop publishing issues. The monthly software "Updates" feature alone is worth the price of a subscription.

Print: America's Graphic Design Magazine, RC Publications, Inc., 6400 Goldsboro Rd., Bethesda, MD 20817. *Bimonthly.*

Covers the techniques and economics of professional graphic design, keeping an eye on advances in desktop publishing. Its yearly regional design and advertising design issues, as well as its book club selections, make it well worth the subscription price.

Publish! PCW Communications, 501 Second St., San Francisco, CA 94107. *Monthly.*

Combines in-depth treatment of the latest hardware and software issues with helpful design- and technique-oriented articles. Of special interest is its monthly typography column.

Step-by-Step Electronic Design: The How-To Newsletter for Desktop Designers. Dynamic Graphics, 6000 North Forest Park Dr., P.O. Box 1901, Peoria, IL 61656. *Monthly.*

This advertising-free, technique-oriented publication is geared to help advanced desktop publishers and others who aspire to greater proficiency in layout and design.

The Weigand Report: The Working Newsletter for Desktop Publishers, Rae Productions International, P.O. Box 647, Gales Ferry, CT 06335. *Eight issues/year.*

The subtitle accurately describes its function: unbiased reporting and analysis on the ever-changing hardware/software, image-scanning and commercial printing scenes, among other timely issues.

U&lc, International Typeface Corp., 2 Hammarskjold Plaza, New York, NY 10017. *Bimonthly.*

An inspiring large-format tabloid, containing features by many of the world's leading graphic and typeface designers; balances a historical, intellectual perspective with down-to-earth treatment of contemporary issues.

WordPerfect: The Magazine, WordPerfect Publishing Corp., 1555 North Technology Way, Orem, UT 84057. *Monthly.*

Useful tips, techniques and features on WordPerfect as a page layout program. Includes reviews of basic formatting commands and features that describe how to integrate WordPerfect with other software.

RESOURCE LIST

ASSOCIATIONS, USERS' GROUPS AND WORKSHOPS

Dynamic Graphics & Education Foundation
6000 North Forest Park Dr.
P.O. Box 1901
Peoria, IL 61656-1901

Workshops on designing for desktop publishing, basic layout and pasteup, typography in design, publication design and more.

Electronic Directions
21 East Fourth St.
New York, NY 10003

Software-specific courses and seminars on Ventura Publisher, PC Pagemaker, using Ready, Set, Go!, using Quark Xpress, using Adobe Illustrator, PostScript for designers and more.

National Association of Desktop Publishers
P.O. Box 508, Kenmore Station
Boston, MA 02215-9998

Performance Seminar Group
204 Strawberry Hill Ave.
Norwalk, CT 06851

Seminars on "Designing Effective Newsletters," "How to Write and Design Sales Literature" and more.

Promotional Perspectives
1955 Pauline Blvd., Ste. 100A
Ann Arbor, MI 48103

Seminars on editing, design and production for desktop publishing. Participants receive an unusually complete set of working tools and handout materials.

Seybold Seminars
6922 Wildlife Rd.
P.O. Box 578
Malibu, CA 90265
(March and September)

WordPerfect Support Group
P.O. Box 1577
Baltimore, MD 21203

GLOSSARY

A

Alignment

The placement of type on a page or in a column. Includes flush-left, flush-right, justified and centered.

Anchoring

Linking an imported graphic to a specific location on a specific page; or linking it to adjacent text, in which case a graphic moves with the text if preceding text is added or removed.

Attribute

Type style or variation within a typeface. Includes bold and italic.

B

Bars

Thick rules—or lines—often used horizontally to separate articles within columns, or the banner from front-page headlines, or to emphasize pull-quotes or visuals.

Baseline

The invisible line upon which a line of type rests.

Base Font

Type specifications that remain the same for a particular document, no matter what type of printer you use. (See also *Font*.)

Byline

Author credit line placed at the beginning or end of an article. Bylines sometimes include the author's title, department or location.

C

Caption

A phrase or sentence that identifies the content of graphics such as charts, graphs or photographs.

Clip art

Previously created illustrations, available as either line art or on disk. Line art can be scanned in or reduced to size by photographic techniques.

Clipboard

A temporary file, used to copy or move text or graphics from one part of your publication to another. Clipboard also lets you share text and graphics between different programs (e.g., WordPerfect and a page layout program) without storing the file.

Color separation

An overlay, or separate layer of a primary color, of an image. Together, separate overlays create four-color images. Many desktop publishing programs let you create separations.

Concordance file

A computer file that simplifies and expedites creating an index, used when a word or phrase appears frequently in a document.

Contrast

The range of black to white tones in a scanned photograph. A low-contrast photo has relatively light blacks and relatively gray whites. A high-contrast photo ranges from full black to full white.

Copy

The text of articles.

Copyfitting

Writing to fit available space. Copyfitting is made easier by "nonsense" files, which are used to determine article length before the story is written. (See also *Nonsense file*.)

Crop mark

Printer mark that brackets the part of a photograph or illustration to be reproduced, which determines its printed size. Crop marks are often placed on tissue paper covering the photograph or illustration.

Cropping

Cutting or manipulating photographs and drawings to eliminate distracting details along the top, bottom or sides. Cropped visuals remain square or rectangular.

Cursor

A blinking rectangle or underscore mark on a computer screen, indicating the position where text or graphics may be entered or edited.

Cursor advance

A command in many word processing programs that lets you use keyboard commands instead of a mouse to position text and graphics. You can move the cursor up, down, left and right by specifying the distance to be moved in inches or points and picas. (See also *Mouse*.)

D

Default

Automatic format setting used by a word processing or desktop publishing program, unless the user changes it. For example, most word processing and desktop publishing programs automatically set line spacing for 12-point type at approximately 14 points. Most programs also let you set up your own custom default files.

Dingbat

A symbol such as a bullet, small box, pointing hand, map symbol or copyright notice. It can be used to emphasize lists, ballot boxes (for forms and surveys) or the end of an article, among other things.

Discretionary hyphen

Used in words such as proper nouns that must be divided in a specific way if they break at the end of a line. Discretionary hyphens allow you to override your software program's built-in hyphenation feature. (See also *Hard hyphen*.)

Dot leaders

Row of periods, often used as a replacement for vertical downrules. (See also *Downrule*.)

Downloadable font

Typeface alphabets and numbers stored on your computer's hard disk that you can transfer to your printer when you need them. (See also *Font cartridge*.)

Downrule

Vertical line used to separate adjacent columns of type. Downrules often are most effective with justified columns in which word spacing is adjusted to achieve lines of equal length.

Drop

White space added to the top of a page, above the columns of type. A drop can add consistency to a newsletter's design and emphasize headlines or visuals. (See also *Sink*.)

Drop cap

Oversized initial capital letter, used to highlight the beginning of a paragraph. It is usually the same height as the tops of ascenders and uppercase letters in the first line of type. (See also *Initial cap* and *Raised cap*.)

Drop shadow

Also called a shadow box, a graphics technique that creates a three-dimensional effect on a page. It involves copying the outline of a box, shading it black, and placing it behind the original image, offset slightly below and to one side.

E

Ellipsis

A three- or four-dot punctuation mark that represents omitted text.

Em dash

A dash used in typeset text to introduce a subordinate phrase. Often expressed as two hyphens in word-processed manuscript copy, an em dash equals the width of a square of the type size, usually an uppercase M.

Em space

A horizontal measure equal in size to a square of the type size, usually an uppercase M. The first line of a new paragraph is often indented one or two em spaces.

En dash

A dash used in typeset text, usually to indicate continuing or inclusive numbers, or in place of a hyphen in a compound adjective that has one element hyphenated. An en dash is equal in width to an uppercase N.

Endnotes

Notes of comment, explanation or citation, appearing at the end of a document. Endnotes are linked to the words or phrases to which they apply by a matching-numbering scheme.

F

Folio

Information that identifies an issue, usually by date, volume and issue number. The folio is generally placed next to the nameplate.

Font

The full alphabet, number and symbol set for a particular version of a typeface. Separate fonts produce bold, italic and bold-italic versions, as well as weight variations of a typeface. Font can also refer to a single type size.

Font cartridge

A plug-in circuit board containing one or more fonts. Font cartridges are cheaper, easier to install and quicker to access than downloadable fonts, but they offer limited typeface and type size options. (See also *Downloadable font*.)

Footnotes

Notes of comment, explanation or citation, appearing at the bottom of the page or table to which they apply. They are usually set in smaller type than the text on which they comment.

Footers

Information appearing at the bottom of each page of a document, such as a date or page number.

Formatting

Choosing consistent typeface, type size, style, margins, line spacing, alignment and indents for each category of type (e.g., headlines, subheads, body copy) in a word-processed file.

G

Graphics monitor

A computer screen that shows text and graphics as they'll appear when a page is printed. (See also *Text monitor*.)

Greeking

Creating files of randomly chosen words forming sentences and paragraphs of varying size, for use in preliminary page design. Greeking also refers to the way that many software programs convert small-size type on a computer screen to rows of symbols, which speeds up screen redraws.

Grid

A matrix of nonprinting vertical and horizontal lines that guide the placement of text and graphics on the page.

Gutter

The vertical space between columns of type. Gutter width should be proportional to typeface, type size and alignment. In two-page spreads, gutter also refers to the space between the right column of the left-hand page and the left column of the right-hand page.

H

Hard hyphen

A special command that prevents awkward hyphenation at line endings. (See also *Discretionary hyphen.*)

Headers

Information appearing at the top of each page of a document, such as a book's title, chapter title and page number.

High-resolution output

Newsletter artwork prepared by image setters, usually phototypesetters, operating at more than 1,200-dot-per-inch resolution. (See also *Low-resolution output.*)

Hyphenation

Breaking a word or compound after a syllable and placing the remainder on the next line.

I

Image scanner

A hardware accessory that converts a glossy photograph into an electronic file, which can be manipulated and placed in a newsletter created with a word processing or page layout program.

Indent

Moving a line of type to the right to indicate the start of a new paragraph or list. Both right- and left-hand indents can be used to adjust the margins of text placed in a box, such as a sidebar or masthead.

Initial cap

An oversized first letter of the first word in an article. Initial caps can be dropped into the copy. (See also *Drop cap* and *Raised cap.*)

Inkjet printers

Printers such as the Hewlett-Packard DeskJet and DeskWriter, which offer much of the quality and flexibility of laser printers at far less cost.

J

Jumpline

A phrase used when an article continues on a following page (e.g., "Continued on page 5," "Continued from page 1," etc.).

Justified text

Copy set flush-left/flush-right in lines of equal length. Copy is justified by increasing or decreasing word spacing within each line.

K

Kerning

Increasing or decreasing letter spacing to improve appearance and readability. (See also *Kerning pairs* and *Tracking*.)

Kerning pairs

Predefined pairs of letters in a particular typeface and size, for which custom letter spacing is specified in advance. Several page layout programs automatically substitute desired letter spacing when these letter pairs are encountered.

Keyboard shortcut

A way to highlight text or quickly access frequently used commands without using a mouse. Often combines COMMAND, CONTROL, SHIFT, ALT or OPTION keys with selected function keys or any other keys. (See *Mouse*.)

Kicker

Descriptive phrase appearing above a headline, intended to stimulate interest in the article it accompanies.

L

Landscape orientation

Type is printed across the 11-inch direction of an 8 1/2- by 11-inch sheet of paper turned sideways to give it a horizontal orientation. Landscape monitors are wider than they are tall and typically display two 8 1/2- by 11-inch pages side by side.

Laser printer

A printer that creates text and graphic images from a grid of 300 dots or more per inch. Similar in operation to photocopiers, laser printers use high heat to bond toner to sheets of paper. High-resolution laser printers operate at 400 to 600 dots per inch.

Leading

Vertical spacing between lines of type. Leading is typically measured from the baseline of one line to the baseline of the next line.

Letter spacing

Adjusting (sometimes adding) space between letters. While some letter combinations need to be tightened, others need to be slightly separated to improve readability and appearance.

Line spacing

See *Leading*.

Linotronic

Popular high-resolution desktop publishing equipment manufactured by the Linotronic Corp. Linotronic image-setters produce camera-ready pages at 1,270 or 2,540 dots per inch. (See also *Phototypesetter*.)

Logo

Your firm or association's name, set in a distinctive typeface, size and style. A logo is often set against a distinct background and accented by horizontal rules and/or other graphic devices.

Low-resolution output

Usually refers to camera-ready artwork prepared with a 300-dots-per-inch laser printer. (See also *High-resolution output*.)

M

Macro

Short computer program of previously stored command sequences. Macros can provide word processing programs with much of the power typically found in page layout programs. (See also *Style*.)

Masthead

The block of information printed in a newsletter that lists staff, publisher's address and subscription information.

Mnemonics

Letters that represent words. For example, the WordPerfect GRAPHICS command Option 1 (HORIZONTAL LINE) can be chosen if you simply enter H for HORIZONTAL.

Mouse

A hand-held device that lets the computer user quickly locate and execute commands and move the cursor to any point on the computer screen. (See also *Keyboard shortcut*.)

N

Nameplate

The title of a newsletter that appears in the same distinctive typeface, size and style in every issue.

Newspaper columns

Text continues from the bottom of one column to the top of the next. Often referred to as "snaking" columns.

Nonsense file

A word-processed file of random letters and syllables that contains the same number of words, sentences and paragraphs found in a typical newsletter article. Nonsense files can be used to try various layouts without using actual text. (See also *Copyfitting*.)

O

Orphan

Less than one-third of a line carried over from the end of one column or page and left isolated at the top of the next. (See also *Widow*.)

P

Paint program

A software program that stores files as collections of dots. Paint-type files can contain numerous levels of gray, but should be produced and reproduced at approximately the same size.

Paragraph spacing

The amount of space between paragraphs. WordPerfect lets you adjust this with the FORMAT command.

PCL

(Printer Command Language) A Hewlett-Packard software protocol that defines how computers exchange information with LaserJet printers.

Phototypesetter

A high-quality output device that creates text and graphics by exposing light-sensitive film at either 1,270 or 2,540 dots per inch. (See also *Linotronic.*)

Pixel

A tiny dot of light that forms the image of a character or picture on a computer monitor. Resolution quality depends on the number of pixels that make up the screen display.

Portrait orientation

Type set on the 8 1/2-inch dimension of an 8 1/2- by 11-inch page. Also refers to vertical monitors that typically display a single page at or near actual size.

PostScript

Adobe's PostScript Page Description Language, which stores text and graphics as lines and arcs that can be filled with a variety of different backgrounds. PostScript files can be previewed on laser printers and later typeset without change on high-resolution typesetters.

Proof

A preliminary printout of your document. Proofs let you make last-minute refinements and check for typographical errors.

Pull-quote

A short phrase or sentence extracted from an adjacent article. A pull-quote can make page design more interesting and spark reader interest in an article.

R

Raised cap

An initial capital letter that extends into the white space above a paragraph. Raised caps add visual interest by adding extra white space to a page. (See also *Drop cap* and *Initial cap*.)

Replace

A command that lets you search for text or formatting commands, and automatically replace them with others. For example, you can quickly replace underlined type with italicized type or abbreviations with spelled-out words, or you can substitute single spaces for double spaces at the ends of sentences. (See also *Search*.)

Resident font

Typeface built into a printer. Times Roman and Helvetica are resident in most PostScript printers. Courier, a typewriter-like font, is often found in non-PostScript laser printers.

Resizing

Increasing or decreasing the size of a graphics file. Proportional resizing maintains the proportions of the original file.

Resolution

The level of detail that an output device can provide. Laser printers, for example, are capable of 300-dot-per-inch resolution. In photography, resolution refers to lines per inch in an electronically reproduced photograph.

Reverse

Text or graphics printed in white against a black background.

Rotation

Text rotated 90 degrees, extending vertically up a page. Text rotation is usually reserved for special effects, such as text set at a 45-degree angle at the upper right-hand corner of the cover page.

Rule

Horizonal or vertical lines used in various thicknesses as borders and separators (e.g., to define adjacent columns of text or articles within a column).

S

Sans-serif

One of the two primary families of typeface design. Sans-serif type lacks serifs—decorative strokes at the end of letters that provide letter-to-letter transition. (See also *Serifs*.)

Scaling

Re-sizing photographs or imported graphics to fit your page layout.

Screen

A shade of gray used for text backgrounds or graphics. Black is 100 percent screening; white is 0 percent. Screening is also the process of breaking up a photograph into dots of black or white for easier printing.

Search

A function that automatically searches the text for specific words or typographic formatting commands and, with the Replace command, automatically modifies or deletes them. (See also *Replace*.)

Serifs

Tiny feet that project from the main strokes of typeface characters. Serifs make a block of text easier to read by providing letter-to-letter transition. (See also *Sans-serif*.)

Sidebar

A short article within an article, usually set off by a box or a screened background.

Sink

A consistent amount of white space between the top of a page and the start of each column of text. (See also *Drop*.)

Small caps

Uppercase letters, set approximately 20 percent smaller than normal, used for emphasis in a headline or text to avoid darkening a page with boldface type.

Soft font

Typeface stored on your hard disk that can be downloaded to a printer as needed.

Spot color

Color applied to isolated graphic accents, such as bars or vertical downrules, or to individual text blocks, headlines or pull-quotes.

Spread

Facing left- and right-hand pages.

Standing head

Distinctive headline that introduces a department or feature repeated in every issue.

Stress

The proportional variation between the thick and thin strokes of a letter. Some typefaces have little or no stress; others are characterized by extreme stress.

Stroke

The thickness of the letters. Some typefaces are available with variations in stroke thickness, ranging from Light (thin) to Black or Heavy (thick). Stroke thickness can also vary within individual letters. (See also *Stress.*)

Style

Electronic file that stores typeface, size, style, letter spacing, alignment, indent and other information. Styles help you maintain consistency and quickly format or reformat your document. (See also *Macro.*)

T

Table

Information, often numerical, displayed in rows and columns within a ruled box. Tables communicate a lot of information at a glance, but require careful alignment of characters.

Table of contents

A listing of articles in a newsletter and the page number where each begins. Newsletters of eight or more pages should contain a front-page table of contents that directs readers' attention to articles inside.

Template

An empty page layout file containing formatting instructions for newsletter copy. Templates can contain a previously created and precisely positioned nameplate and masthead, as well as defined positions for columns of text.

Text monitor

A monitor that displays all letters and numbers in characters of equal size on the computer screen. A text monitor isn't as suitable for desktop publishing applications as is a graphics monitor, since it can't show different typefaces, type sizes or graphic elements. Nor can it preview the appearance of finished pages. (See also *Graphics monitor*.)

Thumbnail

A small, hand-drawn view of a newsletter page. Thumbnails can also be created with PostScript laser printers; you can preview up to 16 pages of a newsletter at reduced size on a single 8 1/2- by 11-inch page.

Tint

A shade of gray used as a background for text or graphics that need to be emphasized.

Tracking

Uniformly increasing or reducing spacing between all characters in a headline or text block. Tightening up letter spacing increases word density; opening up letter spacing improves readability. (See also *Kerning*.)

Trim size

The final size of a printed newsletter page. If the newsletter contains bleeds, the trim size will be smaller than the paper the newsletter was originally printed on, allowing space to trim off the gripper area of the printing press.

Typeface

A particular design interpretation of the letters of the alphabet, numerals and other character symbols.

Type style

Manipulated typeface weight and angle, used to emphasize key words. Boldface, italic and bold italic are common type styles.

Type weight

A typeface's degree of thickness. Heavy, or black, versions of a typeface have thick horizontal and vertical strokes. Light weights have thinner strokes than medium—the face normally used for body copy.

W

Widow

A portion of a word, a single word or less than a third of a line at the end of a page or column of type. (See also *Orphan*.)

Word spacing

The space between words in a heading or text. It affects readability and visual appeal. When justified, WordPerfect subtly adds or reduces word spacing within the lines.

Wraparound

Lines of varying length that flow around an illustration or silhouetted photograph that extends into an adjacent column of type.

WYSIWYG

A slightly overworked acronym for "What You See Is What You Get." It refers to the ability to see text and graphics on your computer screen the same way they'll appear when the page is printed.

INDEX

A

B

C

D

E

F

G

H

I

J

K

L

N

O

P

Q

R

S

T

Looking Good in Print
(100,000 in print!)
$23.95
230 pages, Illustrated
ISBN: 0-940087-05-7

The most widely used reference book for desktop design offers dozens of tips and tricks that help you add style and appeal to your documents. For use with any hardware and software.

Desktop Publishing with WordPerfect — Windows Edition
$21.95
350 pages, Illustrated
ISBN: 0-940087-76-6

Filled with helpful design advice and examples, this book explores the desktop publishing potential of the new Windows version of the world's leading word processing package. Desktop design guru Roger Parker offers readers a thorough overview of the software's features.

Newsletters from the Desktop
$23.95
290 pages, Illustrated
ISBN: 0-940087-40-5

Now the millions of desktop publishers who produce newsletters can learn how to improve the design of their publications.

The Makeover Book: 101 Design Solutions for Desktop Publishing
$17.95
245 pages, Illustrated
ISBN: 0-940087-20-0

"Before-and-after" desktop publishing examples demonstrate how basic design revisions can dramatically improve a document.

The Gray Book
$22.95
224 pages, Illustrated
ISBN: 0-940087-50-2

This "idea gallery" is filled with tips, techniques and visual cues for creating the most interesting black, white and gray graphic effects from laser printers, scanners and high-resolution output devices.

Type from the Desktop
$23.95
290 pages, Illustrated
ISBN: 0-940087-45-6

Learn the basics of designing with type from a desktop publisher's perspective.

The Presentation Design Book
$24.95
280 pages, Illustrated
ISBN: 0-940087-37-5

How to design effective, attractive slides, overheads, graphs, diagrams, handouts and screen shows with your desktop computer.

TO ORDER additional copies of *Desktop Publishing With WordPerfect* or any of the other books in our desktop design series, please fill out this order form and return it to us for quick shipment.

	Quantity		Price		Total
Desktop Publishing With WordPerfect	______	×	$21.95	=	______
Type From the Desktop	______	×	$23.95	=	$______
The Presentation Design Book	______	×	$24.95	=	$______
Newsletters From the Desktop	______	×	$23.95	=	$______
Looking Good in Print	______	×	$23.95	=	$______
The Makeover Book	______	×	$17.95	=	$______
The Gray Book	______	×	$22.95	=	$______
Desktop Publishing With WordPerfect—Windows Edition	______	×	$21.95	=	$______

Shipping: Please add $4.10/first book for standard UPS, $1.35/book thereafter; $7.50/first book for UPS "two-day air," $2.25/book thereafter. For Canada, add $8.10/book. = $______

Send C.O.D. (add $3.75 to shipping charges) = $______

North Carolina residents add 6% sales tax = $______

Total = $______

Name ______________________________

Company ______________________________

Address (No P.O. Box) ______________________________

City ______________________ State ______ Zip ______________

Daytime Phone ______________________________

______ Payment enclosed (check or money order; no cash please)

____VISA ____MC Acc't # ______ - ______ - ______ - ______

Expiration date ______ Signature ______________________________

Please mail or fax to:

Ventana Press, P.O. Box 2468, Chapel Hill, NC 27515

919/942-0220, FAX: 919/942-1140

TO ORDER additional copies of *Desktop Publishing With WordPerfect* or any of the other books in our desktop design series, please fill out this order form and return it to us for quick shipment.

	Quantity		Price		Total
Desktop Publishing With WordPerfect	________	×	$21.95	=	________
Type From the Desktop	________	×	$23.95	=	$________
The Presentation Design Book	________	×	$24.95	=	$________
Newsletters From the Desktop	________	×	$23.95	=	$________
Looking Good in Print	________	×	$23.95	=	$________
The Makeover Book	________	×	$17.95	=	$________
The Gray Book	________	×	$22.95	=	$________
Desktop Publishing With WordPerfect—Windows Edition	________	×	$21.95	=	$________

Shipping: Please add $4.10/first book for standard UPS, $1.35/book thereafter; $7.50/first book for UPS "two-day air," $2.25/book thereafter. For Canada, add $8.10/book. = $________

Send C.O.D. (add $3.75 to shipping charges) = $________

North Carolina residents add 6% sales tax = $________

Total = $________

Name ____

Company ____

Address (No P.O. Box) ____

City ______________________________ State ________ Zip ______________

Daytime Phone ____

__________ Payment enclosed (check or money order; no cash please)

____VISA ____ MC Acc't # ________ - ________ - ________ - ________

Expiration date __________ Signature ______________________________

Please mail or fax to:

Ventana Press, P.O. Box 2468, Chapel Hill, NC 27515

919/942-0220, FAX: 919/942-1140

TO ORDER additional copies of *Desktop Publishing With WordPerfect* or any of the other books in our desktop design series, please fill out this order form and return it to us for quick shipment.

	Quantity		Price		Total
Desktop Publishing With WordPerfect	________	×	$21.95	=	________
Type From the Desktop	________	×	$23.95	=	$________
The Presentation Design Book	________	×	$24.95	=	$________
Newsletters From the Desktop	________	×	$23.95	=	$________
Looking Good in Print	________	×	$23.95	=	$________
The Makeover Book	________	×	$17.95	=	$________
The Gray Book	________	×	$22.95	=	$________
Desktop Publishing With WordPerfect—Windows Edition	________	×	$21.95	=	$________

Shipping: Please add $4.10/first book for standard UPS, $1.35/book thereafter; $7.50/first book for UPS "two-day air," $2.25/book thereafter. For Canada, add $8.10/book. = $________

Send C.O.D. (add $3.75 to shipping charges) = $________

North Carolina residents add 6% sales tax = $________

Total = $________

Name ____

Company ____

Address (No P.O. Box) ____

City ______________________________ State ________ Zip ____________

Daytime Phone ____

__________ Payment enclosed (check or money order; no cash please)

_____VISA _____ MC Acc't # ________ - ________ - ________ - ________

Expiration date __________ Signature ______________________________

Please mail or fax to:

Ventana Press, P.O. Box 2468, Chapel Hill, NC 27515

919/942-0220, FAX: 919/942-1140

MORE ABOUT VENTANA PRESS BOOKS . . .

If you would like to be added to our mailing list, please complete the card below and indicate your areas of interest. We will keep you up-to-date on new books as they're published.

_____Yes! I'd like to receive more information about Ventana Press books. Please add me to your mailing list.

Name ____

Company ____

Street address (no P.O. box) ______________________________

City ______________________ State __________ Zip ________

Please check areas of interest below:

______	AutoCAD	______	Newsletter publishing
______	Desktop publishing	______	Networking
______	Desktop design	______	Facsimile
______	Presentation graphics	______	Business software

Return to: Ventana Press, P.O. Box 2468, Chapel Hill, NC 27515, 919/942-0220, FAX 919/942-1140. (Please don't duplicate your fax requests by mail.)

NO POSTAGE
NECESSARY
IF MAILED
IN THE
UNITED STATES

BUSINESS REPLY MAIL
FIRST CLASS PERMIT #495 CHAPEL HILL, NC

POSTAGE WILL BE PAID BY ADDRESSEE

Ventana Press
P.O. Box 2468
Chapel Hill, NC 27515